GRAMMAR
AND BEYOND
ESSENTIALS

2

Randi Reppen

CAMBRIDGE
UNIVERSITY PRESS

Shaftesbury Road, Cambridge CB2 8EA, United Kingdom

One Liberty Plaza, 20th Floor, New York, NY 10006, USA

477 Williamstown Road, Port Melbourne, VIC 3207, Australia

314–321, 3rd Floor, Plot 3, Splendor Forum, Jasola District Centre, New Delhi – 110025, India

103 Penang Road, #05-06/07, Visioncrest Commercial, Singapore 238467

Cambridge University Press & Assessment is a department of the University of Cambridge.

We share the University's mission to contribute to society through the pursuit of education, learning and research at the highest international levels of excellence.

www.cambridge.org
Information on this title: www.cambridge.org/9781009212991

First published 2019
Update published 2022

20 19 18 17 16 15 14 13 12 11 10 9 8 7

Printed in Malaysia by Vivar Printing

A catalogue record for this publication is available from the British Library

ISBN   978-1-009-21299-1   Student's Book with Digital Pack

Additional resources for this publication at www.cambridge.org/essentials

Scope and Sequence

Unit	Theme	Grammar	Topics	Avoid Common Mistakes
PART 1 The Present				
UNIT 1 page 2	Are You Often Online?	Simple Present	Simple Present (p. 4) Time Clauses and Factual Conditionals (p. 9)	Avoiding *amn't*; remembering a comma after a time clause at the beginning of a sentence
UNIT 2 page 14	Brainpower	Present Progressive and Simple Present	Present Progressive (p. 16) Simple Present and Present Progressive Compared (p. 19)	Remembering a form of *be* with the present progressive; remembering *-ing* for the present progressive
UNIT 3 page 24	What's Appropriate?	Imperatives	Imperatives (p. 26) *Let's* . . . (p. 30)	Avoiding *No* in imperatives; remembering an apostrophe in *Don't* and *Let's*
PART 2 The Past				
UNIT 4 page 34	Entrepreneurs	Simple Past	Simple Past (p. 36) Simple Past of *Be* and *There Was / There Were* (p. 42)	Avoiding the past form after *did not* and *didn't*; avoiding putting a time expression between the subject and the verb
UNIT 5 page 46	Science and Society	Simple Past, Time Clauses, *Used To*, and *Would*	Time Clauses and the Order of Past Events (p. 48) Past with *Used To* and *Would* (p. 51)	Remembering a subject in time clauses; remembering the *-d* in *used to* for affirmative statements
UNIT 6 page 58	Memorable Events	Past Progressive	Past Progressive (p. 60) Using *When* and *While* with Past Progressive (p. 64)	Avoiding a time clause as a complete sentence; remembering a comma when the time clause comes first in a sentence

Unit	Theme	Grammar	Topics	Avoid Common Mistakes
PART 5 Adjectives, Adverbs, and Prepositions				
UNIT 13 page 130	A Good Workplace	Adjectives	Adjectives (p. 132) More About Adjectives (p. 135)	Avoiding misspelling adjectives ending in -ful; remembering to put opinion adjectives first
UNIT 14 page 140	Learn Quickly!	Adverbs of Manner and Degree	Adverbs of Manner (p. 142) Adverbs of Degree (p. 145)	Remembering to use adverbs to describe how something happened; avoiding putting an adverb between the verb and the object; remembering that some adverbs have the same form as adjectives
UNIT 15 page 150	Food on the Table	Prepositions	Prepositions of Place and Time (p. 152) Prepositions of Direction and Manner (p. 156) Phrasal Prepositions and Prepositions After Adjectives (p. 160)	Using prepositions correctly
PART 6 The Future				
UNIT 16 page 166	Life Lists	Future (1)	*Be Going To*, Present Progressive, and Simple Present for Future Events (p. 168)	Remembering *be* with *going to*; remembering *be* before the subject in *Wh-* questions with *be going to*
UNIT 17 page 174	Getting Older	Future (2)	Future with *Will* (p. 176) Future with *Will*, *Be Going To*, and Present Progressive (p. 180)	Remembering *will* before the main verb with the future; remembering the base form of the verb after *will*
UNIT 18 page 186	Learning to Communicate	Future Time Clauses and Future Conditionals	Future Time Clauses (p. 188) Future Conditionals; Questions with Time Clauses and Conditional Clauses (p. 192)	Avoiding *will* in the conditional clause; avoiding *will* in the time clause

Unit	Theme	Grammar	Topics	Avoid Common Mistakes
PART 10 Gerunds and Infinitives				
UNIT 28 page 292	Managing Time	Gerunds and Infinitives (1)	Verbs Followed by Gerunds or Infinitives (p. 294) Verbs Followed by Gerunds and Infinitives (p. 297)	Using infinitives and gerunds after verbs; remembering *to* in infinitives
UNIT 29 page 302	Civil Rights	Gerunds and Infinitives (2)	More About Gerunds (p. 304) More About Infinitives (p. 307)	Avoiding plural verbs with gerund subjects; avoiding infinitives after prepositions; remembering *It* and *to* in *It* sentences
PART 11 Clauses and Conjunctions				
UNIT 30 page 312	Sleep	Subject Relative Clauses (Adjective Clauses with Subject Relative Pronouns)	Subject Relative Clauses (p. 314) More About Subject Relative Clauses (p. 318)	Avoiding a subject pronoun after a subject relative pronoun; remembering the relative pronoun in a subject relative clause
UNIT 31 page 322	Viruses	Object Relative Clauses (Adjective Clauses with Object Relative Pronouns)	Object Relative Clauses (p. 324) More About Object Relative Clauses (p. 328)	Avoiding *who* in possessives; avoiding *whom* in subject relative clauses; avoiding an object pronoun at the end of an object relative clause
UNIT 32 page 332	Special Days	Conjunctions and Adverb Clauses	Conjunctions (p. 334) Adverb Clauses (p. 338)	Remembering a comma after the adverb clause when it is first

Appendices

Introduction to *Grammar and Beyond Essentials*

Grammar and Beyond Essentials is a research-based and content-rich grammar series for beginning- to advanced-level students. The series focuses on the most commonly used English grammar structures and practices all four skills in a variety of authentic and communicative contexts. It is designed for use both in the classroom and as a self-study learning tool.

Grammar and Beyond Essentials Is Research-Based

The grammar presented in this series is informed by years of research on the grammar of written and spoken English as it is used in college lectures, textbooks, academic essays, high school classrooms, and conversations between instructors and students. This research, and the analysis of over one billion words of authentic written and spoken language data known as the *Cambridge International Corpus*, has enabled the authors to:

- Present grammar rules that accurately represent how English is actually spoken and written
- Identify and teach differences between the grammar of written and spoken English
- Focus more attention on the structures that are commonly used, and less on those that are rarely used in writing and speaking
- Help students avoid the most common mistakes that English language learners make
- Choose reading topics that will naturally elicit examples of the target grammar structure
- Introduce important vocabulary from the Academic Word List

Special Features of *Grammar and Beyond Essentials*

Realistic Grammar Presentations

Grammar is presented in clear and simple charts. The grammar points presented in these charts have been tested against real-world data from the *Cambridge International Corpus* to ensure that they are authentic representations of actual use of English.

Data from the Real World

Many of the grammar presentations and application sections include a feature called Data from the Real World. Concrete and useful points discovered through analysis of corpus data are presented and practiced in exercises that follow.

Avoid Common Mistakes

Each unit features an Avoid Common Mistakes section that develops students' awareness of the most common mistakes made by English language learners and gives them an opportunity to practice detecting and correcting these errors. This section helps students avoid these mistakes in their own work. The mistakes highlighted in this section are drawn from a body of authentic data on learner English known as the *Cambridge Learner Corpus*, a database of over 35 million words from student essays written by non-native speakers of English and information from experienced classroom teachers.

Academic Vocabulary

Every unit in *Grammar and Beyond Essentials* includes words from the Academic Word List (AWL), a research-based list of words and word families that appear with high frequency in English-language academic texts. These words are introduced in the opening text of the unit, recycled in the charts and exercises, and used to support the theme throughout the unit. By the time students finish each level, they will have been exposed several times to a carefully selected set of level-appropriate AWL words, as well as content words from a variety of academic disciplines.

Series Levels

The following table provides a general idea of the difficulty of the material at each level of *Grammar and Beyond Essentials*. These are not meant to be interpreted as precise correlations.

	Description	TOEFL IBT	CEFR Levels
Level 1	Beginning	20 – 34	A1 – A2
Level 2	Low Intermediate to Intermediate	35 – 54	A2 – B1
Level 3	High Intermediate	55 – 74	B1 – B2
Level 4	Advanced	75 – 95	B2 – C1

Student Components

Student's Book with Digital Pack

Levels 1 through 3 teach all of the grammar points appropriate at each level in short, manageable cycles of presentation and practice organized around a high-interest unit theme. Level 4 focuses on the structure of the academic essay in addition to the grammar rules, conventions, and structures that students need to master in order to be successful college writers. Please see the Tour of a Unit on pages xvi–xix for a more detailed view of the contents and structure of the units.

Digital Workbook

The Digital Workbook provides extra practice to help students master each grammar point. Automatically-graded exercises give immediate feedback. Each unit offers practice correcting the errors highlighted in the Avoid Common Mistakes section in the Student's Book. Self-Assessment sections at the end of each unit allow students to test their mastery of what they learned. Look for ⬚ in the Student's Book to see where additional practice in the Digital Workbook is available.

Kahoot!

Kahoot! is a game-based learning platform that makes it easy to create, share, and play learning games and quizzes in minutes. Kahoot! can be played on any mobile device or laptop with an Internet connection.

Kahoots can be used for review, formative assessment, or homework.

Cambridge has developed a number of Kahoot! quizzes for *Grammar and Beyond Essentials* - see cambridge.org/kahoot/grammarandbeyond. You can play these Kahoot quizzes before starting a unit as a diagnostic, during a unit as formative assessment, or at the end of a unit to test student knowledge.

Teacher Resources

A variety of downloadable resources are available on Cambridge One (cambridgeone.org) to assist instructors, including the following:

Teacher's Manual

- Suggestions for applying the target grammar to all four major skill areas, helping instructors facilitate dynamic and comprehensive grammar classes
- An answer key and audio script for the Student's Book
- Teaching tips, to help instructors plan their lessons

Assessment

- Placement Test
- Ready-made, easy-to-score Unit Tests, Midterm, and Final in .pdf and .doc formats
- Answer Key

Presentation Plus

Presentation Plus allows teachers to digitally project the contents of the Student's Books in front of the class for a livelier, interactive classroom. It is a complete solution for teachers because it includes the answer keys and audio.

Communicative Activity Worksheets

Downloadable, photocopiable worksheets organized by grammar topic provide communicative activities to facilitate more in-class speaking practice. Each worksheet has an instructor's page and a student's page.

Lesson Mapping Guides

Grammar and Beyond Essentials is designed to be used easily alongside academic English titles from Cambridge University Press. These include: *Academic Encounters, Final Draft, Making Connections, Prism,* and *Prism Reading.*

Academic Encounters   FINAL DRAFT   Making CONNECTIONS   PRISM   PRISM READING

About the Author

 Randi Reppen is Professor of Applied Linguistics and TESL at Northern Arizona University (NAU) in Flagstaff, Arizona. She has over 20 years' experience teaching ESL students and training ESL teachers, including 11 years as the Director of NAU's Program in Intensive English. Randi's research interests focus on the use of corpora for language teaching and materials development. In addition to numerous academic articles and books, she is the author of *Using Corpora in the Language Classroom* and a co-author of *Basic Vocabulary in Use*, 2nd edition, both published by Cambridge University Press.

Corpus Consultants

Michael McCarthy is Emeritus Professor of Applied Linguistics at the University of Nottingham, UK, and Adjunct Professor of Applied Linguistics at Pennsylvania State University. He is a co-author of the corpus-informed *Touchstone* series and the award-winning *Cambridge Grammar of English*, both published by Cambridge University Press, among many other titles, and is known throughout the world as an expert on grammar, vocabulary, and corpus linguistics.

Jeanne McCarten has over 30 years of experience in ELT/ESL as a teacher, publisher, and author. She has been closely involved in the development of the spoken English sections of the *Cambridge International Corpus*. Now a freelance writer, she is co-author of the corpus-informed *Touchstone* series and *Grammar for Business*, both published by Cambridge University Press.

Advisory Panel

The ESL advisory panel has helped to guide the development of this series and provided invaluable information about the needs of ESL students and teachers in high schools, colleges, universities, and private language schools throughout North America.

Neta Simpkins Cahill, Skagit Valley College, Mount Vernon, WA
Shelly Hedstrom, Palm Beach State College, Lake Worth, FL
Richard Morasci, Foothill College, Los Altos Hills, CA
Stacey Russo, East Hampton High School, East Hampton, NY
Alice Savage, North Harris College, Houston, TX

Acknowledgments

The publisher and author would like to thank these reviewers and consultants for their insights and participation:

Marty Attiyeh, The College of DuPage, Glen Ellyn, IL

Shannon Bailey, Austin Community College, Austin, TX

Jamila Barton, North Seattle Community College, Seattle, WA

Kim Bayer, Hunter College IELI, New York, NY

Linda Berendsen, Oakton Community College, Skokie, IL

Anita Biber, Tarrant County College Northwest, Fort Worth, TX

Jane Breaux, Community College of Aurora, Aurora, CO

Anna Budzinski, San Antonio College, San Antonio, TX

Britta Burton, Mission College, Santa Clara, CA

Jean Carroll, Fresno City College, Fresno, CA

Chris Cashman, Oak Park High School and Elmwood Park High School, Chicago, IL

Annette M. Charron, Bakersfield College, Bakersfield, CA

Patrick Colabucci, ALI at San Diego State University, San Diego, CA

Lin Cui, Harper College, Palatine, IL

Jennifer Duclos, Boston University CELOP, Boston, MA

Joy Durighello, San Francisco City College, San Francisco, CA

Kathleen Flynn, Glendale Community College, Glendale, CA

Raquel Fundora, Miami Dade College, Miami, FL

Patricia Gillie, New Trier Township High School District, Winnetka, IL

Laurie Gluck, LaGuardia Community College, Long Island City, NY

Kathleen Golata, Galileo Academy of Science & Technology, San Francisco, CA

Ellen Goldman, Mission College, Santa Clara, CA

Ekaterina Goussakova, Seminole Community College, Sanford, FL

Marianne Grayston, Prince George's Community College, Largo, MD

Mary Greiss Shipley, Georgia Gwinnett College, Lawrenceville, GA

Sudeepa Gulati, Long Beach City College, Long Beach, CA

Nicole Hammond Carrasquel, University of Central Florida, Orlando, FL

Vicki Hendricks, Broward College, Fort Lauderdale, FL

Kelly Hernandez, Miami Dade College, Miami, FL

Ann Johnston, Tidewater Community College, Virginia Beach, VA

Julia Karet, Chaffey College, Claremont, CA

Jeanne Lachowski, English Language Institute, University of Utah, Salt Lake City, UT

Noga Laor, Rennert, New York, NY

Min Lu, Central Florida Community College, Ocala, FL

Michael Luchuk, Kaplan International Centers, New York, NY

Craig Machado, Norwalk Community College, Norwalk, CT

Denise Maduli-Williams, City College of San Francisco, San Francisco, CA

Diane Mahin, University of Miami, Coral Gables, FL

Melanie Majeski, Naugatuck Valley Community College, Waterbury, CT

Jeanne Malcolm, University of North Carolina at Charlotte, Charlotte, NC

Lourdes Marx, Palm Beach State College, Boca Raton, FL

Susan G. McFalls, Maryville College, Maryville, TN

Nancy McKay, Cuyahoga Community College, Cleveland, OH

Dominika McPartland, Long Island Business Institute, Flushing, NY

Amy Metcalf, UNR/Intensive English Language Center, University of Nevada, Reno, NV

Robert Miller, EF International Language School San Francisco – Mills, San Francisco, CA

Marcie Pachino, Jordan High School, Durham, NC

Myshie Pagel, El Paso Community College, El Paso, TX

Bernadette Pedagno, University of San Francisco, San Francisco, CA

Tam Q Pham, Dallas Theological Seminary, Fort Smith, AR

Mary Beth Pickett, GlobalLT, Rochester, MI

Maria Reamore, Baltimore City Public Schools, Baltimore, MD

Alison M. Rice, Hunter College IELI, New York, NY

Sydney Rice, Imperial Valley College, Imperial, CA

Kathleen Romstedt, Ohio State University, Columbus, OH

Alexandra Rowe, University of South Carolina, Columbia, SC

Irma Sanders, Baldwin Park Adult and Community Education, Baldwin Park, CA

Caren Shoup, Lone Star College – CyFair, Cypress, TX

Karen Sid, Mission College, Foothill College, De Anza College, Santa Clara, CA

Michelle Thomas, Miami Dade College, Miami, FL

Sharon Van Houte, Lorain County Community College, Elyria, OH

Margi Wald, UC Berkeley, Berkeley, CA

Walli Weitz, Riverside County Office of Ed., Indio, CA

Bart Weyand, University of Southern Maine, Portland, ME

Donna Weyrich, Columbus State Community College, Columbus, OH

Marilyn Whitehorse, Santa Barbara City College, Ojai, CA

Jessica Wilson, Rutgers University – Newark, Newark, NJ

Sue Wilson, San Jose City College, San Jose, CA

Margaret Wilster, Mid-Florida Tech, Orlando, FL

Anne York-Herjeczki, Santa Monica College, Santa Monica, CA

Hoda Zaki, Camden County College, Camden, NJ

We would also like to thank these teachers and programs for allowing us to visit:

Richard Appelbaum, Broward College, Fort Lauderdale, FL

Carmela Arnoldt, Glendale Community College, Glendale, AZ

JaNae Barrow, Desert Vista High School, Phoenix, AZ

Ted Christensen, Mesa Community College, Mesa, AZ

Richard Ciriello, Lower East Side Preparatory High School, New York, NY

Virginia Edwards, Chandler-Gilbert Community College, Chandler, AZ

Nusia Frankel, Miami Dade College, Miami, FL

Raquel Fundora, Miami Dade College, Miami, FL

Vicki Hendricks, Broward College, Fort Lauderdale, FL

Kelly Hernandez, Miami Dade College, Miami, FL

Stephen Johnson, Miami Dade College, Miami, FL

Barbara Jordan, Mesa Community College, Mesa, AZ

Nancy Kersten, GateWay Community College, Phoenix, AZ

Lewis Levine, Hostos Community College, Bronx, NY

John Liffiton, Scottsdale Community College, Scottsdale, AZ

Cheryl Lira-Layne, Gilbert Public School District, Gilbert, AZ

Mary Livingston, Arizona State University, Tempe, AZ

Elizabeth Macdonald, Thunderbird School of Global Management, Glendale, AZ

Terri Martinez, Mesa Community College, Mesa, AZ

Lourdes Marx, Palm Beach State College, Boca Raton, FL

Paul Kei Matsuda, Arizona State University, Tempe, AZ

David Miller, Glendale Community College, Glendale, AZ

Martha Polin, Lower East Side Preparatory High School, New York, NY

Patricia Pullenza, Mesa Community College, Mesa, AZ

Victoria Rasinskaya, Lower East Side Preparatory High School, New York, NY

Vanda Salls, Tempe Union High School District, Tempe, AZ

Kim Sanabria, Hostos Community College, Bronx, NY

Cynthia Schuemann, Miami Dade College, Miami, FL

Michelle Thomas, Miami Dade College, Miami, FL

Dongmei Zeng, Borough of Manhattan Community College, New York, NY

Tour of a Unit

GRAMMAR IN THE REAL WORLD

presents the unit's grammar in a realistic context using **contemporary** texts.

UNIT
5 Simple Past, Time Clauses, *Used To*, and *Would*
Science and Society

1 Grammar in the Real World

A What is your favorite ice cream flavor? Read the article from a textbook. How is ice cream today different from ice cream in the past?

B Comprehension Check Circle the correct answer.

1 Persians made a frozen dessert with noodles / buffalo milk.
2 In ancient Rome, people mixed snow with fruit / cream.
3 A duchess brought sorbet to Italy / France.
4 British chemists invented ice cream that lasted longer / had no air in it.

C Notice Find the sentences in the article. Complete them with *after*, *before*, or *as soon as*.

1 _____ refrigeration existed, people needed ice to make frozen desserts.
2 _____ scientists found better processes for freezing things, ice cream became popular with all classes, rich and poor.
3 _____ ice cream became more available, people began to buy it more often.

In each sentence, two events happen. Circle the event that happened first.

Simple Past, Time Clauses, *Used To* and *Would*

Ice Cream: A **Food Revolution**

Science can have a great effect on society. Take ice cream, for example. Today, people all over the world, rich or poor, eat ice cream. **Before there were modern refrigerators**, however, ice cream was a luxury food.

The history of ice cream goes back to ancient times. In 400 BCE,[1]
5 Persians made a frozen dessert with noodles and fruit. There are early records of frozen milk and rice in China from around 200 BCE. In 618 CE, King Tang of Shang (China) ate frozen buffalo milk.

Before refrigeration existed, people needed ice to make frozen desserts. For example, in ancient Rome, people would go into the
10 mountains and collect snow. They would bring it to the city and mix the snow with fruit. This was later called "sorbet."

When an Italian duchess[2] moved to France, she brought sorbet and other frozen desserts with her. **After sorbet and ice cream became popular in France**, they spread to the rest of Europe. However, only the rich
15 ate them.

In the twentieth century, ice cream became easier to make and keep. **After scientists found better processes for freezing things**, ice cream became popular with all classes, rich and poor. Then, in the 1940s and
20 1950s, British chemists discovered a new way to make ice cream. They put air into it. This made the ice cream bigger and softer. Now, ice cream was less expensive. It lasted longer, too. **As soon as ice cream became more available**, people
25 began to buy it more often.

Today, almost anyone, rich or poor, can buy ice cream and keep it at home. Ice cream is a universal dessert, popular all over the world. Together, traditional ice cream makers and
30 scientists created a food revolution.

[1]**BCE:** before common era
[2]**duchess:** a woman of very high social rank in some European countries

46

Science and Society **47**

NOTICE ACTIVITIES

draw students' attention to the structure, guiding their own analysis of form, meaning, and use.

GRAMMAR PRESENTATION

begins with an overview that describes the grammar in an **easy-to-understand** summary.

GRAMMAR APPLICATION

keep students engaged with a wide variety of exercises that introduce new and stimulating content.

2 Time Clauses and the Order of Past Events

Grammar Presentation

| Time clauses can show the order of events in the past. | *After* scientists developed better processes for freezing things, ice cream became popular with everyone. |

2.1 Time Clauses

A	A time clause can come first in a sentence. When it comes first, use a comma after it. A time clause can also come second in a sentence. No comma is needed.	┌─TIME CLAUSE─┐ ┌─MAIN CLAUSE─┐ *After* sorbet became popular in France, it spread to the rest of Europe. ┌─MAIN CLAUSE─┐ ┌─TIME CLAUSE─┐ Sorbet spread to the rest of Europe after it became popular in France.
B	Use *after* to introduce the first event.	FIRST EVENT SECOND EVENT *After* an Italian duchess brought ice cream to France, it became popular. SECOND EVENT FIRST EVENT Ice cream became popular *after* an Italian duchess brought it to France.
C	Use *before* to introduce the second event.	SECOND EVENT FIRST EVENT *Before* there were freezers, people needed ice to make frozen desserts. FIRST EVENT SECOND EVENT People needed ice to make frozen desserts *before* there were freezers.
D	Use *when* to refer to the time that something started.	When scientists found new ways to make ice cream, it became cheaper. Ice cream became cheaper *when* scientists found new ways to make it.
E	Use *as soon as* to refer to something that happened right after or immediately after.	FIRST EVENT SECOND EVENT *As soon as* scientists found ways to freeze things, people began buying more ice cream. (Scientists invented ways to freeze things. Soon after, people started buying ice cream more often.)

🖥 Grammar Application

Exercise 3.1 Used To: Statements and Questions

A Complete the article. Use the correct form of *use to* or *used to* and the verbs in parentheses.

The Wisdom of Our Grandparents

College Weekly spoke to Joseph Green, an 87-year-old retired teacher, about the old days.

College Weekly What _did_ people _use to do_ (do) for fun before there was television?

Joseph Green Well, we _____ (listen) to the radio in the evening.

CW How _____ you _____ (spend) your free time?

JG Well, because there was no television, we _____ (play) games a lot.

CW Who _____ (play) with you?

JG My brothers.

CW It seems like people _____ (have) more free time in those days . . .

JG Not really. In fact, people _____ (not have) a lot of free time. For example, my parents _____ (work) six days a week.

CW What was school like?

JG We _____ (write) with pencils and paper. And when I was in college, we _____ (take) notes in real notebooks, not on notebook computers!

CW _____ you _____ (type) your papers?

JG No, I didn't. Typewriters were too expensive. I _____ (write) all my papers in ink on lined paper. I _____ (get) so frustrated if I made a mistake because I had to start all over again!

B Write three affirmative sentences and one negative sentence about Mr. Green's life before computers and TV. Compare your sentences with a partner.

1 *He used to play games in the evenings.*
2 _____
3 _____
4 _____
5 _____

DATA FROM THE REAL WORLD

takes students beyond traditional information and teaches them how the unit's grammar is used in authentic situations, including differences between spoken and written use.

QR CODES

give easy access to audio at point of use.

Exercise 2.3 Answering Questions with Time Clauses

Data from the Real World

We often answer information questions about time (e.g., *When . . . ?, What time . . . ?,* and *How long . . . ?*) with time clauses. In conversation, these answers do not usually contain a main clause.

A *When did you start studying English?*
B *After I got my job at the museum.*

A *How long did you study at a community college?*
B *Until I got my degree.*

A Listen to a radio interview with an inventor of a new printer. Match the interview questions with the answers.

1 When did you come to the United States?   _d_
2 So, when did you get the idea for your invention?   ____
3 And how long did you study at college?   ____
4 When did you build your first printer?   ____
5 And when did you start your printer company?   ____
6 So, when did you get the money for your company?   ____
7 And when did the company start making a profit?   ____

a As soon as my first printer reached the stores.
b After I graduated from college.
c As soon as we got the money to start.
d After I graduated from high school.
e Until I got my degree.
f When I was a student in college.
g After I presented my idea to some banks and investors.

B Listen again and check your answers.

Exercise 2.4 More Time Clauses

A Write sentences in the simple past about inventions and discoveries. Use an event in Column A, an event in Column B, and *after, before, when, until,* or *as soon as.*

	A		B
1	TV / exist	a	people / start to fly more
2	cheap air travel / become possible	b	credit cards / become popular
3	everyone / have a cell phone	c	families / listen to the radio together
4	people / pay for things with cash or checks	d	millions of people / learn to drive
5	free education / be available	e	roads / become safer
6	traffic lights / come into our cities	f	people / buy food from small local stores
7	Ford / make the first mass-produced car	g	people / make calls from pay phones
8	the first supermarket / open	h	most people / not read or write

50 Unit 5 Simple Past, Time Clauses, *Used To,* and *Would*

HOW TO USE A QR CODE

1 Open the camera on your smartphone.

2 Point it at the QR code.

3 The camera will automatically scan the code. If not, press the button to take a picture.

* Not all cameras automatically scan QR codes. You may need to download a QR code reader. Search "QR free" and download an app.

Exercise 3.2 Would, Used To, or Simple Past?

Complete the article about life before electricity. Use *used to* or *would* and the verbs in parentheses, or use the simple past form of the verbs. Sometimes more than one answer is correct.

Alessandro Volta ___invented___ (invent) the first battery in 1800.
(1)
How ___did___ people ___use to live___ (live) in the days before electricity?
(2)   (2)
Most people _____ (burn) oil lamps or candles for light.
(3)
When it got cold, they _____ (make) open fires to keep
(4)
warm. People _____ (not travel) long distances. Most people
(5)
only _____ (visit) neighbors or nearby relatives.
(6)
Before Volta's battery, many scientists _____ (not think)
(7)
that electricity was useful. And in the early days of electricity, some people
_____ (think) it was dangerous. They _____ (be) afraid of
(8)   (9)
it. Some people even _____ (believe) that electricity had a bad effect on
(10)
society. They _____ (prefer) the simple life of the past. Soon, however,
(11)
electricity _____ (make) the world brighter, faster, and more comfortable.
(12)
Electricity in homes and industry _____ (change) the world in many ways.
(13)

Exercise 3.3 Would: Questions and Statements

A Imagine that you can talk to a person who lived before there was electricity. Use the words to make questions with *would*. Then add two questions of your own with *would*.

1 how / heat / your house?   *Before electricity, how would you heat your house?*
2 how / light / your house?   _____
3 how / clean / your house?   _____
4 what / do / in the evenings? _____
5 what / play / with?   _____
6 how / get / to work or school? _____
7 _____
8 _____

B Over to You Now write answers with *would* to the questions. Use your imagination. When you finish, compare your answers with a partner.

We would build a fire to heat our house.

C Group Work Discuss how people used to live before the following inventions changed society. Was life better or worse? Was it safer or more dangerous? In what ways?

- computers
- cold medicine
- cars
- microwave ovens
- airplanes
- TV

A *Before computers existed, students used to write everything down with a pencil or pen.*
B *And they would copy everything again when they revised their papers.*
C *Student life was hard!*

4 Avoid Common Mistakes ⚠

1 Use a subject in the time clause.
            they
      Before. invented electricity, people used candles.

2 Do not forget the *-d* in *used to* in affirmative statements.
                              used
      When I was living in New York, I use to play in a rock band.

3 Use *use to* (without *-d*) in negative statements and in questions with *did*.
                                              use
      How did you used to heat your home?

Editing Task

Find and correct six more mistakes in this article from a magazine.

A New Invention

            use
How did people used to wash dishes? People did not used to have dishwashers before invented electricity, so they would wash dishes by hand. But did men and women used to share the dishwashing equally? Not usually. Mostly it was women who did it. Before there was electricity, women use to heat up water on the stove and use it for washing dishes. It took hours and hours, and dishes often broke
5 or chipped.

In 1886, one woman finally got tired of washing dishes by hand. "If nobody else is going to invent a dishwashing machine," she said, "I'll do it myself." Her name was Josephine Cochrane, a housewife and engineer's daughter who was tired of washing – and sometimes breaking – her favorite dishes after dinner parties. Cochrane worked and worked on her invention until 1893 when finally created a
10 machine that washed dishes. She showed the machine at the World's Fair that year. People operated it by hand, so it was still hard work. After the fair ended, she started a company to make the machines. When first tried to sell dishwashers, only restaurants and hotels bought them from her. However, after electricity became more easily available, her company built electric dishwashers for people to use in their homes. Today, homes around the world have electric dishwashers.

1 Simple Present

Are You Often Online?

1 Grammar in the Real World

A What kinds of things do you do on the Internet? Read the magazine article. What is one good thing and one bad thing about spending time online?

B Comprehension Check Answer the questions.

1 What do sociologists disagree about?

2 How much time does the average person in the United States spend online per week?

3 What is face-to-face time? What are some examples of face-to-face time?

4 Does the article say not to use computers?

C Notice Find the sentences in the article and complete them.

1 In today's busy world, people _____ a lot of time with computers, and they _____ less and less time with people.

2 Sociologists _____ about this.

3 In the United States, the average person _____ 24 hours a week online.

4 Sometimes technology _____ people improve their relationships with others.

Look at the words you wrote in the blanks. Which of the verbs end in -s?

Balancing TIME ONLINE and TIME WITH PEOPLE

[1]**sociologist:** someone who studies people and society

[2]**face-to-face:** meeting with someone in the same place directly

In today's busy world, people **spend** a lot of time with computers, and they **spend** less and less time with people. **Does** this **change** how people interact with family and friends? **Does** it **help** or **hurt** people and relationships? Sociologists[1] **disagree** about this. Some **worry** about the
5 Internet's effect on our friends and family. Others **think** this is not a problem.

Studies **show** that people spend less face-to-face[2] time with family and friends than they did a few years ago. Instead, they **play** online games, **shop** online, and also **look** at social networking sites. In the
10 United States, the average person **spends** 24 hours a week online. They **interact** face-to-face less, and this sometimes has bad effects. For example, some people **do not spend time** together as a family very often. They talk less because they spend more time online.

Sometimes technology **helps** people improve their relationships
15 with others. For example, social networking sites **help** people stay in touch with friends and family who live far away. They enable people to reconnect with old friends and classmates.

Are you worried about the time you spend online? If so, try to make a schedule. Schedule time away from the computer to be with family
20 and friends. Try to balance online time with face-to-face time.

2 Simple Present

Grammar Presentation

The simple present describes habits, general truths, feelings, or thoughts.	Many people *spend* up to 24 hours a week online. I *play* games online every night. My sister *loves* to shop online.

2.1 Affirmative and Negative Statements

AFFIRMATIVE

Subject	Verb	
I You We They	**shop**	online.
He/She/It	**shops**	

NEGATIVE

Subject	Do/Does + Not	Base Form of Verb	
I You We They	**do not** **don't**	**shop**	online.
He/She/It	**does not** **doesn't**		

2.2 Affirmative and Negative Statements with *Be*

AFFIRMATIVE

Subject	*Be*	
I	**am**	
You We They	**are**	online.
He/She/It	**is**	

NEGATIVE

Subject	*Be + Not*	
I	**am not**	
You We They	**are not**	online.
He/She/It	**is not**	

CONTRACTIONS

Affirmative	Negative	
I**'m**	I**'m** not	
You**'re** We**'re** They**'re**	You**'re** not We**'re** not They**'re** not	You **aren't** We **aren't** They **aren't**
He**'s** She**'s** It**'s**	He**'s** not She**'s** not It**'s** not	He **isn't** She **isn't** It **isn't**

Data from the Real World

Research shows the contractions 's not and 're not are more common after pronouns (he, she, you, etc.) than isn't and aren't.

's not / 're not	
isn't / aren't	

Be careful not to use contractions in formal writing.	Say: "He's not feeling well today." Write: He is not feeling well today.

2.3 Yes / No Questions and Short Answers

Do/Does	Subject	Base Form of Verb	
Do	I you we they	shop	online?
Does	he / she / it		

Short Answers

Yes, I **do**.	No, I **don't**.
Yes, you **do**.	No, you **don't**.
Yes, we **do**.	No, we **don't**.
Yes, they **do**.	No, they **don't**.
Yes, he / she / it **does**.	No, he / she / it **doesn't**.

2.4 Information Questions and Answers

Wh- Word	Do/Does	Subject	Base Form of Verb
Where When How often	do	I you we they	shop?
	does	he / she / it	

Answers

I **shop** online.
You **shop** at night.
We **shop** once a week.
They **shop** every day.

He **shops** every night.

Wh- Word	Verb	
Who	uses	e-mail?
What	helps	people reconnect?

Answers

Everyone **uses** e-mail!

The Internet **helps** people reconnect.

2.5 Using Simple Present Statements

A Use the simple present to describe habits and routines (usual and regular activities).

I usually read the news online.
We eat together as a family on weekends.

B Use the simple present to describe facts, general truths, feelings, or thoughts.

The average person spends 24 hours a week online.
Some people worry about the effects of the Internet.

C Use the simple present with adverbs of frequency to say how often something happens.

0%					100%
never	seldom	occasionally	often	usually	always
	hardly ever*	sometimes		almost always	
	rarely			normally	

*ever: at any time

D Adverbs of frequency come before the main verb in affirmative statements but after the verb *be*.

I occasionally play online games.
I am hardly ever free.

E Do not use *sometimes* after *not*.

Note that meaning can change in negative statements with adverbs of frequency.

Sometimes people do not check e-mail.
People ~~do not sometimes~~ check e-mail.
I don't always check e-mail.
(Does *not* mean "I never check e-mail.")

F *Sometimes, occasionally, normally, often, usually,* and *almost always* can come before the verb or at the beginning or end of a sentence.

I usually check my e-mail at home.
Usually, I check my e-mail at home.
I check my e-mail at home usually.

G Adverbs of frequency come before the main verb in questions.

Do you always study at night? Yes, I do.
Do you ever watch YouTube? No, I don't.

H Do not use negative adverbs of frequency in negative sentences.

I don't usually shop online.
~~I don't never shop online.~~

2.6 Using Simple Present Questions

A Answer *when* or *what time* questions with **time expressions**.	What time do you shop online? I shop online *at night*. When do you check e-mail? I check e-mail *during the day*. When do you call your family? I call my family *on Sunday night*. When do you shop at the mall? I shop at the mall *in December*.
B Answer *how often* questions with **frequency expressions**.	How often do you shop? I shop *once a week*. How often do you check e-mail? I check e-mail *three times a day*.

Grammar Application

Exercise 2.1 Statements

A Complete the sentences. Use the correct form of the verbs in parentheses. Use contractions when possible.

1 My family and friends _____ *use* _____ (use) the computer for all sorts of things.

2 I _____ (use) an online dictionary for my classes.

3 My friend Mark _____ (shop) for clothes online.

4 Our classmates Marta and Raul _____ (check) their e-mail at the library.

5 My best friend Ana _____ (not be) on any social networking sites.

6 Ana and her sister Claudia _____ (not buy) groceries online.

7 My family _____ (spend) a lot of time online.

8 My brother Sam is online a lot, but he also _____ (interact) with our family.

9 Technology _____ (not hurt) my relationships.

B Over to You Rewrite three sentences in A so they are true about you. Then compare your sentences with a partner.

A *I don't use an online dictionary. How about you?*

B *No, I don't, but I shop for clothes online.*

Exercise 2.2 Frequency Adverbs

Listen to Alex and Karen talk about their online activities. Complete the sentences with the correct adverb of frequency.

1 Karen ___*hardly ever*___ goes to the mall.

2 Karen is _____ studying.

3 Karen _____ reserves library books online.

4 Alex _____ goes to the library on the weekend.

5 Karen _____ studies in the library.

6 Karen _____ studies at home.

7 Alex _____ meets up with friends.

8 Karen needs a break _____ .

Exercise 2.3 Time Expressions and Frequency Adverbs

Look at the things Brandon does online. Then complete the sentences. Circle the correct answer.

	Sun.	Mon.	Tue.	Wed.	Thu.	Fri.	Sat.
Watch videos	✓						
Read the news	✓	✓	✓	✓	✓	✓	
Shop for groceries	✓	✓					
Play games						✓	✓
Check e-mail	✓	✓	✓	✓	✓	✓	✓
Shop for clothes							

1 Brandon **occasionally** / **never** watches videos online.

2 He checks e-mail **sometimes** / **every day**.

3 He **seldom** / **often** reads the news online.

4 Brandon always plays games **on Thursday** / **on Saturday**.

5 He shops for groceries online **twice** / **once** a week.

6 He **hardly ever** / **never** plays games.

7 Brandon **always** / **rarely** checks e-mail.

8 He **never** / **sometimes** shops for clothes online.

Exercise 2.4 Questions

A Unscramble the words to make questions. Then write two questions of your own.

1 own / Do / a computer? / you   *Do you own a computer?*

2 the news / Do / read / you / online?   _____

3 often / shop online? / do / How / you   _____

4 usually / check / do / you / your / Where / e-mail?   _____

5 website? / your / favorite / is / What   _____

6 music? / you / Do / download / sometimes   _____

7 _____

8 _____

B Group Work Ask three classmates the questions in A. Answer your classmates'
questions. Give extra information.

A *Do you own a computer?*
B *No, I don't. But I use the computers at the library. They're free!*

C Pair Work Tell a partner some things you learned in B.

I own a computer, but Peter doesn't. He uses the computers at the library.
Peter doesn't shop online, but I do.

3 Time Clauses and Factual Conditionals

Grammar Presentation

Time clauses in the present tense show the sequence of events. Factual conditionals describe things that are generally true in a certain situation.

When I get home, I check my e-mail.
If it's late, I don't stay online for a long time.

3.1 Time Clauses

Time Clause		Main Clause
Before **After** **As soon as** **When**	I get to work,	I check my e-mail.

Main Clause	Time Clause	
I check my e-mail	**before** **after** **as soon as** **when**	I get to work.

3.2 Factual Conditionals

Condition		Main Clause	Main Clause	Condition	
If	I get an e-mail,	I feel great!	I feel great	if	I get an e-mail.

3.3 Using Time Clauses

A	Use time clauses to say when the main clause happens. Use *after* to introduce the first event.	SECOND EVENT FIRST EVENT *I check my e-mail **after** I get home.*
B	Use *as soon as* to introduce the first event when the second event happens immediately after.	FIRST EVENT SECOND EVENT ***As soon as** I change my password, I forget it.*
C	Use *while* when events happen at the same time.	***While** I'm online, I check my e-mail.*
D	*When* means "at almost the same time." Use *when* to introduce the first event.	SECOND EVENT FIRST EVENT *I visit social networking sites **when** I get home.*
E	Use *before* to introduce the second event.	SECOND EVENT FIRST EVENT ***Before** I go to work, I check my e-mail.*
F	Use a comma if the time clause comes first.	*Before I go out, I check my e-mail.* *After I check my e-mail, I read the news.*
G	A time clause by itself is not a complete sentence.	*Before I go out, I turn off my computer.* ~~*Before I go out.*~~ *I turn off my computer.*

3.4 Using Factual Conditionals

A	Use factual conditionals to describe things that are generally true in certain situations. The condition describes a situation. The main clause describes the result of the situation.	CONDITION MAIN CLAUSE (RESULT) *If I need a recipe, I go to a cooking site.*
B	Use *if* when one event depends on another one happening.	*If I need directions, I go to a map site.* (I go to a map site only because I need directions.)
C	A condition by itself is not a complete sentence.	*If I need directions, I go to a map site.* ~~*If I need directions.*~~ *I go to a map site.*

Grammar Application

Exercise 3.1 Time Clauses

A Read about Dave. Then complete the sentences. Circle the correct words.

- Dave gets out of bed and immediately turns on his computer.
- Then he checks his e-mail.
- He plays an online game. Then he goes to work.
- At work, Dave checks his e-mail many times a day.
- He gets home and immediately turns on his computer.
- He stays at home all evening and plays online games.
- He sometimes eats dinner and sits in front of his computer.
- He visits a social networking site. Then he goes to bed.

1 **As soon as**/ Before he gets out of bed in the morning, Dave turns on his computer.

2 **After**/**Before** he turns on his computer, he checks his e-mail.

3 He plays an online game **when**/**before** he goes to work.

4 **As soon as**/**While** he is at work, Dave checks his e-mail many times a day.

5 **Before**/**As soon as** Dave gets home, he turns on his computer again.

6 Dave usually plays online games **after**/**while** he is at home in the evening.

7 Dave sometimes eats dinner **while**/**after** he sits in front of his computer.

8 Dave visits a social networking site **before**/**as soon as** he goes to bed.

B Pair Work **Compare your behavior with Dave's. Discuss it with a partner.**

A *As soon as I get out of bed in the morning, I turn on my computer. How about you?*

B *I turn my computer on after I make coffee.*

Read the sentences about Internet research. Underline the time clause or condition. Circle the main clause.

1 <u>When Dani has a school assignment,</u> (she often does research on the Internet.)

2 She usually starts with a search engine when she does research.

3 If the topic is general, Dani thinks about the best words to put into the search engine.

4 For example, if the topic is "How to avoid identity theft," Dani uses *avoid identity theft*.

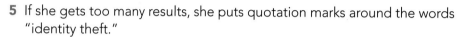

5 If she gets too many results, she puts quotation marks around the words "identity theft."

6 She clicks on a result if it comes from a useful site.

7 When she gets to the page, she usually skims the information first.

8 She reads the entire page if the information seems useful.

A Match the task with the website you go to.

If you . . .	you go to . . .
1 forget the actors in an old movie, __*e*__	**a** a sports site.
2 need the definitions of some words, _____	**b** an online encyclopedia.
3 want to know the score of a soccer game, _____	**c** a recipe site.
4 need to know the temperature in Chicago today, _____	**d** your library's website.
5 need a book at the library, _____	**e** a movie site.
6 drive to a new friend's house, _____	**f** an online dictionary.
7 want to cook something new for dinner, _____	**g** a weather site.
8 forget the birth date of a famous person, _____	**h** a map site.

B Over to You Write conditional sentences about your own Internet research. Use the ideas in A or your own ideas. Then compare your sentences with a partner.

1 If I __*forget the title of a book,*__ I __*go to an online bookstore*__ .

2 If I _____
   I _____ .

3 If I _____
   I _____ .

4 I _____
   If I _____ .

5 I _____
   if I _____ .

4 Avoid Common Mistakes ⚠

1 **Do not contract *not* with *am*.**

I'm not
~~I amn't~~ online every day.

2 **Use the correct form of *do* with singular and plural subjects.**

doesn't
He ~~don't~~ own a computer.

3 **Remember to form information questions correctly.**

does the professor
Where ~~the professor does~~ post his comments?

4 **Do not use *sometimes* after *not*.**

Sometimes I do not check
~~I do not sometimes check~~ e-mail on the weekends.

5 **Always use a comma if a time clause or a condition clause begins a sentence.**

When I change my password, I write it down.
~~When I change my password I write it down.~~

Editing Task

Find and correct 10 more mistakes in this blog entry.

doesn't
My roommate Mark plays online games. He ~~don't~~ own a computer, so he goes
to a computer lab. How often he does play? He plays every night! As soon as he
finishes his homework he goes to the lab. He does not sometimes come home until
midnight. He usually plays with people from around the world. He don't know the
5 other players, but it doesn't matter. When Mark gets home he always has stories
about the games he plays. Why people play these games? I do not understand.
I amn't like Mark. I always play with people face-to-face when I play a game. When I
play a game I know the people. Does many people play online games? How often you
do play online games?

Present Progressive and Simple Present

Brainpower

1 Grammar in the Real World

A What do you do to improve your brain? Read the article from a health magazine. How are the people in the article improving their brains?

B Comprehension Check Match each item with its benefit.

1 Chemicals in blueberries _*b*_   **a** helps the brain, not just the body.

2 Calm thoughts _____   **b** improve your memory and ability to learn.

3 Word puzzles _____   **c** are good for your memory.

4 Exercise _____   **d** make your brain younger.

C Notice Find the sentences in the article. Circle the answer you find in the article.

1 It is 9:00 a.m. in Portland, Oregon. Hannah Lewis **sits / is sitting** at her computer.

2 They all **live / are living** in Portland, of course.

3 Exercise **helps / is helping** the brain, not just the body.

Which sentences describe things that are true in general? Which describe things in progress now or around the present time?

A HEALTHY BRAIN

It is 9:00 a.m. in Portland, Oregon. Hannah Lewis is **sitting** at her computer. She **is looking** at websites that interest her. Bill Green **is doing** a word puzzle at his kitchen table. Kelly South **is eating** a bowl of cereal with blueberries. Nina Ritch **is brushing** her teeth after breakfast.
5 Anthony Owens **is jogging** in the park. Olga Prince **is sitting** on the floor of her apartment with her eyes closed. She **is thinking** beautiful, calm thoughts.

What do these people have in common? They all **live** in Portland, of course. In addition, they **are** all **improving** their brains. We **are**
10 **learning** more about the brain every day. Do things like word puzzles and blueberries help your brain? Many scientists **think** so. They **believe** that exercise, food, and other activities give people sharper memory and stronger, healthier brains.

These things **help** the brain in different ways. For example, the
15 **chemicals** in blueberries **improve** your memory and your ability to learn. Calm thoughts **are** also good for your memory. Using interesting websites **makes** your brain stronger, and word puzzles **make** it younger. Take Bill Green, the word-puzzle
20 lover. He **is** 60, but his brain is like the brain of a 40-year-old. Exercise **helps** the brain, not just the body. Even oral health is connected to the health of the brain, so don't forget
25 to brush your teeth!

Improving your brain **does not stop** at any particular time. It can continue for life.

2 Present Progressive

Grammar Presentation

The present progressive describes things that are in progress now or around the present time.

Hannah *is sitting* at her computer.
She *is exercising* a lot these days.

2.1 Affirmative and Negative Statements

AFFIRMATIVE

Subject	Be	Verb + -ing
I	am	
You We They	are	thinking.
He / She / It	is	

NEGATIVE

Subject	Be + Not	Verb + -ing
I	am not	
You We They	are not	working.
He / She / It	is not	

CONTRACTIONS

Affirmative	Negative	
I'm	I'm not	
You're We're They're	You're not We're not They're not	You aren't We aren't They aren't
He's She's It's	He's not She's not It's not	He isn't She isn't It isn't

▶▶ Spelling Rules for Verbs Ending in *-ing*: See page A4.

Data from the Real World

Isn't *and* aren't *are more common after nouns than* 's not *and* 're not.

Bill and Olga aren't *exercising.*

2.2 Yes / No Questions and Short Answers

Be	Subject	Verb + -ing
Am	I	
Are	you we they	thinking?
Is	he she it	

Short Answers

Yes, I **am**.	No, I'm **not**.	
Yes, you **are**. Yes, we **are**. Yes, they **are**.	No, you're **not**. No, we're **not**. No, they're **not**.	No, you **aren't**. No, we **aren't**. No, they **aren't**.
Yes, he **is**. Yes, she **is**. Yes, it **is**.	No, he's **not**. No, she's **not**. No, it's **not**.	No, he **isn't**. No, she **isn't**. No, it **isn't**.

⊞ Data from the Real World

The 's not and 're not contractions are more common in short answers than the isn't and aren't contractions.

Are they exercising?
No, they're not.

2.3 Information Questions and Answers

Wh- Word	Be	Subject	Verb + -ing
Who	are	you	**helping**?
What	is	your brother	**reading**?
Why	are	you	**jogging**?

Answers
I'm **helping** my brother.
He's **reading** a news article.
Because I'm **trying** to improve my brainpower.

Wh- Word	Be	Verb + -ing
Who	is	**doing** a word puzzle?
What		**happening** at Kelly's house?

Answers
Bill **is doing** a word puzzle.
She's **eating** blueberries.

2.4 Using Present Progressive

A Use the present progressive for things in progress now or around the present time.

Lorna's doing a puzzle right now.
I'm reading a great book about brain training exercises.

B You can use the present progressive with time expressions that mean "right now" and "around now": now, right now, at the moment, this week, these days, this month.

She's working on her essay right now.
He's exercising at the gym now.
What's Felipe reading these days?
I'm not doing anything interesting this week.

C Use the full forms when writing in class. Use contractions in everyday speaking.

Anthony is not running today.
I'm improving my brainpower.

D You can contract Wh- words + is in informal speaking and writing.

Who's she working for?
Why's the printer not working?

You can contract Wh- words + are in speaking but **not** in formal writing.

Say: "What're you doing?"
Write: What are you doing?

Grammar Application

A Complete the article about improving brainpower. Use the correct form of the verb in parentheses. Use full forms.

There are a lot of ways to improve brainpower, such as doing word puzzles and exercising. Here are a few more things our readers are doing.

Jane R., from Chicago, usually wears her watch on her right arm. This week she _is wearing_ (wear) it on her
(1)
left arm. Jane uses her right hand a lot, but now she
_____ (use) her left hand more.
(2)

Joe M., from Dallas, usually drives to work. This month he _____ (not drive). Instead, he
(3)
_____ (walk) to work every day. Also, he
(4)
_____ (run) three times a week this month.
(5)

Isabel and Max V., from Los Angeles,
_____ (go) to the gym together every day this week.
(6)
They _____ (try) to improve their mental and physical health, too.
(7)

Mario S., from Boston, always goes to bed after midnight, but this week
he _____ (not go) to bed so late. Also, he _____
(8)   (9)
(not eat) junk food this week.

B Over to You Here are more things people do to improve their brainpower. Are you or people you know doing any of these things? Use the words to write sentences about you and people you know.

1 I / learn / a musical instrument   _I'm not learning a musical instrument._

2 My best friend / learn / a musical instrument   _____

3 I / improve / my vocabulary   _____

4 My friends / improve / their vocabulary   _____

5 I / eat / less junk food   _____

6 My family / eat / less junk food   _____

7 I / study / math   _____

8 My co-workers / study / math   _____

Exercise 2.2 Questions and Answers

A Complete the questionnaire with the present progressive. Then write true answers.

1 a _Are_ you _doing_ (do) anything to improve your brainpower right now?
   Yes. I am. _____
   b If yes, what _____ you _____ (do)? _____
2 a _____ you _____ (try) to improve your health? _____
   b If yes, what _____ you _____ (do)? _____
3 a _____ you _____ (read) an interesting book? _____
   b If yes, what _____ you _____ (read)? _____
   c If no, _____ you _____ (read) anything else? _____
4 a _____ you _____ (get) enough exercise right now? _____
   b _____ you _____ (eat) the right kinds of food? _____
5 a _____ your friends also _____ (take) classes? _____
   b If yes, what _____ they _____ (study)? _____
6 a _____ you and your classmates _____ (work) hard this semester?

   _____

   b _____ you all _____ (get) good grades?

B Pair Work Ask and answer the questions with a partner. How many of your answers are the same?

C Pair Work Change partners. Ask and answer questions about your first partner.

   A *Is Andrea doing anything to improve her brainpower right now?*
   B *Yes, she is. She's doing a lot! She's . . .*

3 Simple Present and Present Progressive Compared

Grammar Presentation

The simple present describes actions that are true in general or that happen regularly. The present progressive describes things that are happening now or around the present time.	He *runs* every evening. He*'s running* right now.

3.1 Using Simple Present and Present Progressive

A Use the simple present to describe habits, routines, facts, or general truths.	He *runs* in the park every day. Physical exercise *improves* the brain.
Use the present progressive when an action is happening right now or around the present time.	Mark *is doing* brain exercises these days. Right now, he*'s improving* his memory. He*'s not running* today.
B Use the simple present for situations that are true in general. The situations are settled, and we do not expect them to change.	Exercise *helps* the brain, not just the body. Many people *don't get* enough exercise.
The present progressive often describes temporary or changing actions.	Lara *is eating* fish this week. (She's trying fish just for this week.) I*'m reading* a lot these days because I have an exam next week. (I'm reading a lot, but it's just for the exam.)
C Use the simple present with stative verbs, such as *like*, *know*, and *want*. Stative verbs do not describe actions. They describe states or situations.	I *like* your new laptop. I don't *know* her e-mail address. I *want* a new cell phone.
D We do not usually use stative verbs in the present progressive, even if we are talking about right now.	~~I'm liking~~ your new laptop. I'm ~~not knowing~~ her e-mail address. I'm ~~wanting~~ a new cell phone.
Exception Some stative verbs can be used in the present progressive. These verbs have an action meaning as well as a stative meaning.	I *have* a new puzzle book. (*have* = own) He's *having* fish for lunch these days. (*have* = eat) I *think* blueberries are good for brain health. (*think* = believe) I'm *thinking* about a word problem. (*think* = using my mind)

📊 Data from the Real World

Research shows that these are the 25 most common stative verbs in spoken and written English:

agree	dislike	hope	love	see
believe	expect	hurt	need	seem
care (about)	hate	know	notice	think
cost	have	like	own	understand
disagree	hear	look like	prefer	want

▸▸ Stative (Non-Action) Verbs: See page A2.

Grammar Application

Exercise 3.1 Simple Present or Present Progressive?

Complete the article. Use the correct form of the verbs in parentheses. Use the simple present or the present progressive.

Rafael Sosa is only 12 years old, but he _is getting ready_ (get ready) to go to college this
(1)
week. At 12 years old, Rafael _____
(2)
(seem) young for college, but Rafael is not a
typical child. He _____ (have)
(3)
high intelligence-test scores, and he easily
_____ (understand) difficult ideas.
(4)
He _____ (love) both science and
(5)
music. Rafael _____ (write) music and _____ (design) electronic
(6)   (7)
devices. He _____ (own) a lot of college textbooks, and he _____
(8)   (9)
(read) engineering textbooks every day. These days, he _____ (study) Japanese
(10)
and Chinese. Rafael _____ (look) like a normal child, and he _____
(11)   (12)
(like) normal activities, too. He _____ (not spend) all his time reading and studying.
(13)
Right now, he _____ (play) soccer with a group of friends and _____
(14)   (15)
(have) a great time.

Exercise 3.2 Stative or Active?

Complete the conversation with the correct form of *have, look,* or *think*. Use the simple present or the present progressive.

Clerk	Can I help you?
Sally	Yes. I _'m looking_ for some brain-training software. What do you have?
	(1)
Clerk	We _____ several good products for brain training. Here's one: *Memory Plus*.
	(2)
Sally	That _____ good. Does it work?
	(3)
Clerk	I _____ all these products work well.
	(4)
Sally	We're also _____ about our eight-year-old son. What do you
	(5)
	_____ for children?
	(6)
Clerk	Here's *Memory Plus Kids*.
Sally	OK . . . I'm _____ for the price . . .
	(7)
Clerk	Here it is: $25.
Sally	That's not bad.
Clerk	And we're _____ a sale this week, too. Twenty percent off all week.
	(8)
Sally	OK. These _____ perfect. I'll take them.
	(9)

A Complete the text about a company's idea for market research with the correct form of the verbs in parentheses. Use the simple present or the present progressive. Then listen and check your answers.

Large corporations often _need_ (need) to make
decisions about new products. _Do_ people _want_
(want) this product? At the present moment, _____
people _____ (look) for a product like this in the
stores? New products _____ (cost) a lot of
money and _____ (need) a lot of research.
Corporations usually _____ (pay) experts
to do market research. But there is another way. One
large corporation _____ (try) a new idea
this year. Every time the company _____
(need) market information for a new product, managers _____ (ask) the
employees for their opinions. The employees _____ (vote) yes or no on
the new idea. They _____ (tell) the managers, "I _____
(like) the idea" or "I _____ (not like) the idea."

Manager Rick Jons said, "Right now we _____ (use) the collective
brain of our employees, and it _____ (seem) to work. The results are
more reliable than expensive market research."

B Imagine you are doing market research for a new dictionary. Write market research questions about dictionary use. Use the simple present or the present progressive.

1 how often / use a dictionary?   _How often do you use a dictionary?_

2 look for / a better dictionary right now?   _____

3 use a dictionary / in this class today?   _____

4 prefer / an online dictionary or a paper one?   _____

5 use a dictionary / when you prepare for tests?   _____

6 prepare / for a test at the moment?   _____

C Group Work Ask and answer the questions in B. Based on the results, what is the best dictionary for your group?

The best dictionary is an electronic one, like the one Sam is using in this class.

4 Avoid Common Mistakes ⚠

1 **Use a form of _be_ with the present progressive.**

am listening
I ~~listening~~ to the radio.

2 **Use the _-ing_ form of the verb with the present progressive.**

is studying
Fred ~~is study~~.

3 **Spell the _-ing_ form of the verb correctly. (See page A4 for more information.)**

planning   _writing_   _enjoying_
plan → ~~planing~~   write → ~~writting~~   enjoy → ~~enjoing~~

4 **Do not use the present progressive with verbs of stative meaning.**

I have
~~I'm having~~ a very smart brother.

5 **Use the simple present for habits, routines, and general truths. Use the present progressive for actions in progress now or around the present time.**

I'm watching
Can you call me back later? I ~~watch~~ the news right now.

improves
Exercise ~~is improving~~ physical and mental health.

Editing Task

Find and correct nine more mistakes in this article about the brain.

resembles
      The human brain ~~is resembling~~ a computer. It stores a lot of information.
But humans are smarter than computers because we store things outside of our brains
that we do not need to store _in_ our brains. For example, we are storing information
in books, newspapers, images, and of course, computers. Another example is this
5   text. At this moment, you are read this text. You are not needing to remember all
the information in it. The book is having the information, and you read it when you
need it. If you are planing an essay, you can make notes on paper or on a computer.
When you are writting the essay, you can read those notes again. If you are studing
a subject, you can go online and find information about it. The information is on the
10   Internet. We do not look into people's brains to see it. When we are enjoing an online
video, we watching something that is outside of the human brain. So computers are
like extensions[1] of our brains.

[1]**extension:** something added or extra

3

Imperatives

What's Appropriate?

1 Grammar in the Real World

A Who do you usually send e-mails to – friends, family, your professors? Do you write the same way to all of them? Read the web article about e-mailing. What are some good rules to follow in an e-mail to a professor?

B Comprehension Check Read the e-mail. Label the parts *A* for appropriate or *NA* for not appropriate.

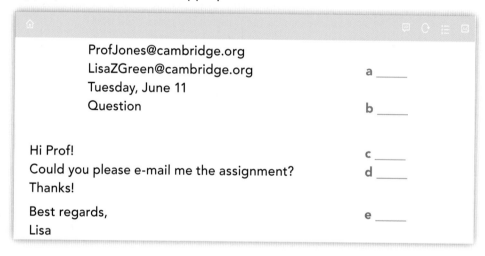

ProfJones@cambridge.org
LisaZGreen@cambridge.org   **a** _____
Tuesday, June 11
Question   **b** _____

Hi Prof!   **c** _____
Could you please e-mail me the assignment?   **d** _____
Thanks!

Best regards,   **e** _____
Lisa

C Notice Find and write the sentences from the article with these meanings.

1 You need an e-mail address that shows your name.

_____

2 You need to write a greeting.

_____

3 It is not good to write pages and pages of text.

_____

4 Text messaging abbreviations are not appropriate.

_____

How to Write an **E-Mail** to a Professor

At some point in the school year, you may need to e-mail a professor. **Make sure** that you create a positive impression[1] by following these simple rules.

1　**Use** an e-mail address that shows your name. A fun e-mail address like soccerfan@cambridge.org does not look professional. Your e-mail may go to
5　the professor's spam folder if there is no name in the e-mail address. **Use** your name or your school e-mail address instead.

2　**Write** the purpose of your e-mail in the subject line. Do not write "Hi" or "Question." **Include** your class name and time so your professor can immediately see this information.

10　3　**Always start** with a greeting, for example, "Dear Prof. Smith." **Never send** an e-mail, especially a request, without one. Your professor might be friendly and informal in class. However, it is not appropriate[2] to be informal in an e-mail to him or her, so **don't start** an e-mail with "Hi there!" or "What's up?"

4　**Be** brief,[3] clear, and specific. **Do not write** pages and pages of text.
15　Remember, your professor is very busy. **Do not write** more than one screen.

5　**Always be** polite. **Say** "please" and "thank you." **Don't tell** your professor what to do. For example, **don't say** "Reply ASAP,[4]" "Please respond immediately," or "Urgent!!!" **Do not write** "I need the assignment. Please send it." Instead, **write** "Could you please e-mail me the assignment?"

20　6　**Don't use** text messaging abbreviations. This is an e-mail to a professor, not a friend, so **avoid** "LOL" (laughing out loud), "TTYL" (talk to you later), or emojis (😊 😖 😀).

7　**Thank** your professor at the end of the e-mail. **Write** something like "Thanks" or "Thanks for your time" and a polite ending like "See you in class on
25　Tuesday" or "Best regards." **Remember** to type your name.

8　Finally, **don't forge**t to check your grammar and spelling. If you follow these rules, you will always communicate appropriately with your professors.

[1]**a positive impression:** a good opinion

[2]**appropriate:** right for a particular situation

[3]**be brief:** do not write a lot

[4]**ASAP:** an abbreviation for "as soon as possible"

2 Imperatives

Grammar Presentation

Imperatives tell people to do things. For example, they can give instructions, directions to a place, or advice.

Write the purpose of your e-mail in the subject line.
Don't use text messaging abbreviations.

2.1 Affirmative and Negative Statements

AFFIRMATIVE			NEGATIVE		
Base Form of Verb			Do + Not	Base Form of Verb	
Avoid	abbreviations.		**Don't**	**make**	demands.
Be	clear.		**Do not**	**write**	pages and pages of text.

Data from the Real World

Don't is much more common than *do not* in conversation. *Do not* is also very strong.

2.2 Using Imperatives in Writing

A	Imperatives are common in rules, road signs, orders, warnings, forms, and directions.	*Stop.* *Do not enter.* *Write clearly.* *Turn left at the next intersection.*
B	They are common in texts with instructions and advice, such as manuals, recipes, and magazine articles.	*Set the date and time.* *Chop the onions.* *Finish your e-mail with something polite.*
C	You can use *always* and *never* to give emphasis in writing.	*Always start with a greeting.* *Never send an e-mail without one.* (= Don't send.)
D	You can use imperatives with time clauses and with *if* clauses.	*Check the e-mail for spelling errors before you send it.*
E	Use a comma when the main clause is second.	*If you e-mail a professor, do not use texting language.*

2.3 Using Imperatives in Speaking and Informal Writing

A Don't use imperatives to tell people you don't know well what to do. It can sound rude. Saying *please* doesn't make it polite.

~~Send me the assignment, please.~~
Could you please send me the assignment?

B When you know people very well, you can use imperatives in everyday situations to ask for things, give instructions or advice, and to make offers or invitations.

Give me that pen.
Call the doctor.
Don't forget.
Have a cookie.
Come over Saturday.

Grammar Application

Exercise 2.1 Forming Imperatives

A Complete the sentences in this advice column about using cell phones. Use the affirmative or negative imperative form of the verbs in the box.

answer	find	keep	leave	let	send	take	turn	use

Rules for Using Cell Phones

What is appropriate use of a cell phone at the office? Here are some simple rules to follow so that you do not upset your friends, co-workers, business clients, and most of all, your boss!

1 __*Turn*__ your cell phone ringer off in the office, or put it on vibrate.

2 __*Don't use*__ a pop song for a ring tone. It is not professional.

3 _____ unimportant calls go to voice mail. Your co-workers do not want to know what you are having for dinner tonight.

4 If your cell phone rings in a restroom, _____ it! People can hear you.

5 _____ your voice down. On a modern cell phone, there is no need to shout.

6 _____ text messages instead of making phone calls in the office. They are less annoying to other people.

7 _____ a quiet, private place to take calls, and be brief.

8 _____ a call in a meeting. Just _____ the room and take the call outside.

B Over to You Rewrite two of the imperatives above using *Always* and two with *Never*. Compare with a partner.

I wrote, "Always turn your cell phone ringer off." How about you?

Use the words to write sentences about appropriate cell phone use.
Use affirmative or negative imperatives. Write each sentence two different ways.

1 go into a meeting / turn your cell phone off

Before ___*you go into a meeting, turn your cell phone off*___ .

___*Turn your cell phone off*___ before ___*you go into a meeting*___ .

2 be in a face-to-face meeting / check your messages

When _____ .

_____ . when _____ .

3 be in a meeting / keep checking your messages

If _____ .

_____ if _____ .

4 be in a presentation / reply to a call or an e-mail

When _____ .

_____ . when _____ .

5 be expecting a call / tell the other people in a meeting

If _____ .

_____ if _____ .

6 take a phone call in a meeting / leave the room to talk

If _____ .

_____ if _____ .

7 leave the room to take a call / be brief

If _____ .

_____ if _____ .

8 finish your call and come back to the room / apologize

After _____ .

_____ after _____ .

Exercise 2.3 Making Rules with Imperatives

A Group Work **Discuss the questions about cell phone use. Do you all do the same things?**

- When do you turn off your phone?
- When do you set it to vibrate?
- Do you take calls during dinner? At a restaurant?
- Do you talk on the phone when you're out with friends?
- Do you sometimes go someplace quiet to talk?
- Do you always answer your phone when someone calls you?

B Group Work **Agree on four rules for using a cell phone appropriately. Write four rules with imperatives. Use time clauses and *if* clauses. Share your ideas with the class.**

When you're in class, turn off your cell phone.

Exercise 2.4 Imperatives with Subject Pronouns

📊 Data from the Real World

You can use *You* with imperatives in informal situations, for example, to decide who does what or to add emphasis and make the imperative stronger.	*You write* the e-mail, and I'll check it. *You take* care now. *Don't you scare* me like that again!
You can use *somebody, someone, everybody,* and *everyone* with imperatives when there are a lot of people, for example, in class or at a party.	*Someone* turn off the lights. *Everybody* please sit down. *Everyone* please take your seats.
Use *someone / somebody* to refer to one person. Use *everyone / everybody* to refer to a group.	

A Complete these sentences people might say while doing group activities in class. Use *you* and the imperative form of the verbs in parentheses.

1 _____*You write*_____ (write) the questionnaire, and I'll write the answers. Does that sound fair?

2 Kate, _____ (do) some research on the Internet.

3 Dale, _____ (be) the salesperson, and Josh, _____ (play) the role of the customer.

4 We'll get a good grade, _____ (not worry).

5 Who's going to be A and B? I'll be A, and _____ (be) B.

6 Binh, _____ (be) the group leader, and Ana, _____ (take) notes.

7 Claudia, _____ (think) of a clever title for our report.

8 Asha, _____ (find) the pictures, and I'll print them.

What's Appropriate? **29**

B Complete the sentences from a student's presentation with *somebody / someone* or *everybody / everyone*.

1 ___*Everybody / Everyone*___ take a seat, please.

2 _____ pass out the worksheet, OK?

3 Now, before I start, _____ choose a partner. We're going to do some pair work.

4 Do you need a pencil, Raffi? _____ hand this pencil to Raffi, please.

5 I want to use the projector now, so _____ turn off the lights, please.

6 _____ please write the answer on the board.

7 Now, _____ go back to your first partner and discuss the questions.

8 Before you leave the room, _____ take a handout.

3 Let's . . .

Grammar Presentation

Let's is a kind of imperative that makes suggestions or gives instructions to other people in a group you are in.	*Let's stop there and talk about this in the next class.*

3.1 Affirmative and Negative Statements

AFFIRMATIVE	NEGATIVE
Let's + Base Form of Verb	*Let's not* + Base Form of Verb
Let's stop there. **Let's be** clear.	**Let's not talk** about that now. **Let's not confuse** writing to friends and writing to professors.

📊 Data from the Real World

In very formal academic writing, people use *Let us*. Research shows that the negative form, *Let's not*, is not very common in academic writing or conversation.	*Let us now look at the use of smartphones.*

3.2 Using Imperatives with *Let's*

A You can use *Let's* to make suggestions to do things with other people.	*Let's meet after class today.*
B You can also use *Let's* to give instructions, for example, in class.	*Let's get started.* *Let's stop there.* *Let's discuss this in the next class.*
C You can soften (say in a nice way) *Let's* imperatives with *just* in speaking.	*Let's just do this exercise, and then we can stop for today.*

📊 Data from the Real World

Research shows that the most common expressions with *Let's* in formal academic speaking are *Let's say*, *Let's see*, and *Let's look at*. *Let's say* often means "imagine." *Let's see* gives you time to think.	*Let's say you're writing to a professor. How do you start your e-mail?* *You can say this in several ways. Let's see, you can say . . .* *Are you still confused? Let's look at page 12.*

🖱️ Grammar Application

Exercise 3.1 Imperatives with *Let's* and *Let's Not*

A Some students are creating a questionnaire on text messaging. Complete the conversation with *Let's* or *Let's not* and the words in the box.

ask	choose a topic	put it first	see	~~start~~	write down

A OK. _____*Let's start*_____.

  (1)

B Right. _____. How about text messaging?

  (2)

A Yeah. That's a good topic for a questionnaire.

B All right. First, _____ some questions. What

  (3)
can we ask?

A _____. Oh, here's one: "Do you ever text

  (4)
friends when you're in class?"

B Yes, that sounds good, but _____. It can

  (5)
be second. The first question can be: "Do you turn off your
cell phone in class?" What do you think?

A OK. So that's two questions. For question three,

 _____: "Do you ever text your instructors?"

  (6)

B Sounds good!

B Listen to the rest of the conversation and write the missing words with *Let's / Let's not.*

A OK, group, _____*let's think*_____ of two more questions.
(1)

B Wait a minute. How will we distribute the questionnaire to everyone?

A _____ about that now. We can ask the teacher for help when we're ready.
(2)

B I have some ideas for the presentation. _____ about that.
(3)

A _____ the questionnaire first. We still need two more questions.
(4)

C _____ . How about: "How many text messages do you send in a day?"
(5)

A Great question. One more.

B What about: "Do you sleep with your cell phone near you?"

A I love it! That's six questions. _____ there for today, OK? Can we meet again
(6)
on Thursday or Friday?

C _____ on Friday. I have to work all day. Thursday's good. Same time?
(7)

A OK, _____ on Thursday.
(8)

Exercise 3.2 Imperatives with *Let's* and *Let's Not*

Read the situations for preparing a group presentation on appropriate work behavior.
Write suggestions using *Let's / Let's not.*

1 You arrive at school to meet with your group. You are the group leader. Everyone is talking.

You want to start the meeting. You say: OK, everybody, ___*let's start the meeting.*___

2 One member wants to talk about handouts. You don't want to think about that until later.

You say: ___*Let's not think about that until later.*___

3 The group isn't sure what to do. You want to try brainstorming ideas. You say:

Well, _____

4 The group thinks of many ideas. You want to divide the ideas up so that everyone presents

something. You say: _____

5 A member thinks that the presentation might be too long. You don't want to worry about

that now. You say: _____

6 Your group is deciding who will introduce the presentation. You want to vote on it.

You say: I have an idea. _____

7 It's getting late and everyone seems tired. You want to stop for now and meet tomorrow.

You say: It's getting late. _____

4 Avoid Common Mistakes

1 **Negative imperatives are *Don't / Do not* + base form. *No* is not used in imperatives.**
Don't use
~~No use~~ text messaging abbreviations.

2 ***Do not* is two words, not one.**
Do not
~~Donot~~ write pages and pages of text.

3 **There are apostrophes in *Don't* and *Let's.***
Don't
~~Dont~~ send text messages during class.

Editing Task

Find and correct four more mistakes in this article about how to set up a professional social networking profile.

> ### YOUR PROFILE
>
> What are the rules for making an appropriate social networking profile? First, ~~dont~~ *don't*
> use a silly photo of yourself. Choose a professional-looking photo. For example, no use a
> picture of yourself at a party or at the beach. And dont use a photo that is too old.
> Update your photo every few years.
>
> 5   For your profile, donot give too much information. Always remember: Strangers are
> looking at your profile. Include details that can give possible employers a good impression.
>   A professional social networking profile is like a résumé, so no lie in your profile.
> Always be honest about your experience and your skills.

Simple Past

Entrepreneurs

1 Grammar in the Real World

A What is the best way to find information today? Read the article from a technology magazine. How did Google start?

B Comprehension Check Answer the questions.

1 Where did Larry Page and Sergey Brin meet?

2 Why did they work in a garage?

3 What other products did Google start?

4 How many people worked at Google after 20 years?

C Notice Look at the article. Find the simple past forms of these verbs.

Group A		Group B	
1 start	_____	5 come	_____
2 move	_____	6 be	_____ ,
3 study	_____		_____ (two forms)
4 happen	_____	7 become	_____
		8 meet	_____

How are the two groups of verbs different?

The **STORY**
OF
Google

Who started Google?

Sergey Brin and Larry Page **started** the company. Sergey **came** from Moscow, Russia. He **moved** to the United States as a young child and later **studied** mathematics and computer science. Larry **was** born in
5 Michigan and **became** interested in computers as a child.

How did they meet?

They **met** in 1995 at Stanford University, in California, where they **were** both computer science students. They **did not get along** at first, but they soon **became** friends.

10 ### What happened next?

They **designed** a new Internet search engine. At first, they **worked** in their rooms in college. Then they **rented** a friend's garage because Sergey's roommate **complained** about the noise from his computers. Three years later, they **started** Google.

15 ### Was it an immediate success?

The company **was** an immediate success. Before Google, **there were** other search engines, but Google soon **became** the most popular one. The company **grew** quickly. They **did not stop** at just one product. Very soon, **there were many** other Google products, including Google
20 Maps, Android phones, and YouTube, of course. Twenty years later, Google **was** one of the top ten most valuable companies in the world and **had** about 60,000 employees.

So what did people do before Google?

Before Google, people **went** to libraries. They **got** information from
25 books. These days, they just "google" for information.

2 Simple Past

Grammar Presentation

You can use the simple past to talk about completed events in the past.	*Brin and Page started Google in 1998.* *They did not get along at first.*

2.1 Affirmative Statements

Subject	Verb + -ed (Regular Verbs)
I You He / She / It We They	**started** in 1998. **employed** 80,000 people.

Subject	Irregular Verb
I You He / She / It We They	**grew** quickly. **became** successful.

▸▸ Spelling Rules for Regular Verbs in Simple Past: See page A4.

▸▸ Irregular Verbs: See page A3.

📊 Data from the Real World				
Research shows that these are six of the most common **regular** simple past verbs.	work start call	work**ed** start**ed** call**ed**	live try plan	liv**ed** tri**ed** plan**ned**
Research shows that these are eight of the most common **irregular** simple past verbs.	have get do say	**had** **got** **did** **said**	go come take make	**went** **came** **took** **made**

2.2 Negative Statements

Subject	*Did + Not*	Base Form of Verb	
I You He / She / It We They	**did not** **didn't**	**start**	slowly.

2.3 Yes/No Questions and Short Answers

Did	Subject	Base Form of Verb	
Did	I you he / she / it we they	**work** **start**	every day? quickly?

Short Answers

Yes, I **did**.	No, I **didn't**.
Yes, you **did**.	No, you **didn't**.
Yes, he / she / it **did**.	No, he / she / it **didn't**.
Yes, we **did**.	No, we **didn't**.
Yes, they **did**.	No, they **didn't**.

2.4 Information Questions

Wh- Word	Did	Subject	Base Form of Verb	
What **Where** **When** **Who** **Why**	did	I you he / she / it we they	**study**?	

Wh- Word	Simple Past Verb	
What **Who**	**happened** **started**	next? the company?

2.5 Using Simple Past

A Use the simple past to talk or write about: • a single action that started and ended in the past.	They started Google in 1998. x ⟶ past now
• a repeated action or habit in the past.	They worked in their rooms every day. xxx ⟶ past now
• a state, situation, or feeling in the past.	They didn't get along. ▬▬▬▬⟶ past now
B Time expressions can come at the start or end of a statement. Examples: *last week / month / year*, *10 years ago*, *in 1998*, *yesterday*.	Last year, I joined a new company. I joined a new company last year. Two years ago, I graduated. I graduated two years ago.
C Remember to use a comma when the time expression comes at the beginning of the sentence.	In 1998, they started Google. They started Google in 1998.
D Adverbs of frequency often come before the main verb in simple past statements. Some examples of adverbs of frequency are *never*, *rarely*, *sometimes*, *often*, *usually*, and *always*.	They often had meetings at a pizza parlor. They sometimes worked in their room.

Research shows that *didn't* is not common in formal writing. Use *did not* instead. Writers sometimes use *didn't* in quotes of people speaking.

Use *didn't* in conversation and informal writing. In conversation, *did not* can sound formal, emphatic, or argumentative.

Formal writing
didn't
did not

Conversation
didn't
did not

🖱 Grammar Application

Exercise 2.1 Statements and Questions

A Complete the article with the simple past form of the verbs in parentheses.

Ben Cohen and Jerry Greenfield __*grew up*__ (grow up) (1) in Merrick, Long Island. They _____ (2) (meet) in middle school, and they _____ (3) (graduate) from high school together. Their connections to ice cream _____ (4) (begin) at an early age. Ben _____ (5) (drive) an ice cream truck in high school. Jerry _____ (6) (work) in his college cafeteria as an ice cream scooper.

Ben _____ (7) (try) different colleges, but he _____ (8) (not graduate). At one time, he _____ (9) (teach) crafts in a school. At the school, he sometimes _____ (10) (make) ice cream with his students. Jerry _____ (11) (want) to be a doctor. After he _____ (12) (graduate) from college, he _____ (13) (apply) to medical school, but he was not successful. During those years, Ben and Jerry _____ (14) (stay) friends.

After a few years, Ben and Jerry _____ (15) (go) into the food business together. At first, they _____ (16) (think) about making bagels, but the equipment was expensive. So they _____ (17) (choose) ice cream and _____ (18) (take) a $5 class on ice cream making.

Ben and Jerry _____ (19) (see) an opportunity in Burlington, Vermont. This college town _____ (20) (not have) an ice cream shop. They _____ (21) (find) an old gas station, and in 1978 they _____ (22) (open) the first Ben & Jerry's store.

Ben & Jerry's quickly _____ (23) (become) popular because it _____ (24) (have) great ice cream and a caring approach to the community. On their first anniversary, they _____ (25) (give) everyone free ice cream as a "thank you." They still give away free ice cream every year on their anniversary.

B Pair Work Complete the *Yes/No* questions and answers about Ben and Jerry. Then ask and answer the questions with a partner. Give more information.

1 _____*Did*_____ Ben and Jerry _____*grow up*_____ (grow up) on Long Island?
  _____*Yes, they did.*_____

2 _____ they _____ (meet) in college?
  _____

3 _____ Ben _____ (graduate) from college?
  _____

4 _____ Ben _____ (teach) in a school?
  _____

5 _____ Jerry _____ (go) to college?
  _____

6 _____ Jerry _____ (apply) to law school?
  _____

7 _____ they _____ (think) about making ice cream at first?
  _____

8 _____ they _____ (open) their first store in 1978?
  _____

A *Did Ben and Jerry grow up on Long Island?*
B *Yes, they did. They grew up in Merrick, Long Island.*

C Complete the information questions about Ben and Jerry. Use the answers to help you.

1 A Where _____*did Ben and Jerry grow up*_____ ? B On Long Island.
2 A Where _____ ? B In middle school.
3 A What _____ ? B Crafts.
4 A What kind of course _____ ? B An ice cream-making course.
5 A How much _____ ? B $5.
6 A When _____ ? B In 1978.
7 A Why _____ ? B The ice cream was good.
8 A What _____ ? B Free ice cream.

D Pair Work Complete the information questions about Ben and Jerry. Write *did* in the blank, if necessary. If *did* is not necessary, write an **✗**. Then take turns asking and answering the questions with a partner.

1 Who ____*✗*____ drove an ice cream truck in high school?
2 Who _____ worked in the college cafeteria?
3 What _____ he do in the cafeteria?
4 Who _____ graduated from college?
5 What _____ he want to study after college?
6 Who _____ taught in a school?
7 What _____ happened on their first anniversary?
8 Why _____ they open a store in Burlington?

Verbs ending in /t/ or /d/	/ɪd/ or /əd/	
If the base form of the verb ends with the sound /t/ or /d/, say -ed as an extra syllable /ɪd/ or /əd/.	/t/ rent – rented	/d/ decide – decided
Verbs ending in voiceless consonants	**/t/**	
If the base form of the verb ends in /f/, /k/, /p/, /s/, /ʃ/, and /tʃ/, say the -ed as /t/.	/f/ laugh – laughed /s/ miss – missed /k/ look – looked /ʃ/ finish – finished /p/ stop – stopped /tʃ/ watch – watched	
Verbs ending in voiced consonants or vowels	**/d/**	
If the base form of the verb ends in a voiced consonant or vowel, say the -ed endings as /d/.	live – lived change – changed	learn – learned play – played

A Listen and repeat the verbs with -ed endings in the chart above.

B Circle the -ed endings that have an extra syllable (/ɪd/ or /əd/) in these sentences. Then listen, check, and repeat.

1 My family moved here six years ago.

2 I needed to earn some money, so I decided to get a job in a factory.

3 I earned a lot of money, but I wanted to be my own boss.

4 I studied business and learned how to start a company.

5 I finished the program and graduated two years ago.

6 Finally, I started my own business.

C Over to You Write six sentences about your own life. Use the ideas in B or your own ideas. Compare sentences with a partner. Ask your partner for more information.

A *My family moved here in 1998.*
B *Really? Where did you live before that?*

A Complete the article with the simple past form of the verbs in parentheses.

Today, Oprah Winfrey is one of the most successful broadcasters, publishers, and entrepreneurs in the world. However, she did not have an easy start in life. Oprah ___had___ (1) (have) a difficult childhood. She _____ (not have) a lot of opportunities as a (2) child, but she was very intelligent. She _____ (learn) to read before the age (3) of three. Her broadcasting career _____ (begin) in high school. In 1971, she (4)

_____ (go) to Tennessee State University.
(5)

During high school and college, she _____
(6)

(work) on a radio show. She also _____ (work)
(7)

at a TV station in Nashville as a student. At the age of 19,

she _____ (become) the first African-American
(8)

woman news anchor[1] at the station.

In 1976, she _____ (graduate) from
(9)

college. That year, she _____ (move) to
(10)

Baltimore. There she _____ (host) a
(11)

TV talk show called _People Are Talking_. Eight years

later, she _____ (start) working on a morning show in Chicago.
(12)

It _____ (become) _The Oprah Winfrey Show_. Oprah's popularity
(13)

_____ (grow) quickly, and in 1986, it _____ (become) a
(14)   (15)

national show.

[1]**anchor:** a person who reports the news

B Pair Work **Complete the questions about Oprah Winfrey. Use the information in the article. Then ask and answer the questions with a partner.**

1 What kind of childhood _____ ?

2 What _____ before the age of three?

3 Which university _____ ?

4 What _____ during high school and college?

5 What else _____ as a student?

6 Where _____ after college?

7 What _____ working on in Chicago?

8 When _____ a national show?

A _What kind of childhood did Oprah Winfrey have?_
B _She had a difficult childhood._

3 Simple Past of *Be* and *There Was / There Were*

Grammar Presentation

The simple past of *be* and *There was / There were* describe people, places, and things in the past.	Oprah Winfrey **was** an intelligent child. **There were** millions of visitors to Oprah's website last month.

3.1 Simple Past of *Be*: Affirmative and Negative Statements

AFFIRMATIVE

Subject	*Was / Were*	
I He / She / It	**was**	at Stanford University.
You We They	**were**	

NEGATIVE

Subject	*Was / Were + Not*	
I He / She / It	**was not** **wasn't**	in Chicago.
You We They	**were not** **weren't**	

📊 Data from the Real World

Research shows that *wasn't* and *weren't* are not common in academic writing. Use *was not* and *were not* instead.

Use *wasn't* and *weren't* in conversation, where they are very common.

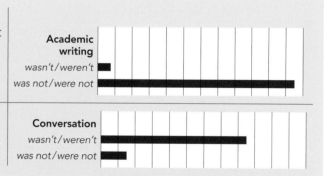

3.2 Simple Past of *Be*: Yes / No Questions and Short Answers

Was / Were	Subject	
Was	I he / she / it	popular?
Were	you we they	

Short Answers

Yes, I **was**. Yes, he / she / it **was**.	No, I **wasn't**. No, he / she / it **wasn't**.
Yes, you **were**. Yes, we **were**. Yes, they **were**.	No, you **weren't**. No, we **weren't**. No, they **weren't**.

3.3 Information Questions with Simple Past of *Be*

Wh- Word	*Was / Were*	Subject
Who **Where** **What** **How**	**was**	I? he / she / it?
	were	you? we? they?

Wh- Word	*Was*	
Who **What**	**was**	there at the beginning? next for the company?

3.4 *There Was / There Were*

There Was / Wasn't + Singular or Noncount Noun	*There Were / Weren't* + Plural Noun
There was a problem. **There wasn't any** software. **There was no** software.	**There were** some problems. **There weren't any** programs. **There were no** programs.

3.5 Using *There Was / There Were*

A Use *There was (not) / There were (not)* to talk about things that did or did not exist in the past.	Before Google, *there were other search engines.* *There was no software.*
📊 Research shows that *There was / were no* is more common than *There wasn't / weren't any.*	
B The form of *be* always agrees with the noun that follows it.	*There were other search engines.* *There ~~was~~ other search engines.*

Exercise 3.1 Statements

A Complete the lecture about Sarah Breedlove McWilliams Walker (1867–1919).
Use the affirmative or negative form of *was*, *were*, *there was*, and *there were*.

    Sarah Breedlove McWilliams Walker __*was*__ the
(1)
first American female self-made millionaire. However,
before she became a millionaire, life _____
(2)
easy for young Sarah. Her parents died, and Sarah

_____ an orphan at the age of seven. For a
(3)
time, Sarah and her sister _____ cotton
(4)
pickers. By the age of 14, Sarah _____ already
(5)
married. Her husband died two years later, and she went to
live with her brothers. They _____ barbers.
(6)
    In the 1890s, Sarah lost some of her hair. At that time,

_____ no good products in the stores for this
(7)
problem. In fact, _____ a lot of hair care
(8)
products for African Americans in those days. Sarah saw that

_____ an opportunity for a new business, so
(9)
she invented "Madam Walker's Wonderful Hair Grower."
The business grew. Soon _____ other
(10)
"Madam Walker" products, such as shampoos and
cosmetics. She _____ very successful and
(11)
eventually became a millionaire.

B Pair Work   Now listen to the lecture. It has some extra information about
Madam Walker. Write down three new things you hear. Then tell your partner.

1 _____

2 _____

3 _____

A *Her brothers were barbers in St. Louis.*

B *Right. And she worked for . . .*

Exercise 3.2 Questions with *Be* and Other Verbs

Pair Work Write the simple past questions. Then interview a classmate.
Ask for more information as you talk.

1 What / be / your first job   *What was your first job?* _____
2 be / it / a good job   _____
3 What / be / your co-workers like   _____
4 What / you / do there   _____
5 Why / you / leave   _____
6 What / be / your best job   _____
7 Why / you / like it   _____
8 Where / be / your worst job   _____

4 Avoid Common Mistakes ⚠

1 **Use the simple past, not the simple present, when you write about the past.**
     started
I start my first job in 2008.

2 **After *did not* or *didn't*, use the base form of the verb, not the past form.**
They didn't earned a lot of money.

3 **Put time expressions at the beginning or end of a statement, not between the subject and the verb, and not between the verb and the object.**
          yesterday   *Yesterday,*
I bought yesterday a computer.   OR   I bought yesterday a computer.

4 **Use *there were* with plural nouns. Use *there was* with singular or noncount nouns.**
   were   *was*
There was a lot of people. There were no information.

Editing Task

Find and correct nine more mistakes in the blog.

>   *moved*
> My family move from Mexico City to the United States in 2018. I went to Hamilton High School in Los Angeles. I did not knew anybody, and I did not had any friends here. I in 2009 met Jun. He became my first friend.
>
> We in 2012 graduated. I got a job at a nice restaurant, but I did not enjoyed my job. Jun drove
> 5 a taco truck, but he did not liked the food. I wanted to be my own boss, and I always liked food and cooking. Jun wanted his own business, too. Jun saw an opportunity. There was hungry office workers downtown at noon, but there weren't a nice place to eat. We bought a food truck and we start Food on the Move in 2014.

Simple Past, Time Clauses, *Used To*, and *Would*

Science and Society

1 Grammar in the Real World

A What is your favorite ice cream flavor? Read the article from a textbook. How is ice cream today different from ice cream in the past?

B Comprehension Check Circle the correct answer.

  1 Persians made a frozen dessert with **noodles / buffalo milk**.

  2 In ancient Rome, people mixed snow with **fruit / cream**.

  3 A duchess brought sorbet to **Italy / France**.

  4 British chemists invented ice cream that **lasted longer / had no air in it**.

C Notice Find the sentences in the article. Complete them with *after*, *before*, or *as soon as*.

  1 _____ refrigeration existed, people needed ice to make frozen desserts.

  2 _____ scientists found better processes for freezing things, ice cream became popular with all classes, rich and poor.

  3 _____ ice cream became more available, people began to buy it more often.

In each sentence, two events happen. Circle the event that happened first.

Ice Cream:
A **Food Revolution**

Science can have a great effect on society. Take ice cream, for example. Today, people all over the world, rich or poor, eat ice cream. **Before there were modern refrigerators**, however, ice cream was a luxury food.

The history of ice cream goes back to ancient times. In 400 BCE,[1]
5 Persians made a frozen dessert with noodles and fruit. There are early records of frozen milk and rice in China from around 200 BCE. In 618 CE, King Tang of Shang (China) ate frozen buffalo milk.

Before refrigeration existed, people needed ice to make frozen desserts. For example, in ancient Rome, people would go into the
10 mountains and collect snow. They would bring it to the city and mix the snow with fruit. This was later called "sorbet."

When an Italian duchess[2] moved to France, she brought sorbet and other frozen desserts with her. **After sorbet and ice cream became popular in France**, they spread to the rest of Europe. However, only the rich
15 ate them.

In the twentieth century, ice cream became easier to make and keep. **After scientists found better processes for freezing things**, ice cream became popular with all classes, rich and poor. Then, in the 1940s and
20 1950s, British chemists discovered a new way to make ice cream. They put air into it. This made the ice cream bigger and softer. Now, ice cream was less expensive. It lasted longer, too. **As soon as ice cream became more available**, people
25 began to buy it more often.

Today, almost anyone, rich or poor, can buy ice cream and keep it at home. Ice cream is a universal dessert, popular all over the world. Together, traditional ice cream makers and
30 scientists created a food revolution.

[1]**BCE:** before common era
[2]**duchess:** a woman of very high social rank in some European countries

2 Time Clauses and the Order of Past Events

Grammar Presentation

Time clauses can show the order of events in the past.	*After scientists developed better processes for freezing things, ice cream became popular with everyone.*

2.1 Time Clauses

A A time clause can come first in a sentence. When it comes first, use a comma after it.

A time clause can also come second in a sentence. No comma is needed.

┌────────── TIME CLAUSE ──────────┐ ┌── MAIN CLAUSE ──┐
After sorbet became popular in France, it spread to the rest of Europe.

┌────────── MAIN CLAUSE ──────────┐ ┌── TIME CLAUSE ──┐
Sorbet spread to the rest of Europe after it became popular in France.

B Use *after* to introduce the first event.

FIRST EVENT   SECOND EVENT
After an Italian duchess brought ice cream to France, it became popular.

SECOND EVENT   FIRST EVENT
Ice cream became popular after an Italian duchess brought it to France.

C Use *before* to introduce the second event.

SECOND EVENT   FIRST EVENT
Before there were freezers, people needed ice to make frozen desserts.

FIRST EVENT   SECOND EVENT
People needed ice to make frozen desserts before there were freezers.

D Use *when* to refer to the time that something started.

When scientists found new ways to make ice cream, it became cheaper.

Ice cream became cheaper when scientists found new ways to make it.

E Use *as soon as* to refer to something that happened right after or immediately after.

FIRST EVENT   SECOND EVENT
As soon as scientists found ways to freeze things, people began buying more ice cream.

(Scientists invented ways to freeze things. Soon after, people started buying ice cream more often.)

2.1 Time Clauses *(continued)*

F Use *until* to refer to things that continued up to a certain time.	*Until* people had refrigerators, it was difficult to keep food for a long time. (Up to the time when people got refrigerators, it was difficult to keep food for a long time.)

Grammar Application

Exercise 2.1 Time Clauses

Read the sentences about Ernest Hamwi, the possible inventor of the ice cream cone. Label the first event *1* and the second event *2*.

1 (Until Ernest Hamwi invented the ice cream cone), (most people ate ice cream in a dish.)

2 Hamwi was a waffle seller at the 1904 World's Fair when he invented the ice cream cone.

3 When an ice cream seller at the fair ran out of dishes, Hamwi rolled up a waffle.

4 The warm waffle turned hard when Hamwi filled it with ice cream.

5 As soon as they saw Hamwi's cones, all the other ice cream sellers started using them.

6 Before Hamwi started an ice cream cone business, he returned from the fair.

7 After Hamwi's story became popular, many people said that *they* invented the ice cream cone.

8 Another man, Italo Marchiony, invented an edible ice cream *cup* before Hamwi invented his cone.

Exercise 2.2 Time Words

Complete the sentences. Circle the correct answer.

1 (Before)/ After people drove cars, they rode horses.

2 **When/Until** the Internet became popular, people wrote letters and sent faxes.

3 **Before/After** the first men landed on the moon in 1969, U.S. astronauts made five more trips to the moon between 1969 and 1972.

4 **As soon as/Before** people used digital cameras, they took photographs using film.

5 Public transportation changed completely **until/when** the first airlines began to operate.

6 People did not understand the solar system **when/until** scientists invented telescopes.[1]

7 **Before/As soon as** telephones existed, communication was very slow.

8 **As soon as/Until** scientists developed medicines such as vaccines,[2] public health improved rapidly.

[1]**telescope:** a device you look through to make objects that are far away look bigger | [2]**vaccine:** a special substance that you take into your body to prevent disease and that has a weak or dead form of the disease-causing organism

Data from the Real World

We often answer information questions about time (e.g., *When . . . ?*, *What time . . . ?*, and *How long . . . ?*) with time clauses. In conversation, these answers do not usually contain a main clause.

A When did you start studying English?

B *After* I got my job at the museum.

A How long did you study at a community college?

B *Until* I got my degree.

A Listen to a radio interview with an inventor of a new printer. Match the interview questions with the answers.

1 When did you come to the United States? *d*

2 So, when did you get the idea for your invention? _____

3 And how long did you study at college? _____

4 When did you build your first printer? _____

5 And when did you start your printer company? _____

6 So, when did you get the money for your company? _____

7 And when did the company start making a profit? _____

a As soon as my first printer reached the stores.

b After I graduated from college.

c As soon as we got the money to start.

d After I graduated from high school.

e Until I got my degree.

f When I was a student in college.

g After I presented my idea to some banks and investors.

B Listen again and check your answers.

A Write sentences in the simple past about inventions and discoveries. Use an event in Column A, an event in Column B, and *after*, *before*, *when*, *until*, or *as soon as*.

A	B
1 TV / exist	a people / start to fly more
2 cheap air travel / become possible	b credit cards / become popular
3 everyone / have a cell phone	c families / listen to the radio together
4 people / pay for things with cash or checks	d millions of people / learn to drive
5 free education / be available	e roads / become safer
6 traffic lights / come into our cities	f people / buy food from small local stores
7 Ford / make the first mass-produced car	g people / make calls from pay phones
8 the first supermarket / open	h most people / not read or write

1 *Before TV existed, families listened to the radio together.*
2 _____
3 _____
4 _____
5 _____
6 _____
7 _____
8 _____

B Pair Work Compare your sentences with a partner. How many different ways are there to say the same thing?

A I wrote, "Before free education was available, most people did not read or write."
What did you write?

B I wrote, "Until free education was available, most people did not read or write."

C Over to You Think of three more sentences like the ones in B. Use your own ideas and the words *after*, *before*, *when*, *until*, or *as soon as*. Share your sentences with a partner.

Before there were microwave ovens, it took a long time to heat up food.

3 Past with *Used To* and *Would*

Grammar Presentation

Used to and *would* describe repeated past actions, habits, and situations.	Before we had the Internet, we used to go to the library a lot. Before there was refrigeration, people would use ice to keep food cool.

3.1 Statements with *Used To*

AFFIRMATIVE

Subject	Used To	Base Form of Verb	
I You He / She / It We They	used to	listen	to the radio.

NEGATIVE

Subject	Did + Not	Use To	Base Form of Verb	
I You He / She / It We They	did not didn't	use to	watch	TV.

3.2 Yes/No Questions and Short Answers with *Use To*

Did	Subject	*Use To*	Base Form of Verb	
Did	I you he/she/it we they	use to	keep	food cool with ice?

Short Answers			
Yes, I **did**.	No, I **didn't**.
Yes, you **did**.	No, you **didn't**.
Yes, he/she/it **did**.	No, he/she/it **didn't**.
Yes, we **did**.	No, we **didn't**.
Yes, they **did**.	No, they **didn't**.

3.3 Information Questions with *Used To*

Wh- Word	*Did*	Subject	*Use To*	Base Form of Verb	
When Why Where How often	did	I you he/she/it we they	use to	keep	food cool with ice?

Wh- Word	*Used To*	Base Form of Verb	
Who	used to	keep	food cool with ice?

3.4 Statements with *Would*

AFFIRMATIVE

	Subject	*Would*	Base Form of Verb	
In the past,	I you he/she/it we they	would	build	a fire to heat water.

3.4 Statements with *Would (continued)*

NEGATIVE

	Subject	*Would + Not*	Base Form of Verb	
In the past,	I you he/she/it we they	**would not** **wouldn't**	**bathe**	often.

Data from the Real World

Research shows that statements about the past with *wouldn't* are not very common. Instead, you can use the negative form of the simple past.

In the past, they didn't bathe often.

3.5 Information Questions with *Would*

Time Context	*Wh-* Word	*Would*	Subject	Base Form of Verb	
In the past,	**how** **where**	**would**	I you he/she/it we they	**heat**	the water?

Time Context	*Wh-* Word	*Would*	Base Form of Verb	
In the past,	**who**	**would**	**heat**	the water?

Data from the Real World

Research shows that *Yes/No* questions with *would* are very rare. Instead, you can use *Yes/No* questions with the simple past.

In the past, did you always get information from the library?

3.6 Using *Used To*

A You can use *used to* for actions that happened regularly in the past. These actions do not happen now.	*My grandmother used to wash clothes by hand.*
B You can use *used to* for states that were true in the past. These states are not true anymore.	*Air travel used to be very expensive. It is less expensive now.*

3.6 Using *Used To* (continued)

C Do not use *used to* for things that happened only once.	*In the 1940s, chemists discovered a new way to make ice cream.* *In the 1940s, chemists* ~~used to discover~~ *a new way to make ice cream.*

3.7 Using *Would*

A You can use *would* for actions that happened regularly in the past.	*When my grandparents were children, they would listen to the radio every night.*
B Before you use *would*, first make the past time clear. Use a time expression, a simple past verb, or *used to*.	*In the old days, people would wash clothes by hand. They would hang them outside to dry.* *It used to be a day or more before the clothes would dry.*
C With stative verbs, use *used to*, not *would*, to talk about the past. Some examples of stative verbs are *be, love, know,* and *want*.	*We used to love to eat ice cream.* *We* ~~would love~~ *to eat ice cream.* *Ice cream used to be a luxury.* *Ice cream* ~~would be~~ *a luxury.*
D Do not use *would* to talk about things that happened only once.	*Last week, Joe made green tea ice cream at home.* *Last week, Joe* ~~would make~~ *green tea ice cream at home.*
E Use full forms in writing. Use contractions in speaking.	*In writing: We would sing songs or play games in the evening.* *In speaking: We'd go to bed early.*

Grammar Application

A Complete the article. Use the correct form of *use to* or *used to* and the verbs in parentheses.

🏠   💬   🔄   ☰   ✉

The Wisdom of Our Grandparents

College Weekly spoke to Joseph Green, an 87-year-old retired teacher, about the old days.

College Weekly   What __*did*__ people __*use to do*__ (do) for
                      (1)   (1)
                   fun before there was television?

Joseph Green   Well, we _____
                                   (2)
                   (listen) to the radio in the evening.

CW   How _____ you _____ (spend)
                 (3)   (3)
       your free time?

JG   Well, because there was no television, we
       _____ (play) games a lot.
                       (4)

CW   Who _____ (play) with you?
                     (5)

JG   My brothers.

CW   It seems like people _____ (have) more free time in
                                       (6)
       those days . . .

JG   Not really. In fact, people _____ (not have) a lot of free
                                      (7)
       time. For example, my parents _____ (work) six days
                                    (8)
       a week.

CW   What was school like?

JG   We _____ (write) with pencils and paper. And when I was
                   (9)
       in college, we _____ (take) notes in real notebooks, not
                         (10)
       on notebook computers!

CW   _____ you _____ (type) your papers?
       (11)   (11)

JG   No, I didn't. Typewriters were too expensive. I _____
                                                       (12)
       (write) all my papers in ink on lined paper. I _____ (get)
                                              (13)
       so frustrated if I made a mistake because I had to start all over again!

B Write three affirmative sentences and one negative sentence about Mr. Green's life before computers and TV. Compare your sentences with a partner.

1 *He used to play games in the evenings.*

2 _____

3 _____

4 _____

5 _____

Complete the article about life before electricity. Use *used to* or *would* and the verbs in parentheses, or use the simple past form of the verbs. Sometimes more than one answer is correct.

Voltaic battery

Alessandro Volta ___*invented*___ (invent) the first battery in 1800.
(1)

How ___*did*___ people ___*use to live*___ (live) in the days before electricity?
(2)   (2)

Most people _____ (burn) oil lamps or candles for light.
(3)

When it got cold, they _____ (make) open fires to keep
(4)

warm. People _____ (not travel) long distances. Most people
(5)

only _____ (visit) neighbors or nearby relatives.
(6)

Before Volta's battery, many scientists _____ (not think)
(7)

that electricity was useful. And in the early days of electricity, some people

_____ (think) it was dangerous. They _____ (be) afraid of
(8)   (9)

it. Some people even _____ (believe) that electricity had a bad effect on
(10)

society. They _____ (prefer) the simple life of the past. Soon, however,
(11)

electricity _____ (make) the world brighter, faster, and more comfortable.
(12)

Electricity in homes and industry _____ (change) the world in many ways.
(13)

A Imagine that you can talk to a person who lived before there was electricity. Use the words to make questions with *would*. Then add two questions of your own with *would*.

1 how / heat / your house?   ___*Before electricity, how would you heat your house?*___

2 how / light / your house?   _____

3 how / clean / your house?   _____

4 what / do / in the evenings?   _____

5 what / play / with?   _____

6 how / get / to work or school?   _____

7 _____

8 _____

B Over to You Now write answers with *would* to the questions. Use your imagination. When you finish, compare your answers with a partner.

We would build a fire to heat our house.

C Group Work Discuss how people used to live before the following inventions changed society. Was life better or worse? Was it safer or more dangerous? In what ways?

- computers
- cold medicine
- cars
- microwave ovens
- airplanes
- TV

A *Before computers existed, students used to write everything down with a pencil or pen.*

B *And they would copy everything again when they revised their papers.*

C *Student life was hard!*

4 Avoid Common Mistakes ⚠

1 **Use a subject in the time clause.**

    they
Before∧invented electricity, people used candles.

2 **Do not forget the *-d* in *used to* in affirmative statements.**

    used
When I was living in New York, I ~~use~~ to play in a rock band.

3 **Use *use to* (without *-d*) in negative statements and in questions with *did*.**

    use
How did you ~~used~~ to heat your home?

Editing Task

Find and correct six more mistakes in this article from a magazine.

A New Invention

        use
How did people ~~used~~ to wash dishes? People did not used to have dishwashers before invented electricity, so they would wash dishes by hand. But did men and women used to share the dishwashing equally? Not usually. Mostly it was women who did it. Before there was electricity, women use to heat up water on the stove and use it for washing dishes. It took hours and hours, and dishes often broke
5 or chipped.

      In 1886, one woman finally got tired of washing dishes by hand. "If nobody else is going to invent a dishwashing machine," she said, "I'll do it myself." Her name was Josephine Cochrane, a housewife and engineer's daughter who was tired of washing – and sometimes breaking – her favorite dishes after dinner parties. Cochrane worked and worked on her invention until 1893 when finally created a
10 machine that washed dishes. She showed the machine at the World's Fair that year. People operated it by hand, so it was still hard work. After the fair ended, she started a company to make the machines. When first tried to sell dishwashers, only restaurants and hotels bought them from her. However, after electricity became more easily available, her company built electric dishwashers for people to use in their homes. Today, homes around the world have electric dishwashers.

Memorable Events

1 Grammar in the Real World

A What were you doing on August 21, 2017? Read the blog. What were the bloggers doing?

B Comprehension Check **Answer the questions.**

1 What were people buying at the store in August 2017?

2 Where was Emily staying when the eclipse happened?

3 What were Steve and his friends doing when the moon blocked the sun?

4 How was Bao feeling when the eclipse happened?

C Notice **Find the sentences in the blog. Circle the correct words.**

1 In 2017, I studied / was studying at Clemson University in Greenville, South Carolina.

2 The total eclipse was at 1:17 p.m. in St Louis, but at 10:30 a.m., we got / were getting ready!

3 When the eclipse happened, I packed / was packing books into boxes.

Do the sentences show an action that was in progress in the past or an action that happened only one time in the past?

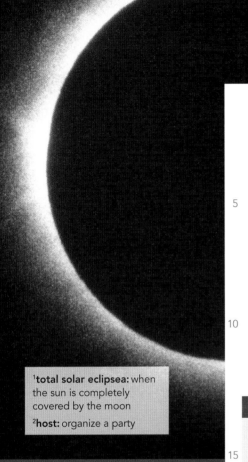

¹**total solar eclipsea:** when the sun is completely covered by the moon

²**host:** organize a party

The Total **Solar Eclipse**¹ – What were you doing?

Hey! Do any of our readers remember the solar eclipse in August 2017? Wasn't it awesome? I remember everyone **was running** to the store to buy special eclipse glasses to protect their eyes. It felt like the whole of North America **was waiting** for that magical moment when
5 the moon passed in front of the sun. Eclipse watchers from Oregon to South Carolina **were preparing** to experience the few short minutes when the moon completely blocked the sun's light. Families **were organizing** eclipse parties, people **were traveling** miles to get the best view, and school children **were doing** all kinds of eclipse projects.

10 **Were you waiting** outside that day? I was! Most people **weren't working**. They were too busy having fun! So, what **were *you doing*** and where were you **when the eclipse happened**?

3 Responses	leave a comment

Emily: I remember it! I **was staying** with my friends in Missouri **when
15 the eclipse happened**. It was fantastic! We **were standing** in the yard and we **were wearing** our special NASA eclipse glasses. My friend Nathan **was playing** the live NASA event on a big computer screen, too. Oh, yeah, and I remember the total eclipse was at 1:17 p.m. in St Louis, but at 10:30 a.m., we **were getting** ready!

20 **Steve:** In 2017, I **was studying** at Clemson University in Greenville, South Carolina so I was lucky! Greenville was right on the path of the eclipse. I **was hosting**² an eclipse party that day. I had over 50 guests. All of us **were taking** pictures **when the moon blocked the sun**. It was amazing.

25 **Bao:** Unfortunately, I **was working** on August 21, so I **wasn't having** fun at all! I had a vacation job in a factory. When the eclipse happened, I **was packing** books into boxes. I remember my friend Jorge called me. He and my brother **were watching** the eclipse just down the block from my apartment. **While I was talking** to Jorge, I **felt** sad because I
30 was alone.

2 Past Progressive

Grammar Presentation

The past progressive describes actions that were in progress at a time in the past.	*On August 21, we were watching the eclipse.*

AFFIRMATIVE

Subject	Was / Were	Verb + -ing	
I He / She / It	**was**	**watching**	the eclipse.
You We They	**were**		

NEGATIVE

Subject	Was/Were + Not	Verb + -ing	
I He / She / It	**was not** **wasn't**	**working**	that day.
You We They	**were not** **weren't**		

Was/Were	Subject	Verb + -ing	
Was	I he / she / it	**watching**	the eclipse?
Were	you we they		

Short Answers

Yes, I **was**. Yes, he/she/it **was**.	No, I **wasn't**. No, he/she/it **wasn't**.
Yes, you **were**. Yes, we **were**. Yes, they **were**.	No, you **weren't**. No, we **weren't**. No, they **weren't**.

2.3 Information Questions

Wh- Word	Was/Were	Subject	Verb + -ing
What **How**	**was**	I he/she/it	**doing?**
	were	you we they	

Wh- Word	Was/Were	Verb + -ing
Who **What**	**was**	**hosting** a party? **happening** at 1:17 p.m.?

2.4 Using Past Progressive

A Use the past progressive to talk about events in progress at a time in the past.	They *were watching* the eclipse at lunchtime.
B Use time expressions with *in, at, on*, and *last* to talk about events in progress at specific times in the past.	*In 2017*, I was studying in Greenville. We were traveling a lot *in August*. I was hosting a party *at 12:00*. He wasn't working *on New Year's Eve*. She wasn't working *on August 21*. They weren't watching TV *last night*.

📊 Data from the Real World

Research shows that these are the verbs most frequently used with the past progressive in formal and informal writing and speaking. The verbs in **bold** are very frequent.

say	**wonder**	try	come	take	make
think	**ask**	look	work	watch	drive
talk	do	get	sit	read	wear

Exercise 2.1 Statements and Questions

A Complete the interview about New Year's Eve activities. Use the words in parentheses with the past progressive.

New Year's Eve Roundup

The *Morning Sun* asked three people:

"What were you doing last New Year's Eve?"

Sandy L., 25, Personal Trainer

Q What were _____**were**_____ you _____**doing**_____ (do) last New Year's Eve?
(1)   (1)

A I was dancing _____**was dancing**_____ (dance) and I __was having__ (have) a
(2)   (3)
great time.

Q Who __were__ you __celebrating__ (celebrate) with?
(4)   (4)

A My best friends and I __celebrated__ (celebrate) New Year's Eve at a party.
(5)

Amir A., 20, Salesperson

Q What __were__ you __doing__ (do) last New Year's Eve?
(6)   (6)

A I __wasn't having__ (not have) fun! I __was sleeping__ (sleep) last New Year's Eve!
(7)   (8)

Q Why __were__ you __sleeping__ (sleep)?
(9)   (9)

A I was tired! At that time, I __was working__ (work) for several hours a day at a
(10)
department store. The store __were having__ (have) a big sale on December 31.
(11)

Roberto R., 34, Computer Technician

Q __Were__ you __doing__ (do) anything fun last New Year's Eve?
(12)   (12)

A Not really. I __was driving__ (drive) from New York to Chicago. My wife and
(13)
I __was moving__ (move) to Chicago. We __started__ (start) new jobs there.
(14)   (15)

Q That's too bad. Who __were driving__ (drive)?
(16)

A I __was__ (be). But we __weren't feeling__ (not feel) bad. In fact, we
(17)   (18)
__were feeling__ (feel) very good about our new life in Chicago.
(19)

B Group Work Talk in groups about what you were doing last New Year's Eve.
Ask *Yes/No* and information questions to get as many details as you can.

Exercise 2.2 Time Expressions

A Over to You **Complete the questions. Circle the correct words. Then answer the questions about yourself.**

1 What were you doing (last)/ in year?
   I was going to school and working part-time.

2 Where were you living **at / in** 2009?

3 What were you doing **on / in** the Fourth of July?

4 What were you doing **at / on** 9:00 a.m. yesterday?

5 Were you studying English **in / last** month?

6 Was your family living in the United States **on / in** 2000?

7 Who were you living with **at / in** the winter of 2010?

8 Were you working **at / on** 6:00 p.m. yesterday?

B Pair Work **Compare the words you circled with a partner. Then discuss your answers to the questions.**

Exercise 2.3 More Statements and Questions

A Listen to people talking about the most important time in their lives. When was the day or time? What were they doing? How were they feeling? Complete the chart.

Name	Day/Time	What he or she was doing	What he or she was feeling or thinking
1 Wei	April 25, 2005	1 2	1 2
2 Nick		1 *getting his driver's license*	1
3 Ana	*the spring of 1999*	1 2	1 *thinking about her family* 2

B Pair Work **Now take turns telling your partner about the people in A.**

A *On April 25, 2005, Wei was . . .*
B *On . . . , Nick was getting his driver's license. He was feeling . . .*

C Over to You **What was an important day or time in your life? What were you doing? What were you thinking or feeling? Tell your partner.**

An important day in my life was in July 2008, the first day of my new job. I was starting a new career, and I was feeling very . . .

3 Using *When* and *While* with Past Progressive

Grammar Presentation

Time clauses with *when* and *while* and the past progressive show something that was in progress; the main clause shows that something happened.	The eclipse happened while I was packing books into boxes. While I was sitting at my desk, I got only one call.

3.1 Past Progressive or Simple Past?

A Use the past progressive for an action in progress in the past.	On the day of the earthquake, we were living in San Francisco.
B Use the simple past for an action that happened one time and was completed.	On the day of the earthquake, the power went out.

3.2 Using Past Progressive with Simple Past with Time Clauses

A Time clauses with *when* or *while* show when events happened.	MAIN CLAUSE TIME CLAUSE The power went out while we were riding the elevator. MAIN CLAUSE TIME CLAUSE We were riding the elevator when the power went out.
B Use *when* or *while* in a past progressive time clause to show an event that was in progress when a second event happened. Use the simple past in the main clause.	MAIN CLAUSE TIME CLAUSE SECOND EVENT EVENT IN PROGRESS The power went out when/while we were riding the elevator. TIME CLAUSE MAIN CLAUSE EVENT IN PROGRESS SECOND EVENT When/While we were riding the elevator, the power went out.
C Use *when*, but not *while*, in a simple past time clause to show an event that happened while an event was already in progress. Use the past progressive in the main clause.	MAIN CLAUSE TIME CLAUSE EVENT IN PROGRESS SECOND EVENT We were riding the elevator when the power went out. TIME CLAUSE MAIN CLAUSE SECOND EVENT EVENT IN PROGRESS When the power went out, we were riding the elevator.
D Time clauses usually come second. When they come first, remember to use a comma. Do not use a period after a time clause. It is not a complete sentence.	We were riding the elevator when the power went out. When the power went out, we were riding the elevator. ~~When the power went out.~~ We were riding the elevator.

3.2 Using Past Progressive with Simple Past with Time Clauses *(continued)*

E You can also use time clauses in questions. Notice that the word order does not change.

SUBJECT   VERB

Were you having fun when the eclipse happened?

What was he doing when the earthquake hit?

Where were you sitting when the power went out?

Grammar Application

Exercise 3.1 Past Progressive or Simple Past?

Complete the paragraph about a memorable event. Circle the correct verb.

My most memorable experience ___**was** / was being___ the solar eclipse of 2009. In the
(1)

summer of 2009, I ___traveled / **was traveling**___ around
(2)

Turkey. One day when I ___read / **was reading**___ the
(3)

newspaper, I ___**saw** / was seeing___ an article about the
(4)

eclipse. I ___**decided** / was deciding___ to go to the town
(5)

of Amasya because the article ___**said** / was saying___ it
(6)

was the best place to see it. I ___**arrived** / was arriving___ in town on the day of the
(7)

eclipse. I ___walked / **was walking**___ down the street when I ___**saw** / was seeing___
(8)   (9)

a group of people in the town square. They ___waited / **were waiting**___ for the
(10)

eclipse to start. I ___**decided** / was deciding___ to join them. Then the eclipse
(11)

___**started** / was starting___ at around 2:00 in the afternoon. The shadow of the
(12)

moon moved across the sun, and the sky started to get dark. By 3:00, the sun was

completely covered. Everyone was quiet and amazed. Unfortunately, while the eclipse

___happened / **was happening**___ , my cell phone rang! I was so embarrassed!
(13)

Exercise 3.2 Time Clauses

Correct the punctuation mistakes in these sentences.

1 When the power went out, I was cooking a big dinner.
2 When the eclipse happened Bao was working in a factory.
3 When the power went out we were riding home on the subway.
4 While we were standing in a doorway the ground started to shake.
5 When the earthquake hit she was driving across the bridge.
6 Asha was standing in the town square. When the sky got dark.
7 Rob was shopping. When the lights went out.
8 While we were working. The hurricane hit.

A Complete the reader stories. Use the past progressive or simple past form of the verbs in parentheses.

Reader Stories: A Day I Will Never Forget

I will never forget the 1989 San Francisco earthquake.

My wife and I ___*were eating*___ (eat) at a restaurant
(1)
when the earthquake _____ (hit).
(2)
We _____ (wait) for our food when the waiter
(3)
_____ (shout), "It's a big one!
(4)
Get under the table!" We _____ (stay) under
(5)
the table and _____ (eat) our dinner while the ground _____ (shake).
(6)   (7)

– Samir N., Oakland, California

I will never forget Hurricane Newton. It wasn't dangerous,
but it was very exciting. I _____ (walk)
(8)
on the beach when a lifeguard _____
(9)
(tell) me to go home. When I _____
(10)
(get) home, my mother _____ (wait)
(11)
for me. She _____ (make) dinner when
(12)
the electricity _____ (go) out.
(13)
We _____ (stay) inside and _____ (play) games by candlelight while
(14)   (15)
the storm _____ (crash) all around us.
(16)

– Luisa F., Acapulco, Mexico

B Use the words to write questions about the stories in A. Use the past progressive.

For Samir N.

1 What/do/? ___*What was Samir doing when the earthquake hit?*___

2 Where/eat/? _____

3 What/eat/? _____

For Luisa F.

4 What/do/? _____

5 Where/walk/? _____

6 What/mother/do/? _____

C Group Work Talk about a memorable event in your life. What happened? What were you doing? Ask and answer questions about the event. Use information questions.

A *My most memorable experience was the snowstorm of 2010.*
B *What were you doing when it started snowing?*
A *When it started snowing, I was . . .*
C *Then what did you do?*

4 Avoid Common Mistakes ⚠

1 **Use the correct form of *be* in the past progressive.**
    were
They ~~was~~ watching fireworks on New Year's Eve.

2 **Use the correct word order in information questions in the past progressive.**
    were the people
Where ~~the people were~~ standing?

3 **Use the past progressive for an event in progress.**
    went   *were riding*
The power ~~was going~~ out while they ~~rode~~ the elevator.

4 **A time clause by itself is not a complete sentence.**
We stayed in the car while the ground was shaking.
We stayed in the car. ~~While the ground was shaking.~~

5 **If the time clause comes first in a sentence, use a comma.**
While they were looking at the map ⌄ they found their hotel.

Editing Task

Find and correct nine more mistakes in this excerpt of an interview with some people who remember the moon landing in 1969.

                    were you
Interviewer Where ~~you were~~ when *Apollo 11* landed on the moon?

Maria Well, in the summer of 1969 I was nine. I was living in Mexico. On July 20, I was playing on
5   the beach with some friends. My parents was listening to the radio. When the speaker was announcing the landing.

Interviewer What you were doing when the astronauts landed on the moon?

10   **Tom** At that time, my wife and I moved from Chicago to San Diego. To save money, we stayed in campgrounds every night. We listened to the car radio at our campsite when the astronauts stepped on the moon. That night, while we was lying on the ground we looked up at the moon. We were being amazed!

Count and Noncount Nouns

1 Grammar in the Real World

A What information about yourself do you want to keep private? Read the article from a website. What are some ways you can protect your personal information?

B Comprehension Check Match the kind of ID theft with the way to avoid it.

ID thieves . . .

1 take information from your garbage. _____

2 steal your credit card number online. _____

3 "phish" for information. _____

But you can . . .

a only pay on secure websites.

b not respond to an unsolicited e-mail.

c shred your bills before you throw them away.

C Notice Find the sentences in the article and complete them with *a* or *an*. If no word goes in the blank, write ✗.

1 Identity theft is the act of using someone's personal information without

_____✗_____ permission.

2 ID thieves go through your garbage and look for _____ papers.

3 They "phish" for _____ information.

4 Phishing is sending _____ e-mail that asks you for your personal information.

5 The e-mail looks like it is from _____ bank.

Which of the nouns are things you can count? Which are things you cannot count? Which noun is plural?

IDENTITY THEFT

Keep your identity private! Here are some facts about identity (ID) theft.

What Is Identity Theft?

Identity theft is the act of using someone's personal **information** without **permission**. ID thieves use the **information** to buy things. They also use it to get

5   credit cards or to open other types of accounts. Personal **information** includes your name and address. It also includes your Social Security number or credit card numbers. You can lose **money** because of ID theft. ID theft also causes **damage** to your reputation. Sometimes, people cannot get **work** or loans for school because of ID theft.

10 ## How Do Thieves Steal Your Identity?

■ ID thieves go through your garbage and look for papers with **information** about you, such as bills.

■ They steal your credit card number when you are buying something. This can happen with online shopping or in stores.

15 ■ They "phish" for **information**. Phishing is sending an e-mail that asks for your personal **information**. The e-mail looks like it is from a bank or credit card company. It often asks you to go to a website and give your personal **information**.

How Can You Avoid ID Theft?

shred: cut into very small pieces
secure: safe
unsolicited: not asked for

20 ■ Shred[1] bills and other documents that have personal **information** before you throw them away.

■ If you shop online, only shop at well-known shopping sites. Only pay on secure[2] Web pages. URLs on secure pages begin with "https." (The s means "secure.")

■ Never answer an unsolicited[3] e-mail. This is especially true if

25   the e-mail looks like it is from a bank or a credit card company.

Follow this advice, and you can protect yourself from ID theft.

2 Count Nouns and Noncount Nouns

Grammar Presentation

Nouns are the names of people, places, and things. You can count most nouns (*an e-mail, three e-mails*); you cannot count certain nouns (*information, money*).

A *website* gave us *information* about ID theft.

2.1 Count Nouns

Count nouns refer to things you can count with numbers. They have a plural form.

I do not have a credit card *account*.
An ID thief opened two *accounts* in my name.
The *bank* on First Street is closed.
There are three *banks* on Oak Street.

2.2 Noncount Nouns

Noncount nouns refer to things you *cannot* count with numbers. They have only one form.

ID theft causes *damage* to your reputation.
The computer records how much *money* you spend.
I need some *advice*.

2.3 Using Count Nouns

A Singular count nouns always have a determiner before them. Determiners are words like *a, an, the, that, this, my,* or *our*.

I have *a brother*.
I have ~~brother~~.
This computer is fast.
~~Computer~~ is fast.

B You can use plural count nouns with or without a determiner. However, do not use *a* or *an* with plural nouns.

Computers are not very expensive nowadays.
These computers are not very expensive.
Credit *cards* are convenient.
I can't find *my* credit *cards*.
I can't find ~~a credit cards~~.

2.4 Using Noncount Nouns

A Do not use plural forms like *-s* with noncount nouns.	*They gave us information about ID theft.* *They gave us ~~informations~~ about ID theft.*
B Do not use numbers with noncount nouns.	*She gave me advice about using my credit card.* *She gave me ~~two advices~~.*
C Do not use *a / an* with noncount nouns.	*Because of ID theft, he can't get work.* *Because of ID theft, he can't get ~~a work~~.*
D You can use other determiners (*my, some, this,* etc.) with noncount nouns.	*They found some information on the Internet.* *Her advice was useful.*
E Use a singular verb form with noncount nouns.	*Safety is important to everyone.* *There was information about ID theft online.*
F Some noncount nouns also have a countable meaning. **Noncount Noun** / **Count Noun** coffee / coffees experience / experiences paper / papers	*Coffee is delicious. (coffee as a drink)* *We ordered two coffees. (two cups or orders of coffee)* *They hired someone with experience. (knowledge about a job)* *He has had a lot of interesting experiences. (things that he did or that happened to him)* *She needed some paper to print on. (material for writing or printing on)* *She threw away some important papers. (individual documents)*

📊 Data from the Real World

Some common noncount nouns in speaking and writing are:

advice	equipment	information	music	research	stuff
bread	evidence	knowledge	news	rice	traffic
cash	fun	luck	permission	safety	water
coffee	furniture	milk	progress	security	weather
damage	health	money	publicity	software	work

Exercise 2.1 Count or Noncount?

A Complete the chart. Check (✓) *Count* or *Noncount*. Then write the plural form of the count nouns.

Noun	Count	Noncount	Plural Form
1 passport	✓		*passports*
2 document			
3 information			
4 research			
5 equipment			
6 computer			
7 software			
8 credit card			
9 identity			
10 safety			
11 privacy			
12 e-mail			

B Complete the article. Where needed, write *-s*, *-es*, or *-ies* to make nouns plural. Write ✗ if a plural form is not needed.

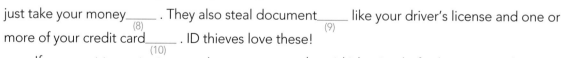

ID thieves use other people's identity _**ies**_ without their (1)
permission _**✗**_ . Some ID thieves look in the garbage for (2)
information_____ about you. Others use software_____ and (3) (4)
high-tech equipment_____ to steal your identity. (This is why Internet (5)
security_____ is so important on home computer_____ today.) In (6) (7)
addition, some ID thieves just steal your bag. These thieves do not
just take your money_____ . They also steal document_____ like your driver's license and one or (8) (9)
more of your credit card_____ . ID thieves love these! (10)

If you want to protect your privacy_____ and avoid identity theft, do not carry these (11)
things in your wallet, pocket, or purse:

- Your Social Security card or number.
- Your passport. If someone steals this, they could use it to commit a serious crime.
  These criminals threaten everyone's safety_____ . (12)
- Your computer, e-mail, and other password_____ . A lot of people keep this (13)
  information in their wallets, but it is a bad idea!
- Your birth certificate. With a little research_____ about you, a thief can use your birth (14)
  certificate to get a driver's license, credit cards, and even bank loans.

C Pair Work Think about an ID card you have (for example, your student ID card or your driver's license), and discuss it with your partner. When do you use this card? What kind of information does it have about you? How easy is it to steal or copy the information on it?

Exercise 2.2 Count and Noncount Meanings

Complete the sentences. Use the correct form of the nouns in the box. Then write C if the noun is a count noun or NC if it is a noncount noun.

crime	experience	life	paper

1 Marc had a bad ____*experience*____ with ID theft. It damaged his reputation.   _C_

2 Now he can't get a job, even though he has a lot of _____ in his field.   ____

3 How did it happen? There were _____ in Marc's garbage that had a lot of personal details about him.   ____

4 In addition, he put his passwords down on _____ instead of memorizing them.   ____

5 Marc is not alone – there is a lot of Internet _____ nowadays.   ____

6 Some _____ affect us financially, but ID theft can hurt us emotionally, too.   ____

7 _____ is difficult for Marc right now.   ____

8 We all have difficult times in our _____ , but we can learn from our mistakes.   ____

Exercise 2.3 More Count Nouns

A Write these count nouns in the correct categories.

backpacks	CDs	jeans	soccer balls	sweaters
basketballs	computer games	movies	sofas	tables
briefcases	~~desks~~	shirts	suitcases	tennis rackets

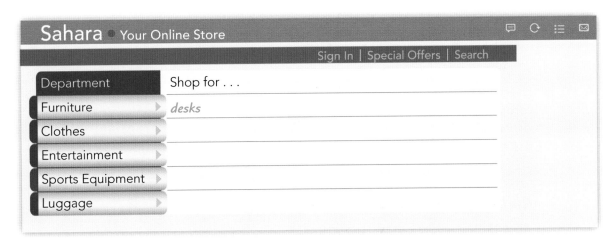

Sahara ● Your Online Store

Sign In | Special Offers | Search

Department   Shop for . . .

Furniture ▶ *desks*

Clothes ▶

Entertainment ▶

Sports Equipment ▶

Luggage ▶

B Pair Work Now ask and answer questions with a partner about where things are in the store.

A *Where do you shop for sofas?*

B *You shop for sofas in the furniture department.*

Exercise 2.4 Common Noncount Nouns

A Complete the conversation about full-body scanners (machines that show what is on a person's body) with the correct form of the words in the box.

airport	fun	person	publicity	traveler
evidence	news	progress	traffic	

A There was a report on the _____news_____ last night about
(1)
those full-body scanners at _____ . People were
(2)
complaining about them. Do you know anything about them?

B Not much, but there's a lot of _____ about them
(3)
these days in the media. I know some people are worried about
the health issues. I mean, is the technology safe?

A Well, so far, there's no _____ that body scanners
(4)
are dangerous. There's no real proof. In fact, I was reading
somewhere that they're pretty safe.

B Hmm. Maybe they're better than what we had before. I guess
we're making _____ in keeping airports safe, but
(5)
what about the privacy issues?

A Right! Scanners can give some pretty personal information about _____ .
(6)
They're like an X-ray. They can show exactly what's on your body.

B And there are millions of _____ these days! With all the _____
(7)   (8)
at airports nowadays, security is taking a lot longer.

A Yeah. I used to like going to the airport, but I guess you aren't supposed to have
_____ at the airport nowadays!
(9)

B Group Work Do you think body scanners are a good idea or a bad idea? Use these words to give your opinion.

Body scanners are good for . . .	security	convenience
Body scanners are bad for . . .	safety	personal information
I worry about . . .	privacy	my health
. . . is important to me.	crime	the government

I think they're a good idea. I worry about privacy, but safety is important to me.

3 Noncount Nouns: Determiners and Measurement Words

Grammar Presentation

You can use certain determiners and measurement words with noncount nouns.	Can you give me *some advice* about spyware programs? She told me two interesting *pieces of news*.

3.1 Noncount Nouns with Determiners

A Use *a lot of*, *some*, and *a little* with noncount nouns in affirmative statements.	There was *a lot of milk* in the refrigerator. I have *some* important *information* for you. Could I have *a little cream* in my coffee, please?
B Use *much*, *a lot of*, and *any* with noncount nouns in questions.	Was there *much furniture* in the apartment? Is there *a lot of traffic* at 5:00 p.m.? Are you making *any progress* with your English these days?
C Use *some* and *a little* for questions that are offers and requests.	Would you like *some tea*? Would you like *a little sugar* in your coffee?
D Use *not much*, *not a lot*, and *not any* with noncount nouns in negative statements.	There's *not much juice* left in your glass. She does*n't* earn *a lot of money* in her present job. We did*n't* do *any work* yesterday.
E Do not use *much* or *a little* with count nouns.	We don't have *much time* left. We don't have ~~much hours~~ left. There's *a little coffee* in the cup. There's ~~a little cups~~ on the table.

3.1 Noncount Nouns with Determiners *(continued)*

F Do not use *many* or *a few* with noncount nouns.	*There is not much news today.* *There is ~~not many news~~ today.* *I sold some furniture that I didn't need.* *I sold ~~a few furniture~~.*
G You can use *a lot of*, *some*, and *any* with both count and noncount nouns.	*There is a lot of Internet crime nowadays.* *They caught a lot of ID thieves last year.* *There's some new furniture at the apartment.* *We bought some new chairs.* *We don't have any new equipment.* *There aren't any new computers at the school.*

3.2 *Too Many / Much* and *Enough*

A Use *too many* with count nouns and *too much* with noncount nouns to say "more than you want."	*Too many people came to the lecture on Internet privacy. Some of them had to stand.* *There is too much information about us on databases. It's scary!*
B Use *enough* with count and noncount nouns to say "the amount you need."	*We have enough eggs in the refrigerator.* *We have enough information on the problem.* *We don't have enough potatoes.* *We don't have enough milk. We need to buy some.*

3.3 Noncount Nouns with Measurement Words

A Containers					**Portions**	
a **box** of	cereal pasta		a **bottle** of	water juice	a **piece** of	cake bread pie candy
a **package** of	sugar rice coffee		a **glass** of	milk juice water	a **slice** of	pizza bread cake cheese turkey
a **can** of	soup tuna		a **carton** of	milk juice	a **scoop** of	ice cream sorbet

3.3 Noncount Nouns with Measurement Words *(continued)*

Measurements		
a **gallon** of	milk gas	
a **pound** of	butter sugar coffee meat	
a **cup** of	sugar milk coffee tea	

Shapes		
a **bar** of	soap chocolate	
a **loaf** of	bread	
a **sheet** of	paper	
a **tube** of	toothpaste	

B You can also use *piece* with non-food items, such as *advice, information, news, music, equipment, evidence, furniture, tape,* and *research.*

He told us an interesting piece of news.
They gave us a helpful piece of advice.

C Measurement words can be singular or plural.

I bought a pound of butter and three loaves of bread.

Grammar Application

Exercise 3.1 Determiners and *Too* and *Enough*

A Complete the web article. Circle the correct words.

What Are Cookies? by Sue Wilder

(Many) / Much computer security experts are concerned about the use of cookies on the Internet. A "cookie" is a piece of
(1)
information stored in your computer. It contains information on all the Internet sites that you look at. **A lot of / Much** websites send
(2)
a cookie to your computer when you visit them. Companies with websites can get **many / a lot of** information about consumers
(3)
with cookies. For example, an online store sends a cookie that gives the store **much / some** details about who you are. The next
(4)
time you visit the store, it remembers your details.

There is **a lot of / many** concern about cookies because they are a privacy issue. However, **some / much** experts do not think
(5)   (6)
that there are **some / any** problems to worry about. These experts say cookies do not have **any / much** harmful effects on your
(7)   (9)
computer; that is, they do not contain **a few / any** viruses.
(9)

You can change a setting on your computer to block cookies. However, one study showed that **not many / a few** computer
(10)
users do this.

B Complete the comments on the article in A with *too much, too many,* or *enough.*

Comments (3)

Tom S., Canada: The writer spent _____*too much*_____ time on cookies. She didn't spend
(1)

_____ time on social networking sites. _____ computer users think those
(2)   (3)

sites are private, but they're not.

Amy G., New York: I agree with Tom. Not _____ computer users understand how social
(4)

networking sites work. Some of those sites give out _____ information. There isn't
(5)

_____ privacy!
(6)

Maria R., Houston: It's not the site's fault if you put up _____ silly pictures of yourself!
(7)

And you can set your profile to "private." It only takes a minute, so everyone has _____ time
(8)

to do that.

Exercise 3.2 Measurement Words

A Match the measurement words and the nouns.

1 a piece of ___*b*___	**a** rice	**5** a cup of _____	**e** chocolate
2 a package of _____	~~**b** cake~~	**6** a bar of _____	**f** paper
3 a glass of _____	**c** pizza	**7** a scoop of _____	**g** coffee
4 a slice of _____	**d** milk	**8** a sheet of _____	**h** ice cream

B Complete the article about privacy issues and shopping. Use the
correct form of the words in the box. Then listen and check your answers.

bar	box	carton	~~loaf~~	pound
bottle	can	gallon	package	tube

A lot of supermarket shoppers have store club cards these days. Club cards give you lower
prices or points for shopping. To get the lower prices, you swipe your card every time you
make a purchase. The card tells the store who you are and what you buy. Here is an example.
Shopper 1 buys three _____*loaves*_____ of bread, two _____ of juice, a
(1)   (2)

_____ of milk, a _____ of toothpaste, a _____
(3)   (4)   (5)

of rice, a _____ of soap, and two _____ of cereal each week.
(6)   (7)
What does that tell the store? It probably tells the store that he has a big family, and he probably
has children. Shopper 2 buys seven _____ of water, seven _____ of
(8)   (9)
tuna, and a _____ of turkey each week. What does this tell the store? Shopper 2 is
(10)
probably single, and she is probably dieting or is concerned with her health. How does the store
use this information? It sends advertising to the shoppers with specific information about the
products that they buy. This gets them back into the store to buy more products.

C Group Work **What did you buy this week? Write three sentences on a piece
of paper. Do not write your name! Read the papers in groups and try to guess who
wrote them.**

This person bought three loaves of bread, so it might be Nicki.

4 Avoid Common Mistakes ⚠

1 **A singular count noun needs a determiner.**
               a
I do not have ∧ card for this store.

2 **Do not use *a/an* with a noncount noun.**
You need a permission to use my credit card.

3 **Do not use a noncount noun in the plural.**
                                information
The supermarket has personal ~~informations~~ about shoppers.

4 **Do not use *many* or *too many* with a noncount noun.**
               a lot of
There was ~~many~~ Internet crime last year.

5 **Do not use *much* with a noncount noun in affirmative statements.**
                 a lot of
She had ~~much~~ cash in her wallet when somebody stole it.

Editing Task

Find eight more mistakes in this article about Internet spyware.

                    a
    Spyware is ∧ type of computer software. Someone sends it to computer
without your knowledges or permissions. It takes control of your computer. It
can make your computer run slowly or even crash. Spyware often records an
information about your computer use. It gives the information to advertisers or
5   other people who want to collect informations on you. Many spyware sneaks
into your computer when you are downloading and installing programs from
the Internet. One way to prevent a spyware is to put security settings on your
Internet browser. Set your browser to a medium or higher setting. There is also
much software you can buy that blocks spyware.

Articles

1 Grammar in the Real World

A Where do you get the news? Read the web article about how people get their news from a website. What are some ways that people get news online?

B Comprehension Check **Answer the questions.**

1 How does Christina Jackson get the news?
2 What is changing about the way people get the news?
3 The article says news is becoming an online social activity. What are some examples of this?
4 What are some very popular news subjects on the Internet right now?

C Notice **Read the sentences from the article and answer the questions.**

1 "They go to **a** news site and list the type of stories they want to read. They tell **the** news site if they want pictures or video."

In the first sentence, do we know which site this is? Is the site in the second sentence the same one?

2 "Many people do not read **a** daily newspaper anymore."

Do we know which newspaper the writer is talking about?

3 "They still have more access to the news they want, thanks to **the** Internet."

Do we know what the article refers to by "Internet"? Is this part of our general knowledge?

GETTING The NEWS

How do you get **the** news? Do you get it from TV, **the** Internet, **the** radio, or **the** newspaper? For many people, this is changing.

Take Christina Jackson, **an** office manager in Dallas, for example. Each morning, she checks her phone for news headlines. Then she
5   checks **a** social networking site and her e-mail to see what news stories her friends are discussing. In other words, friends are becoming **the** new news editors.

A recent study analyzed how people get their news. It found that news is becoming **an** online social activity. Seventy-one percent of
10   adults get their news online, and many of them leave comments for other people to read. They write their reactions to news stories on social networking sites, and they e-mail their friends links to interesting stories on news sites.

The study also showed that people like to customize their news.
15   For example, they go to **a** news site and list **the** type of stories they want to read. They tell **the** news site if they want pictures or video, and they also get news stories sent to them by e-mail. A lot of people go to **a** wide range of sites to get their news. Fifty-seven percent visit between two and five different news sites each day. Some popular news subjects
20   online are **the** weather, health, business, and international events.

Even though many people do not read **a** daily newspaper anymore, they still have more access to **the** news they want, thanks to **the** Internet.

2 Articles

Grammar Presentation

Articles are used with nouns. The indefinite article is *a* or *an*. The definite article is *the*.

A recent study analyzed how people get *the* news. *The* study found that news is becoming *an* online social activity.

2.1 Using *A* and *An*

A Use *a / an* with singular count nouns. It means "one."	*A study* analyzed news trends.
Use *a* with consonant sounds. Use *an* with vowel sounds.	I went to *a website*. I wrote *an e-mail*.
B *A / An* can go before a noun or an adjective and a noun.	It's *a study*. It's *a new study*. It's *an interesting study*.
C Do not use *a / an* with plural nouns or noncount nouns.	I watch (*some*) *TV news shows* every day. I watch a̶ *TV news shows* every day.
You can use no article or *some* with plural or noncount nouns instead.	Wei gets (*some*) *information* from the Web. Wei gets a̶n̶ *information* from the Web.
D Use *a / an* with a person, place, or thing when you and your listener are not familiar with it or when the specific name of it is not important.	I go to *a news site* each day. (We do not know which news site it is.) Raul bought *a newspaper* yesterday. (We do not know which newspaper it is.)

2.2 Using *The*

A Use *the* with singular nouns, plural nouns, and noncount nouns.	*The study* showed Internet news habits. *The news stories* were interesting. *The information* was useful.
B *The* can go before a noun or an adjective + noun.	I read *the news* online every morning. Did you hear *the big news*? Tom got married!

2.2 Using *The (continued)*

C Use *the* with people, places, and things that are familiar to you and your listener. For example, when:

1 The noun is unique – there is only one (*the sun*, *the moon*, *the Internet*).

People walked on the moon in 1969.
(We know that there is only one moon.)

2 The noun is part of your and your listener's everyday world or general knowledge (*the dog*, *the newspaper*).

I read the newspaper every day.
(The newspaper is part of our everyday life.)

3 There is additional information that explains which noun you are talking about (*the building on the left*, *the computer in the lab*).

I watch the news show that's on at 11:00 p.m. (It is a specific news show, the one that is on at 11:00 p.m.)

D People often use *a / an* the first time they speak or write about a new noun, and then use *the* every time after that.

A recent study analyzed how people get their news.
(We do not know which study it is.)
The study found that not many people read newspapers.
(Now we know that it is the study you just mentioned.)

Grammar Application

Exercise 2.1 A or An?

Complete the sentences about people's media habits. Circle the correct words.

1 A / An recent study showed **a / an** change in media habits.

2 Sara Cameron, a business student, used to read **a / an** newspaper every day, but now she visits **a / an** Internet news site several times a day.

3 Last night, her friend Rachel sent her **a / an** interesting news story from **a / an** business blog.

4 Rachel also put **a / an** link to **a / an** news video in **a / an** e-mail to all her friends.

5 Rachel used to write articles for **a / an** fashion magazine, but now she posts articles on **a / an** online fashion blog.

6 Last month, Sara bought **a / an** book at **a / an** used bookstore. Yesterday, she downloaded **a / an** ebook instead.

7 When she misses **a / an** episode of her favorite TV show, she watches it on **a / an** TV website the next day.

Look at the pictures. What are the people saying? Circle the correct answer.

1 a Did you see a movie?
  b Did you see the movie?

2 a My laptop's on a chair.
  b My laptop's on the chair.

3 a I want to buy a phone.
  b I want to buy the phone.

4 a Let's watch a news show.
  b Let's watch the news show.

A Read an excerpt from a report on jobs in new media. Write *a*, *an*, *the*, or Ø (no article).

Public relations (PR) firms create _____Ø_____ publicity for companies. For example,
(1)
_____ PR person writes _____ interesting story about _____ company
(2)   (3)   (4)
and tries to get _____ story into a newspaper. PR firms also try to get people on
(5)
TV or on _____ radio to talk about the company. PR firms like to use these media.
(6)
However, today, they also get their stories into new media, for example, on _____
(7)
social networking sites or in _____ blogs. PR firms often hire young people to help
(8)
them do this. For example, while Ali Lewis, a 25-year-old from Boston, was in college,
he wrote _____ popular blog about the media. _____ public relations firm
(9)   (10)
read his blog and asked him to come in for _____ job interview. Ali is _____
(11)   (12)
good writer, and he understands how new media work, so they gave him _____
(13)
job. In his new job, Ali helps companies work with social networking sites and blogs.

B Now listen to the report and check your answers.

Exercise 2.4 *The*: Only One or General Knowledge

People often use *the* with these nouns. There is only one of these nouns (e.g., the *moon*), or it is clear which one is meant.

the government	the media	the past	the environment	the moon
the president	the Internet	the future	the weather	the sky
the public	~~the radio~~		the world	the sun
	the press		the Earth	

A Complete the blog and follow-up comments with a word from the word box above. Sometimes, more than one answer is possible.

The News Today

February 11 by Claire Sanchez

I'm so bored with the news these days! Everything in the media – including TV, the Internet, magazines, and newspapers, and even ___*the radio*___ – is about celebrities. It seems that the only stories that we see in the media
(1)
are about celebrities and their personal problems! There are a lot of serious issues in _____
(2)
today, and we don't see much in _____ about them. What's your opinion?
(3)

3 Comments

Emily: I agree. For example, climate change is a serious issue. We need more stories about how global warming is affecting the environment. _____ is in danger, and the public isn't interested. I mean, it's
(4)
great to see the blue sky and _____ every day, but ice is melting in the Arctic! Why aren't
(5)
people interested in this?

NewsBoy: I agree, too. There isn't enough news about education, in my opinion. In _____ ,
(6)
when I was a kid, schools had enough money and classes weren't crowded. Today, it's getting very hard to get into a class at the community college. _____ won't be better, unless we do something in the present.
(7)

Erkan: Actually, _____ was talking about education on TV last night, NewsBoy.
(8)
But even though the president thinks we need more money for education, that doesn't mean that
_____ is doing anything about it. I don't think _____ really cares about
(9)   (10)
education. I mean, think about the average person – your neighbors, for example. Do they really care about crowded college classes?

B Group Work Discuss these questions in groups.

1 What's a recent news story that you were really interested in? Why did it interest you?
2 What kind of news stories do you hate reading? Why?
3 What do you think is the best (or worst) way to get the news?

3 Generalizing: More About Articles

Grammar Presentation

Generalizations are true statements about all or most members of a group.	*Teens usually get their news from the Internet.* (= Almost all teens do this; this is true in general.)

3.1 Using Articles in Generalizations and Definitions

A To make generalizations, you can use: **1** a plural noun with no article **2** a noncount noun with no article **3** *a / an* or *the* + a singular count noun	*Young people don't read newspapers.* *Information on new media habits is available.* *A good journalist covers all sides of an issue.*
B Do not use *the* with a plural count noun or a noncount noun when you make generalizations.	*Society* ~~The society~~ needs people with ~~the~~ good communication skills.
C You can also use quantifiers like *most*, *a lot of*, and *some* in generalizations.	*Most Internet users visit more than one news site each day.* *A lot of teenagers get the news from the Internet.* *Some people get the news on their phones.*
D You can use *a / an* with definitions to say what something is.	*A PR firm creates publicity for companies.*

Grammar Application

Exercise 3.1 Generalizations

Complete the report on a survey. Circle the correct words.

A recent study analyzed the media habits of American teens. The study showed that **the / Ø** American teens are not giving up TV for new media. In fact, they are watching more (1) TV than before. For **the / Ø** TV viewers aged 13–20, the top show was *American Idol* in the (2) year of the survey. This was the same for **the / Ø** parents, too. The survey found that teens (3) also play **the / Ø** video games, and not always **the / Ø** violent games. (4) (5)

According to the study, **a / Ø** typical U.S. teen remembers **the / Ø** TV (6) (7) advertisements well and does not have a negative attitude toward them. **Most / The** (8) young people also love the Internet, but they spend less time on it than **the / Ø** adults. (9) They download **the / Ø** music and spend about two or three hours a day listening to it. (10)

Exercise 3.2 Definitions

Complete the definitions. Use *a*, *an*, or Ø (no article) and the correct form of the words in the box.

adult	parent	senior	tween
minor	preteen	~~teenager~~	twenty-something

1 ____*A teenager*____ is a young person between 13 and 19 years old.
2 _____ is a person over the age of 18.
3 According to the law, _____ is a person below the age of 18.
4 _____ are people with children.
5 _____ are people over the age of 65.
6 _____ is a person between the ages of 20 and 29.
7 _____ is like a preteen – a child aged 8 to 12 years old. It's a new word in marketing.
8 _____ are young people under the age of 13.

4 Avoid Common Mistakes ⚠

1 **Use *a / an* the first time you mention a new idea.**
Do you have∧*a* social networking site?

2 **Use *the* with a noun when there is only one or when the noun is part of your and your listener's everyday world or general knowledge.**
∧*The* Internet is a good source of news.

3 **Use plural nouns without *the* in generalizations.**
~~The~~ *Online* ~~online~~ news consumers go to many different websites.

4 **Use noncount nouns without *the* in generalizations.**
~~The~~ *Communication* ~~communication~~ is changing.

Editing Task

Find and correct 10 more mistakes in this article on microblogging.

Microblogging is∧*a* way of keeping in touch with other people. The people write microblogs for their friends and families. They use microblogging sites to publish information about their activities. It is an economical way to give a lot of information to a lot of people.

5 Microblogs are very useful method of communicating for companies, too. The companies advertise their products with microblogs. They send the information in short messages to customers.

In education, some teachers use microblogging with the students. Students write down all their study activities, and teachers send the advice. Some people use audio blogs in the
10 education. They record the spoken messages and upload them to a microblogging site.

People first started using microblogs in 2005. By 2007, there were 111 microblogging sites around world. The microblogs are becoming more and more popular.

Pronouns;
Direct and Indirect Objects

Challenging Ourselves

1 Grammar in the Real World

A What challenges do you face in your life? Read the online article about ways people challenge themselves. What are some reasons to challenge yourself every day?

B Comprehension Check Answer the questions.

1 According to the text, what are some reasons to challenge yourself?
2 How does challenging yourself help you when you have real problems?
3 If you want to challenge yourself, what are some steps to follow?

C Notice Read the sentences from the article and answer the questions.

1 "Mari is afraid to speak in public, so **she** challenges **herself** by taking a public speaking class."

Who does *she* refer to? _____

Who does *herself* refer to? _____

2 "Ken wants to improve **his** critical thinking skills."

Who does *his* refer to in this sentence? _____

Challenging Ourselves

We all face challenges in **our** lives. For example, people lose **their** jobs, or **they** deal with health problems. These challenges are difficult for all of us. However, if **you** challenge **yourself**, even when **your** life is going well, **you** can be ready
5 to handle tough situations in the future. **You** will become more confident and more creative. **You** will also improve **your** problem-solving skills.

Challenging **yourself** means trying new things. These things will help **you**, but **they** may also be difficult or scary.
10 People have **their** own needs and goals, so other people's challenges may be different from **yours**. Here are some examples:

- Alison wants to be more fit. To challenge **herself**, **she** works out an extra half hour each day.

15 - Dan wants to improve **his** performance at work. He challenges **himself** by volunteering to do difficult tasks that no one else wants to do.

- Mari is afraid to speak in public, so **she** challenges **herself** by taking a public speaking class.

20 - Ken wants to improve **his** critical thinking skills. **He** now reads articles with opinions that are different from **his**.

Do **you** want to challenge **yourself**? Follow these three easy steps:

1 Write down **your** goal. Give **your** plan a start and a
25 finish date.

2 Tell people about **your** goal. This helps **you** stick to **your** plan.

3 Go one step further than **you** originally planned. For example, do **you** want to save $25 a week to buy a
30 car someday? Then save $30.

Take on small challenges every day. Small challenges give people strength. **They** help people handle life's *big* challenges when **they** happen.

2 Pronouns

Grammar Presentation

Pronouns replace or refer to nouns.	(= MARI) (= MARI) *Mari is afraid to speak in public, so she challenges herself by taking a public speaking class.*

2.1 Pronouns

Subject	Object	Possessive Determiner + Noun	Possessive	Reflexive	Reciprocal
I	me	my + noun	mine	myself	
you	you	your + noun	yours	yourself	
he	him	his + noun	his	himself	
she	her	her + noun	hers	herself	each other one another
it	it	its + noun	—	itself	
we	us	our + noun	ours	ourselves	
they	them	their + noun	theirs	themselves	

2.2 Using Pronouns

A Use subject pronouns to replace nouns in the subject position.	*Alison wants to be more fit. She is taking an exercise class.*
B Use object pronouns to replace nouns in the object position.	*Sara loves exercise classes. She takes them three times a week.*
C Use a possessive pronoun to replace a possessive determiner + singular or plural noun. The possessive pronoun agrees with the subject that it replaces.	*My exercise class is at night. Hers is on the weekend. (hers = her exercise class)* *Amy's classes meet in the afternoon. His meet in the morning. (his = his classes)*
D Use reflexive pronouns when the object of the sentence is the same as the subject. Use them in the object position.	*I taught myself to speak Japanese.* *Ken challenges himself by reading different opinions.* *The students didn't hurt themselves in the exercise class.*

2.2 Using Pronouns *(continued)*

E Use *by* + a reflexive pronoun to mean "alone" or "without any help."	*My son can ride a bike by himself.* (He does not need any help.) *Lara works out by herself.* (She works out alone.)
F Use reciprocal pronouns when two or more people give *and* receive the same action or have the same relationship.	*Mari and I have the same challenges. We help each other.* (I help Mari, and Mari helps me.) *Tom and his sisters e-mailed one another about the news.* (Each person e-mailed the other people.)
G You can use *one* to replace a singular noun. Use *ones* to replace a plural noun.	*I need an exercise class. That one looks good.* **A** *The white running shoes are nice.* **B** *I like the black ones.*

📊 *Each other* is about four times more frequent than *one another*.

A Complete the interview. Circle the correct pronouns.

How Do You Challenge Yourself?

Town Talk asked people: What is difficult for you in life? How are you challenging yourself to improve?

Q   How do you challenge ___ **your / (yourself)** ?
(1)

Al   I never finish my work on time, so I'm challenging

___ **mine / myself** ___ to use time better. I made a study schedule.
(2)

I did it all by ___ **myself / me** ___. No one helped ___ **it / me** ___!
(3)   (4)

The schedule is very tight, but I'm staying on ___ **him / it** ___.
(5)

My friends and my teachers all say that I'm doing well!

Q   People are telling us how they are improving ___ **their / theirs** ___
(6)

lives. How are you improving ___ **your / yours** ___?
(7)

Kay   I'm afraid of flying, so travel is difficult. I got help from a friend.

She was also afraid of flying, and she got better by ___ **herself / her** ___.
(8)

Now she's helping ___ **I / me** ___. My first flight is next week. I feel very
(9)

good about ___ **it / her** ___. I feel strong and confident now.
(10)

Q   We're asking people about their challenges in life.

What's ___ **your / yours** ___?
(10)

Tim   ___ **Ours / Our** ___ is saving money. Daniela and I want to buy a
(12)

house, so ___ **our / we** ___ challenge is not spending too much
(13)

money. ___ **We / Us** ___ are challenging ___ **us / ourselves** ___ to
(14)   (15)

make a budget and save money each week.

Daniela   We remind ___ **one another / us** ___ to be careful about money.
(16)

We help ___ **each other / ourselves** ___ think about ways to spend
(17)

less money.

B Pair Work Discuss these questions with a partner.

1 What is difficult for you?

2 What do you challenge yourself to do?

A *I'm afraid of public speaking. I'm challenging myself to speak in class whenever I can. How about you?*

B *I'm challenging myself . . .*

Exercise 2.2 *One* and *Ones*

Complete the conversations. Use *one* or *ones*.

1 A Do you want the large box of cereal?

 B No. I'm saving money. I want the small ___*one*___ .

2 A Which exercise class are you taking?

 B The _____ at 3:00 p.m. looks good.

3 A I'm making a budget. Can I borrow your calculator?

 B Sorry, I don't have _____ .

4 A Which sports do you like to do?

 B I like the challenging _____ , like skiing and rock climbing.

5 A Being a parent is challenging! I need some books to help me.

 B Sure. The _____ on the shelf over there are very useful.

6 A Do you want to return these running shoes?

 B Yes. The _____ that I ordered were white.

7 A Do you want to sign up for a credit card with our store?

 B No. I don't want _____ . I'm challenging myself to get out of debt.

8 A I need to go downtown. Which bus stop should I go to?

 B The _____ on Oak Street.

Exercise 2.3 Prepositions with Reflexive Pronouns

⊞ Data from the Real World

Research shows that reflexive pronouns frequently follow these verbs with *for*, *to*, and *about*:
do (something) *for*, *make* (something) *for*
talk to + (someone)
talk about, think about, feel + adjective + *about*
(something / someone)

I made a schedule for myself.
Sometimes I talk to myself.
Tim never thinks about himself.
She feels good about herself.

A Complete the article about controlling your nerves in an uncomfortable situation. Circle the correct preposition.

Do You Get "the Jitters"?

When people do challenging activities, they get nervous. Sometimes this is called "the jitters." Getting nervous is a normal reaction. Like an athlete before an event, maybe you get the jitters before a class presentation or a test. Here are some tips from successful students to help you control the jitters when you have to take a test or speak in front of the class.

- Be well prepared. For example, for a test, make a study schedule **for** / to yourself and stick to it. (1) For a presentation, make an outline **about / for** yourself and memorize it. (2)

- Be positive. Think **to / about** yourself and how well prepared you are. (3) Talk **for / to** yourself before the event. Tell yourself that you are smart (4) and well prepared.

- Focus on the task. If you are taking a test, focus on the test. If you are speaking, think about the topic of your talk. Don't think **about / for** yourself during (5) the event.

- Reward yourself. After the event, feel good **for / about** yourself! You did (6) something very challenging! Now, do something nice **for / about** yourself. (7) Make a nice meal **for / to** yourself, or go out with friends and celebrate! (8)

B Pair Work Discuss these questions with a partner.

1 How do you prepare for a challenging activity? What do you think about?

2 How do you reward yourself afterward?

I prepare by practicing a lot with my friends. I think about how much I practiced, and I try not to think about myself. I also make a schedule for myself. …

3 Direct and Indirect Objects

Grammar Presentation

Objects are nouns that receive the action of a verb. Some sentences have two objects after the verb: an indirect object (IO) and a direct object (DO).	IO DO *They gave the winner an award.*

3.1 Using Direct and Indirect Objects

A The direct object is the person or thing that receives the action of the verb.

> DO
> *The teacher gave the student a test.*
> (What did the teacher give? A test.)

B The indirect object is the person or thing that receives the direct object.

> IO   DO
> *The teacher gave the student a test.*
> (The student received the test.)

C You can use indirect object + direct object.

You can also use direct object + preposition + indirect object.

These sentences have the same meaning.

Do not use *to* and *for* with indirect object + direct object.

> IO   DO
> *The teacher gave the student a test.*
>
> DO PREP   IO
> *The teacher gave a test to the student.*
>
> ~~The teacher gave to the student a test.~~

D The pronouns for indirect objects are *me, you, him, her, it, us,* and *them*.

You can replace both the direct and the indirect objects with pronouns when you use direct object + preposition + indirect object.

Do not replace both the direct and the indirect objects with pronouns when you use indirect object + direct object.

> IO   DO
> *The teacher gave her a test.*
>
> DO   IO
> *The teacher gave a test to her.*
>
> DO   IO
> *The teacher gave it to her.*
> (it = the test; her = the student)
>
> IO DO
> *The teacher gave ~~her it~~.*

Grammar Application

A Read the text. For each numbered sentence, write *DO* above the direct object and *IO* above the indirect object. Then label the sentences *IO + DO* (indirect object + direct object) or *DO + PREP + IO* (direct object + preposition + indirect object).

Vu Tran wanted to go to college, but he did not have any money. However, Vu had a very helpful counselor in high school, Mrs. Ramirez.

          IO   *DO*

1 Mrs. Ramirez gave Vu some good advice.   *IO + DO*

2 Mrs. Ramirez gave Vu the names
of 10 scholarship organizations.   _____

3 Vu and Mrs. Ramirez sent the
completed applications to the
scholarship organizations.   _____

4 A few months later, Vu told
Mrs. Ramirez the good news.   _____

5 Five of the 10 organizations offered
a scholarship to Vu.   _____

6 Vu chose one organization, and it sent
a check to his college.   _____

Today, Vu is a successful computer technician. He overcame a great challenge with help from Mrs. Ramirez.

B Rewrite each sentence in A. Change the IO + DO sentences to DO + PREP + IO sentences. Then change the DO + PREP + IO sentences to IO + DO.

1 *Mrs. Ramirez gave some good advice to Vu.*

2 _____

3 _____

4 _____

5 _____

6 _____

Exercise 3.2 *To* and *For* with Direct Objects

📊 Data from the Real World

Research shows that the following verbs and prepositions are frequently used together in sentences with the pattern: verb + direct object + preposition + indirect object.

verb + DO + *to* + IO *e-mail, give, lend, offer, owe, read, sell, send, show, teach, tell* *To* emphasizes the direction of the action.	*I **e-mailed** pictures **to** you.* *The teacher **gave** a test **to** the student.* *(The test went from the teacher to the student.)*
verb + DO + *for* + IO *bake, buy, cook, do, find, get, keep, leave, make, order, save* *For* means that the subject does the action to please or help the other person or thing.	*I got tickets **for** my friends.* *The students baked a cake **for** the teacher.* *(The students baked a cake to please the teacher.)*
verb + DO + *to* / *for* + IO *bring, take, write* These verbs use either *for* or *to*.	*He took a schedule **for** his friend.* *(He took it to give to his friend as a favor.)* *He took a schedule **to** his friend.* *(He carried or gave it to his friend.)*

A Complete the text with *to* or *for*.

   Is it possible to change the way you think? Sometimes. Take Ken, for example.

Ken had very strong opinions about a lot of things. One day, Ken's teacher, Mrs.

Green, gave an exam __*to*__ the class. When Mrs. Green showed the test results
                    (1)

_____ Ken, he was shocked. The results showed that he didn't always base his
    (2)

ideas on correct information. Ken then decided to challenge himself and Mrs. Green

helped Ken. First, she found a website _____ Ken. It published articles on ideas
                                          (3)

that were different from Ken's. Ken discussed the articles with Mrs. Green. Mrs. Green

also made quizzes _____ Ken on the articles he read. In addition, Mrs. Green
                    (4)

found a critical thinking skills class _____ Ken. He also e-mailed some reports on
                                        (5)

the class _____ Mrs. Green. Today, Ken has excellent critical thinking skills.
           (6)

B Pair Work Listen to the text. There is additional information about Ken. Write down three new things you hear. Then tell your partner.

1 _____

2 _____

3 _____

A *Ken was a biology student at a community college.*

B *Right. And the exam was about . . .*

Exercise 3.3 Object Pronouns

Complete the answers in the conversations with the correct indirect object pronoun for the underlined word. Then rewrite each answer using a different pattern.

1 A Where did <u>Ken</u> get that course schedule?

  B Mrs. Green gave the schedule to _him_. _Mrs. Green gave him the schedule._

2 A What did Mrs. Green give <u>Ken</u>?

  B She gave _____ an exam. _____

3 A What did Mrs. Green find for <u>Ken</u>?

  B She found a critical thinking skills class for _____ . _____

4 A What did Mrs. Ramirez do for <u>Vu</u>?

  B She wrote _____ a letter of recommendation. _____

5 A Did Vu mail the applications to <u>the scholarship organizations</u>?

  B Yes, he e-mailed _____ the applications. _____

6 A Did the scholarship organization send some of the scholarship money <u>to Vu's parents</u>?

  B No, it didn't mail the money to _____ . _____

7 A Did your school give <u>you and your sister</u> scholarships?

  B No, our school gave _____ a loan. _____

8 A Can you give <u>me</u> $200 for books this semester?

  B No, but I can give _____ $100. _____

Exercise 3.4 More Object Pronouns

A Write six sentences about nice things that people have done for you or given to you.

1 _My brother gave me some money for my birthday._

2 _____

3 _____

4 _____

5 _____

6 _____

B Pair Work Exchange information with a partner. Ask questions as you talk.

A *My brother gave me $20 for my last birthday.*

B *That's nice. My brothers don't give me presents, but we go out together on our birthdays.*

4 Avoid Common Mistakes ⚠

1 **Do not confuse subject and object pronouns.**

me
She gave the schedule to Ken and ~~I~~.

2 **Do not use *to* or *for* in sentences with the pattern verb + indirect object + direct object.**
Tom gave ~~to~~ his brother a skateboard.   Tom bought ~~for~~ his brother a skateboard.

3 **Some verbs take *to*. Some verbs take *for*.**

to
I e-mailed the assignment ~~for~~ you. Did you get my message?
for
I made a cake ~~to~~ you.

4 **In sentences with verb + indirect object + direct object, do not replace both the direct and the indirect objects with pronouns.**

her the test
The teacher gave ~~her it~~.

Editing Task

Find and correct eight more mistakes in this story about a personal challenge.

her
Lara was afraid of heights. The fear caused many problems for ~~she~~. Her life was
very difficult. For example, her was very uncomfortable on airplanes. She also did not
like to take elevators in tall buildings. Lara's husband gave to her some advice.
He told to Lara a secret: If she deals with her fears, she can improve in all areas of her
5 life. Then her husband found a skydiving class to her. He found a schedule online,
and he gave her it. Then he gave Lara money to pay for the class. He also bought the
equipment to her. Lara took the class. It was hard, but she challenged herself.
After Lara finished the class, her husband gave a present for her. He baked for her
a cake, and they celebrated together.

1 Grammar in the Real World

A Where do you think new medicines come from? Read the article about a scientist who looks for new medicines. Where does Dr. Smith find new medicines?

B Comprehension Check Who went to these places? According to the article, did they find medicines or chemicals there? Check (✓) the correct boxes. Sometimes more than one answer is correct.

	Did Dr. Smith go there?	Did other scientists go there?	Did people find medicines or chemicals there?
1 the Amazon	☐	☐	☐
2 the Arctic Ocean	☐	☐	☐
3 Africa	☐	☐	☐
4 the Pacific Ocean	☐	☐	☐
5 an underwater volcano	☐	☐	☐

C Notice Find the sentences in the article and complete them.

1 We _____ chemicals all around the world.

2 I _____ around the world twice.

3 I _____ more than 50 countries for my work.

4 About two years ago, we _____ a submarine inside an underwater volcano.

In which sentence do we know when the action happened? In which sentences is the time indefinite?

Interview with Jane Smith, Ph.D.,

Marine Biologist[1]

[1]**marine biologist:** someone who studies plants and animals that live in the ocean
[2]**expedition:** a long journey with a special purpose, e.g., to discover something
[3]**submarine:** a boat that travels underwater

So, Dr. Smith, what exactly do you do?

We look for new medicines. We go to the ocean and discover chemicals in marine organisms – deep-sea animals and plants. We use these chemicals to develop drugs to treat human diseases.

5 **That's amazing. I didn't know medicines came from under the sea! Tell me more.**

Over the years, scientists **have** also **found** a lot of important drugs on land. For example, they **have developed** useful drugs from plants and animals in the Amazon rain forest in Brazil. Our work is similar. However, 10 we look for medicines in the ocean.

Where exactly do you find these chemicals?

We **have discovered** chemicals all around the world. Scientists **have found them** in warm water and in cold water, like in the Arctic Ocean. We**'ve found** them in shallow water and in very deep water, sometimes 15 tens of thousands of feet under the surface.

It sounds like you get to travel a lot for your work. Where have you been?

I**'ve been** around the world twice. My team **has led** underwater expeditions[2] in Africa, the Caribbean, the Pacific Ocean, off the coast 20 of South America, and in Asia. I**'ve been** very lucky with this job! I**'ve visited** more than 50 countries for my work.

What are some of the most exciting things you have seen or done?

I**'ve made** hundreds of very deep dives and **had** some exciting adventures. For example, about two years ago, we took a submarine[3] 25 inside an underwater volcano. However, we didn't know it was a volcano. Suddenly, the volcano erupted. The submarine shot up 200 feet a minute! That was really exciting!

2 Present Perfect

Grammar Presentation

The present perfect describes past events that are important in the present, but the specific time that the events happened is not important or is unknown.

*We **have found** chemicals all over the world.*
(We found them sometime in the past, and this is still important now.)

2.1 Statements

Subject	Have/Has (+ Not)	Past Participle	
I You We They	**have** **have not** **haven't**	**visited**	50 countries.
He She It	**has** **has not** **hasn't**		

Contractions

I have	→	I**'ve**
You have	→	You**'ve**
We have	→	We**'ve**
They have	→	They**'ve**
He has	→	He**'s**
She has	→	She**'s**
It has	→	It**'s**

2.2 Yes/No Questions and Short Answers

Have/Has	Subject	Past Participle	
Have	I you we they	**found***	new medicines?
Has	he/she/it		

Short Answers

Yes, I **have**. Yes, you **have**. Yes, we **have**. Yes, they **have**.	No, I **haven't**. No, you **haven't**. No, we **haven't**. No, they **haven't**.
Yes, he/she/it **has**.	No, he/she/it **hasn't**.

*Found is an irregular past participle. Irregular Verbs: See page A3.

2.3 Information Questions and Answers

Wh- Word	Have/Has	Subject	Past Participle	
Where	have	I	**traveled**?	
Why	have	you	**gone**	to the Amazon?
What	have	we	**discovered**?	
How	have	they	**studied**	life under the sea?
How often	has	he/she/it	**traveled**	in a submarine?

Answers

You **have traveled** around the world.

I **have gone** to look for medicines.

We**'ve discovered** chemicals in plants.

They**'ve studied** it in submarines.

He**'s traveled** in a submarine many times.

Wh- Word	Has	Past Participle	
Who	has	**been**	to Africa?

Answer

Dr. Smith **has been** to Africa.

2.4 Using Present Perfect

A Use the present perfect to talk about past events that are still important now.

People have discovered medicines in the Amazon.
(This began in the past and is important now.)

B Use the present perfect to describe actions or events that happened once or repeatedly at indefinite times in the past.

She has traveled to Mexico.
She has traveled around the world many times.
(We don't know exactly when she did these things.)

C Use the present perfect to give the number of times something happened up to now.

I've been to Africa twice.
(Before now, I went there two times.)

D Use the present perfect to give lists of past experiences.

I've been to France, Spain, and England.

You can also use the present perfect with "been" to mean "go and come back again."

A *Where have you been?*
B *I've just been to the store.*
(I went to the store and have come back again.)

E Use *ever* in present perfect questions to ask if something happened at any time in the past.

A *Have you ever traveled to Africa?*
B *Yes, I have./No, I haven't.*

A *Have you ever been inside a volcano?*
B *Yes, I have./No, I haven't.*

Verbs that are often used with the present perfect in speaking and writing include *agree, be, do, experience, find, go, say, see, show, talk,* and *think.*

Scientists *have done* experiments in space.
Researchers *have found* useful chemicals under the sea.
Research *has shown* there is water on Mars.
Have you *thought* about that?

🖱 Grammar Application

Exercise 2.1 Statements

Complete the sentences about a biotech company, a company that develops medicines. Use the present perfect form of the verbs in parentheses.

A number of drug companies ___*have found*___ (find) medicines in the rain forest.
(1)
In fact, over 120 medicines _____ (come) from rain forest plants. Some companies
(2)
_____ (get) information about these plants from the local people. In many cases,
(3)
the people _____ (live) there for hundreds of years, and they know all about the
(4)
plants. However, they _____ (not receive) money or other benefits for their help.
(5)
Some drug companies _____ (not think) about the rights of the local people who
(6)
help them. Also, some companies _____ (not take) care of the local environment.
(7)
One drug company, Rain Forest Biotech, _____ (take) steps to improve
(8)
things. Rain Forest Biotech _____ (develop) a new way to find drugs and respect
(9)
the people and land at the same time. Rain Forest Biotech also _____ (set) up
(10)
programs to help the local people they work with.

Exercise 2.2 Questions and Answers

A Complete the interview with the president of Rain Forest Biotech. Use the present perfect form of the verbs in parentheses. Then listen and check your answers.

Chris Green My guest today is Dr. Marty Robles. Dr. Robles is the president of Rain Forest Biotech. Rain Forest Biotech has made some exciting discoveries in the rain forests of the Amazon. Dr. Robles, you have an exciting company, and you ___*'ve had*___ (have)
(1)
an exciting life, too, I think. Tell us a little bit about your life. How many times _____ you
(2)
_____ (be) to the Amazon?
(2)

Dr. Robles I _____ (make) 100 trips to the
(3)
Amazon region.

Chris Green	Who _____ (go) with you?
Dr. Robles	My team.
Chris Green	And who else _____ you _____ (work) with there?
Dr. Robles	Well, I _____ (meet) many traditional healers on my trips. These people _____ (teach) me how they use local plants to cure diseases. I _____ (learn) a great deal about their lives and about their land, too.
Chris Green	_____ you _____ (be) to Africa?
Dr. Robles	No, I _____ (not be) to Africa, but my team _____ (visited) New Guinea, and I _____ (do) research in Australia.

B Listen again. What else do you learn about Dr. Robles? Circle the correct words.

1 Dr. Robles has traveled to rain forests in **Central America / Central Asia**.

2 His team has discovered medicines for **heart / brain** disease.

3 He's brought his children with him on **some / all** of his expeditions.

Exercise 2.3 More Questions

A Unscramble the words to make questions.

1 lived / have / How many / places / different / you / ?

How many different places have you lived?

2 Chicago / you / in / lived / Have / ?

_____

3 Where / traveled / you / have / ?

_____

4 Have / New York City / visited / you / ever / ?

_____

5 with / Who / you / traveled / have / ?

_____

6 your family / you / helped / has / How / ?

_____

7 Has / advice / you / your family / life / given / about / ?

_____

8 learned / have / this class / in / you / What / ?

_____

B Pair Work Ask and answer the questions in A with a partner. Give true answers about yourself. Ask follow-up questions and add extra information.

A *How many different places have you lived?*
B *Two.*
A *Where have you lived?*
B *I've lived in El Salvador and the United States.*
A *Have you ever visited . . . ?*

3 Present Perfect or Simple Past?

Grammar Presentation

<table>
<tr>
<td>The present perfect describes events that happened at an indefinite time in the past and may still be happening in the present. These events are still important or still have an effect in the present. The simple past is for finished events that happened at a specific time in the past.</td>
<td>*She has visited the rain forest many times. She went there last year.*</td>
</tr>
</table>

3.1 Present Perfect or Simple Past?

<table>
<tr>
<td>A Use the present perfect for things that happened at an indefinite time (or times) in the past.</td>
<td>*She has been to Costa Rica.*
Scientists have discovered medicines in the Amazon.</td>
</tr>
<tr>
<td>Use the simple past for things that happened at a specific time (or times) in the past.</td>
<td>*She went to Costa Rica in 2010.*
Scientists discovered a new medicine in the Amazon last year.</td>
</tr>
<tr>
<td>B Use the present perfect for things that have happened in an unfinished time period (e.g., today, this morning, this year).</td>
<td>*He has traveled to Africa twice this year.* (This year is not finished. He may travel there again.)
I have visited three cities for my current job. (My job is not finished. I may visit more cities for it.)</td>
</tr>
<tr>
<td>Use the simple past for things that happened in a time period that is finished (e.g., yesterday, last night, a year ago).</td>
<td>*He traveled to Indonesia twice last year.* (Last year is finished. He cannot go to Indonesia again in that time period.)
I visited three cities for my old job. (That job is finished. I can't travel for it again.)</td>
</tr>
</table>

3.1 Present Perfect or Simple Past? *(continued)*

| C | Use the present perfect to introduce a topic, and then use the simple past to give the details. | *We've had* a lot of exciting experiences. For example, we *took* a submarine into an underwater volcano *last year.* |

⬚ Grammar Application

Exercise 3.1 Present Perfect or Simple Past?

A Complete the article about Amanda Lewis, an astronaut. Circle the correct verbs.

She **has wanted /(wanted)** to be an astronaut when she
(1)
was a child. She **has grown up / grew up** in Texas and
(2)
has studied / studied biology and engineering at the University
(3)
of Texas. After college, she **has been / was** a pilot in the Navy.
(4)
She **has joined / joined** NASA in 1999 and **has become / became**
(5)   (6)
an astronaut. Since then, she **has orbited / orbited** the Earth
(7)
230 times and **has gone / went** on three spacewalks in the last
(8)
mission. She also participates in science experiments as part
of her job, and she **has studied / studied** the effects of radiation
(9)
on plants for the past six months. The most exciting thing she
has seen / saw as a pilot is the Northern Lights. She **has seen / saw**
(10)   (11)
them on a mission last year.

B Pair Work Compare your answers with a partner. Discuss the time that the actions in each sentence happened. Decide if the time is definite or indefinite, finished or unfinished.

A Complete the text with the present perfect or simple past form of the verbs in parentheses.

SCIENCE TALK

Three scientists answer the question, "What is the most interesting or exciting thing you have seen or done in your work?"

ERICA SALAZAR, Marine Archaeologist

I _____*have seen*_____ (see) a lot of amazing things under
(1)
the sea. For example, in 2013, my team _____
(2)
(discover) some Roman ships in the Mediterranean. The ships
probably _____ (sink) around 100 BCE.
(3)

JOE COSTA, Biologist

I _____ (have) some very exciting experiences
(4)
in the Amazon rain forest. On a trip last year, a local person
_____ (tell) us about a plant for treating stomach
(5)
problems. My stomach _____ (be) upset, and I _____
(6)   (7)
(try) a traditional healer's plant. I _____ (feel) better immediately!
(8)

JENNY LEE, Astronaut

We _____ (see) many wonderful sights from the
(9)
International Space Station. On our last mission, we
_____ (look) out a window and
(10)
_____ (see) a meteor shower.
(11)
Some of the meteors _____ (hit) the station.
(12)
It _____ (be) spectacular!
(13)

B Over to You What is one exciting or interesting thing you have seen or done in your life? Tell your partner. Use the present perfect to begin, and give the details in the simple past.

A *I've had a lot of exciting adventures. For example, last summer I climbed Mount Whitney.*

B *The most interesting thing I've seen is an eclipse. I saw it when I was a child.*

4 Avoid Common Mistakes ⚠

1   **Use the correct word order in present perfect information questions.**

has he
Where ~~he has~~ gone?

2   **Use the correct form of the past participle in the present perfect.**

found
I have ~~finded~~ many useful plants in the Amazon.

3   **Use the simple past for finished actions or events.**

graduated
She ~~has graduated~~ from the University of Texas in 2011.

4   **Use the simple past to say exactly when something happened.**

went
They ~~have gone~~ on an expedition last year.

5   **Use the present perfect for actions or events in the indefinite past that are still important now.**

have gone
I ~~went~~ to three different countries on my trip so far.

Editing Task

Find and correct nine more mistakes in this interview with a rain forest explorer.

Claire Smith   How did you decide to become a rain forest explorer?

Bettie Silva   *was*
I ~~have been~~ interested in the rain forest when I was a child. I have grown up in Brazil, and I heard many stories about the rain forest regions in my country as a child.

5   **Claire Smith**   When did you go on your first expedition?

Bettie Silva   I have gone on my first expedition in 2005. I have seen a lot of amazing sights on that first trip.

Claire Smith   Where have you gone on your first trip?

Bettie Silva   I went to rain forests in the Amazon and in Asia.

10   **Claire Smith**   Who you have traveled with?

Bettie Silva   I've traveled with teams of scientists and other explorers at different times.

Claire Smith   Have you ever had any dangerous experiences in the rain forest?

Bettie Silva   Yes. Sadly, I have loosed team members. For example, last year, a poisonous snake has bitten one of my group members. But I had many wonderful

15   experiences on trips so far, too. I have helped scientists discover new medicines, and I have meeted many interesting local people.

Adverbs with Present Perfect; *For* and *Since*

Unsolved Mysteries

1 Grammar in the Real World

A In your opinion, what has been the most important scientific discovery? Read the article from a science magazine. What are some mysteries that science has not yet solved?

B Comprehension Check **Answer the questions.**

1 What is one theory about why birds do not get lost when they migrate?
2 How do we know earthquake lights exist?
3 How many bees have died since the 1980s?
4 What are some situations in which people yawn?

C Notice **Read the sentences from the article and answer the questions.**

1 "They have not figured out the cause **yet**."

Did scientists figure out the cause? Does the writer think that they will figure it out in the future?

2 "They have **already** given the problem a name: Colony Collapse Disorder."

Did scientists give the problem a name?

3 "Why do we yawn? Scientists **still** have not solved this mystery."

Did scientists solve the mystery? Does the writer want them to solve it?

Unsolved MYSTERIES

Humans have learned many things over the years. For example, we have discovered DNA, and we have cured many diseases. We have visited the moon and sent robots to Mars. However, scientists **still** have not solved these mysteries.

5   **Bird migration**[1] How do birds travel thousands of miles over land and sea without getting lost? Scientists have **never** understood this. There are some theories. One idea is that birds have magnetic particles[2] in their brains to help them find their way. However, science has **never** proven this.

10   **Earthquake lights** Blue and white lights flash in the sky just before an earthquake occurs. People have reported this for hundreds of years. Photographs from the 1960s prove the lights exist, but researchers **still** have not found the cause. One explanation is that the lights are gas escaping from openings in the earth.

15   **Disappearing bees** Scientists have **recently** said that billions of bees have died since the 1980s. Why? They have not figured out the cause **yet**. However, they have **already** given the problem a name: Colony Collapse Disorder.

Yawning Why do we yawn? Scientists **still** have not solved this 20   mystery. People yawn when they are tired, but they also yawn in other situations, such as during exercise. Another mystery is why yawning is "contagious" – we yawn when other people yawn. In fact, you may have **just** yawned from reading this sentence!

These and other mysteries are a challenge for scientists. Although 25   we have not **yet** solved them, we are making progress every day.

[1]**migration:** movement from one place to another
[2]**particles:** a technical term for very small pieces

2 Adverbs with Present Perfect

Grammar Presentation

Adverbs *already*, *still*, and *yet* with the present perfect show how a past event relates to the present.	He has *already* given a name to the disease, but he has not discovered the cause *yet*. He *still* has not found a cure for it. (This is the situation right now, up to this point in time.)

2.1 Adverbs with Present Perfect

A Use *already* when something happened sooner than expected.	*Scientists have already given the disease a name.* *It is only 8:00 p.m., but they have already gone home.*
Use *already* in affirmative statements and in questions. It usually comes before the past participle.	PAST PARTICIPLE *Have they already solved the problem?*
B Use *yet* with things that have not happened. It often means you expected something to happen or expect something to happen soon.	*There are many mysteries scientists have not figured out yet.*
Use *yet* in negative statements and in questions. It usually comes at the end of the sentence.	*Have they discovered the cause yet?*
C Use *still* with things that have not happened. It often means you want something to happen, but it has not.	*Scientists are still looking for an explanation.*
Use *still* in negative statements, but avoid it in questions. It usually comes before *have / has*.	*It is past midnight, and she still has not gone home.*
D Use *never* and *not ever* to mean "not at any time" or "zero times." They usually come before the past participle.	PAST PARTICIPLE *Scientists have never understood the cause.* *They haven't ever understood the cause.* (These sentences have the same meaning.)
You can use *ever* in Yes / No questions.	*Have you ever thought about these mysteries?*
E Use *just*, *lately*, and *recently* when something happened a short time ago. *Just* usually comes before the past participle. *Lately* usually comes at the end of a sentence. *Recently* can go in either position.	PAST PARTICIPLE *We have just discovered a new type of fish.* *She has been sick lately.* *Scientists have recently studied the issue.* *Scientists have studied the issue recently.*

Grammar Application

Complete the statements about earthquake prediction with the present perfect form of the verbs in parentheses. Then check the correct statement about the action.

	The action has happened.	The action has not happened.
1 People _*have not been*_ (not be) able to predict earthquakes **yet**.	☐	☑
2 However, many people _____ **already** _____ (notice) that animals behave strangely before an earthquake.	☐	☐
3 The United States Geological Survey (USGS) _____ **already** _____ (do) a few studies on animal behavior and earthquakes.	☐	☐
4 However, the USGS _____ (not prove) that animals can predict earthquakes **yet**.	☐	☐
5 As a result, Western scientists **still** _____ (not be) able to develop a warning system for earthquakes.	☐	☐
6 However, Asian scientists _____ **already** _____ (determine) the connection between animal behavior and earthquakes.	☐	☐
7 In fact, Chinese researchers _____ **already** _____ (use) animal behavior to save many people during earthquakes.	☐	☐
8 Many people think that we **still** _____ (not do) enough animal studies in the West.	☐	☐

A Complete the article about cow behavior. Circle the correct adverb.

Have you ever noticed that groups of cows all face the same way? Scientists have ever /(never) been able to explain this. Satellite
(1)
photos have **recently / yet** shown that cows
(2)
around the world all face either north or south. Scientists have **already / still** not learned why
(3)
cows do this. One theory involves magnets. The Earth is like a huge magnet, and magnets

point to the north. Studies have **already / yet** shown that this helps some small animals, such as
(4)
bats, find their way. In addition, researchers have **never / already** found that fish and whales have
(5)
tiny magnetic particles in their brains. Therefore, some researchers have **recently / yet** guessed
(6)
that cows also have magnetic particles in their brains. However, they have not found any proof
already / yet. They **still / lately** have not done any tests to see if cows have magnetic particles in
(7)   (8)
their brains.

B Now listen and check your answers.

Put the adverb in parentheses into the correct place in these sentences about the mystery of aging. Sometimes more than one answer is possible.

still
1 Medical researchers ˄ have not discovered the causes of aging. (still)

2 We have seen that humans are living longer and longer. (already)

3 However, we have not seen many people live beyond the age of 100. (still)

4 So far, humans have not lived past the age of 130. (ever)

5 Researchers have begun to understand the processes that occur in the body as we age. (just)

6 Scientists have discovered chemicals in the body that tell it to start aging. (recently)

7 Many people wonder what we can do to extend our lives, but science has not found the answers. (yet)

8 Some say that eating a low-calorie diet can extend life, but science has not proven this. (still)

Exercise 2.4 Questions and Answers

A Unscramble the words to make questions. Use the present perfect form of the verbs and add *have* or *has* where needed. Sometimes more than one answer is possible.

1 scientists / another planet like Earth / yet / find / ?

   Have scientists found another planet like Earth yet?

2 already / we / what planets / send spaceships to / ?

   _____

3 find / ever / people / a cure for the common cold / ?

   _____

4 what medicines / recently / discover / researchers / ?

   _____

5 people / already / where / look / for new medicines / ?

   _____

6 figure out why we dream / yet / anyone / ?

   _____

7 any scientists / recently / in the news / be / ?

   _____

8 you / wonder about a scientific mystery / ever / ?

   _____

B Group Work Discuss the questions in A. Try to give extra information and ask follow-up questions.

   A *Have scientists found another planet like Earth yet?*
   B *I don't know. If they've already found a planet like Earth, I want to visit it!*
   C *I don't think they've found a planet like Earth yet. But one is probably out there somewhere.*

3 Present Perfect with *For* and *Since*

Grammar Presentation

<table>
<tr>
<td>

For and *since* with the present perfect describe the length of time that an action or event from the past continues into the present.

</td>
<td>

She has not exercised for more than 30 years.

She has not exercised since 1987.

</td>
</tr>
</table>

3.1 *For* and *Since*

<table>
<tr>
<td>

A Use the present perfect with *for* and a period of time (*20 years, three days, an hour, a long time*) to show the length of time of an action or event.

</td>
<td>

He has lived here for 20 years.

They have studied this problem for a long time.

</td>
</tr>
<tr>
<td>

B Use the present perfect with *since* and a point in time in the past (*2009, last year, May 15*) to show when an action or event started.

</td>
<td>

Humans have kept bees since 4000 BCE.

We have known about Colony Collapse Disorder since the 1990s.

</td>
</tr>
<tr>
<td>

C You can also use *since* before a clause.

</td>
<td>

I have eaten chocolate since I was a child.

</td>
</tr>
<tr>
<td>

D You can use *for* and *since* in negative sentences to show when something happened for the last time.

</td>
<td>

We have not gone to the moon since the 1970s. (The last time we went there was the 1970s.)

There has not been an eclipse for five years. (The last eclipse was five years ago.)

</td>
</tr>
<tr>
<td>

E You can ask about periods of time with *How long . . . ?*

</td>
<td>

A *How long have you lived here?*
B For four years.
A *How long has this been a problem?*
B Since the 1980s.

</td>
</tr>
</table>

📊 Data from the Real World

<table>
<tr>
<td>

In conversation, people often omit *for* with these verbs: *live, work, be, know* (a person), and *play*.

</td>
<td>

Say: *"She's lived here a long time."*

</td>
</tr>
<tr>
<td>

In conversation, people also often say *in* instead of *for* in negative statements.

</td>
<td>

Say: *"I haven't exercised in years."*

</td>
</tr>
<tr>
<td>

Always use *for* in writing.

</td>
<td>

Write: *She has lived here for a long time.*
Write: *I have not exercised for years.*

</td>
</tr>
</table>

Grammar Application

Exercise 3.1 *For or Since?*

A Complete the paragraph from an article about another scientific mystery: people who have bad lifestyle habits but live very long lives. Circle the correct words.

Experts have agreed (for) / since many years that exercise, a good diet, and other
(1)
healthy lifestyle habits lead to a long life. However, why do some people with bad

lifestyle habits live long lives? Scientists do not know. Take Sarah Baines, for example.

She is 99 years old, and she is in good health. However, Sarah has had unhealthy habits

for / since her entire life. For example, Sarah has not exercised for / since she was a
(2)   (3)
child. She has smoked for / since 75 years, for / since she was a young woman.
(4)   (5)

Sarah also loves to eat. She has not been on a diet for / since 1952. She does not
(6)
like vegetables, and she has not eaten any salads for / since the last 40 years. She also
(7)
loves fatty food. She has eaten high calorie meals such as steak, potatoes with butter,

and ice cream almost every day for / since her entire life. In addition, Sarah does not
(8)
get much sleep. She has not gone to bed before midnight for / since she was 13 years
(9)
old. This lifestyle is incredibly unhealthy, and Sarah often does not feel well, but she is

stubborn and will not change.

B Pair Work Compare your lifestyle habits with Sarah's. Try to use *for* and *since*. Tell a partner.

A *I've exercised three times a week since 2015. How about you?*

B *I haven't exercised for many years, but I've eaten healthy food since I was a child.*

A Complete the interview with Mel Green, who is 85 years old. Use the present perfect form of the verbs in parentheses. Write *for* or *since* before each time expression.

Andy Jones We're at the Corner Café, and I am speaking with the chef and owner, Mel Green. Mel is 85 years old today. He's in excellent health. He has a sharp mind, and he still works! Happy birthday, Mel! So, tell us a little about your long life. Have you lived here a long time?

Mel Green Well, I _'ve lived_ (live) in California
(1)
_____ 50 years,
(2)
and I _____ (be) here in San
(3)
Miguel _____ 1972.
(4)

Andy Jones How do you spend your days?

Mel Green I work! I _____ (work) as a chef _____ 1945.
(5)   (6)

Andy Jones How long _____ you _____ (own) the Corner Café?
(7)   (7)

Mel Green I _____ (own) this restaurant _____ 1980.
(8)   (9)

Andy Jones What else do you do?

Mel Green I love to learn languages. I _____ (learn) Spanish, and I speak
(10)
a little Chinese, too.

Andy Jones Wow!

Mel Green Yeah. Now I can speak Spanish with some of my customers.

Andy Jones What _____ you _____ (do) to stay healthy
(11)   (11)
_____ so many years?
(12)

Mel Green I _____ (not do) anything special to stay healthy, but I
(13)
_____ (not eat) sweets _____ I was in
(14)   (15)
my twenties.

Andy Jones What are some of your other lifestyle habits?

Mel Green I get up early. I _____ (get) up at 5:00 a.m. every morning
(16)
_____ about 30 years.
(17)

Andy Jones What about exercise?

Mel Green I _____ (not exercise) _____ a long time, but my
(18)   (19)
work keeps me active. I'm on my feet all day.

Andy Jones What are your recommendations for a long life?

Mel Green Keep busy!

B Find one place in the interview in A where you can omit *for* and circle it. Then find one place where you replace *for* with *in* and write *in* above *for*.

C Pair Work Ask about your partner's life and answer questions about your life. Use the questions in A or your own ideas. Use the present perfect and time expressions with *for* and *since*.

A *How long have you lived here?*
B *I've lived here (for) a long time.*

A *How do you spend your days?*
B *I work. I've worked at a repair shop since last year.*

A *Do you work out at the gym?*
B *Yes, but I haven't worked out in / for months.*

4 Avoid Common Mistakes

1 **Use *never* in affirmative statements, not negative statements.**
                    never
Science has ~~ever~~ been able to explain this.

2 **Use *ever* in negative statements, not affirmative statements.**
                  ever
They have not ~~never~~ been able to explain this.

3 **Use the correct word order with adverbs and present perfect.**
        He   just
~~Just he~~ has ⌃returned from his trip.

4 **Use *since* with a point in time in the past. Use *for* with a period of time.**
                            for   *since*
I have not exercised ~~since~~ three years. I have not exercised ~~for~~ last month.

5 **Do not use *for* or *since* with the simple present or present progressive.**
      have studied   *have studied*
We ~~study~~ this problem for 30 years. We ~~are studying~~ this problem since the 1960s.

Editing Task

Find and correct eight more mistakes in this article about blushing.

Max is a drama major. Today, he is presenting a scene from a play in one of his
                          has taken
classes. He ~~is taking~~ acting classes since he was a child. He is acting, in front of people
since many years, and he has been in the drama department since three years.
He has ever felt uncomfortable on the stage. However, for some reason, Max just has
5 forgotten his lines, and his face has become red. Max is blushing.

Many people blush when they are embarrassed, but science has not never been
able to explain why we blush. Researchers know how we blush: The nervous system
causes the blood vessels in our face to dilate. This increases blood flow to the face,
and this makes it look red. Researchers know for many years that teenagers blush more
10 than adults do, but still there has not been much research on blushing.

1 Grammar in the Real World

A What do you like about big cities? What don't you like? Read the online article about problems caused by the growth of cities. How is city life improving?

B Comprehension Check Answer the questions.

1 Why do people migrate to cities?

2 What happens when cities grow too fast?

3 Who has found solutions to some of these problems? What are the solutions?

4 What examples of green buildings and green belts does the article mention?

C Notice How does the writer express these ideas in the article? Write the sentences from the article.

1 Environmental problems are now worse than they were.

_____

2 Urban planners started creating green belts in cities, and they are still doing this.

_____

CITY LIFE

Half of the world's population now lives in cities – that is over 3 billion people. Cities are growing at a faster and faster rate because people around the world **have been leaving** the countryside in search of jobs and a better life in urban areas. Current estimates are that 180,000
5 people migrate to cities each day.

This trend **has caused** problems in some countries. Cities are growing too fast. For example, the population of Mumbai, India, increases by 4.2 percent each year. Beihai, China, **has been growing** by 10.6 percent every year. There often isn't enough housing for all of the
10 new people. As a result, the number of people living in slums[1] **has risen** in many cities. Environmental problems **have been getting worse**, too.

Luckily, architects and urban planners **have found** solutions to some of these problems. In many cities around the world, architects **have designed** "green" buildings. They use solar power, and they use
15 less water.

In addition, urban planners **have been creating** green belts in cities. Green belts are large pieces of natural land that offer fresh air and places for recreation for people in cities. Planners **have reclaimed**[2] green belts, too. In Seoul, South Korea, for example, planners uncovered a small river
20 in the middle of the city that was under a highway and built a park on both sides of the river.

These ideas **have not solved** all of the problems of big cities. There is still not enough housing, for example. Also, green buildings and green belts are too expensive for some cities. However, these
25 ideas **have made** life better for many people around the world.

[1]**slum:** a poor and crowded area of a city

[2]**reclaim:** take something back

Cities **121**

2 Present Perfect Progressive

Grammar Presentation

The present perfect progressive usually shows something that started in the past and continues into the present time.	Environmental problems *have been getting worse*. (This started in the past and continues into the present time.)

2.1 Statements

Subject	Has/Have (+ Not)	Been	Verb + -ing	
I You We They	**have** **have not** **haven't**	**been**	**working** **migrating** **living**	here.
He She It	**has** **has not** **hasn't**			

Contractions	
I have → I**'ve** You have → You**'ve** We have → We**'ve** They have → They**'ve**	
He has → He**'s** She has → She**'s** It has → It**'s**	

2.2 Yes/No Questions and Short Answers

Has/Have	Subject	Been	Verb + -ing
Have	I you we they	**been**	**working?**
Has	he/she/it		

Short Answers	
Yes, I **have**. Yes, you **have**. Yes, we **have**. Yes, they **have**.	No, I **haven't**. No, you **haven't**. No, we **haven't**. No, they **haven't**.
Yes, he/she/it **has**.	No, he/she/it **hasn't**.

2.3 Information Questions

Wh- Word	Has/Have	Subject	Been	Verb + -ing
Where **When** **Why** **How**	**have**	I you we they	**been**	**working?**
How long	**has**	he/she/it		

2.3 Information Questions *(continued)*

Wh- Word	Has / Have	Been	Verb + -ing	
What	has	been	**happening**?	
Who			**migrating**	to cities?

2.4 Using Present Perfect Progressive

A Use the present perfect progressive for actions and events that started in the past and continue into the present time or for actions that have just stopped.	*Environmental problems have been getting worse.* *We've been talking about these problems for years.*
B Use the present perfect progressive with *for* and *since* to show the duration of an action or event. Remember: Use *for* + a length of time and *since* + a specific time.	*I've been living here for a year.* *He hasn't been working since last May.*
C Use the present perfect progressive for actions or events that are new, temporary, or changing.	*He's been staying with a friend until he finds his own apartment.* *We've been talking about the news all day.*
D Use the present perfect progressive with time expressions and adverbs, such as *this week / month / year, these days, nowadays, recently,* and *lately.*	*The city planners have been working hard this week.* *A lot of people have been coming into the cities lately.*
Do not use the present perfect progressive with time expressions that describe finished time periods, such as *last year* or *three days ago.*	*The city built a lot of new housing last year.* *The city ~~has been building~~ a lot of new housing last year.*

Exercise 2.1 Statements

Complete the blog post on city improvements. Use the present perfect progressive form of the verbs in parentheses.

⌂   💬 ↻ ☰ ✉

Jen's Bay City Blog

New Report Has Good News on City Improvements
May 25

   If you're like most Bay City residents these days, you
___*have not been feeling*___ (not feel) happy about garbage
      (1)
pickup, safety, transportation, and the libraries for a long time. However,
a new report from the city this week has some good news. According
to the report, people _____ (notice)
      (2)
a lot of improvements lately. Here are just a few:

• The garbage collection service

_____ (pick) up
      (3)
trash on time. In addition, the garbage collection service

_____ (not leave) garbage
      (4)
around the pickup areas. I haven't noticed this one on my block, but I'm glad some of you have.

• People _____ (feel) safer in the park at night. This is because
      (5)
more police _____ (patrol) the park after dark. This is one that
      (6)
I've definitely experienced. I walked through the park the other night, and it felt much better.

• Public transportation _____ (improve). People
      (7)
_____ (not complain) about rude bus drivers lately. I guess
      (8)
those lucky people aren't on my bus line!

• The libraries _____ (stay) open on weeknights. As a result,
      (9)
more families and working people _____ (use) them. I
      (10)
haven't been to the library recently, but I want to check this out.
What do you think? Leave a comment below with your opinion!

Exercise 2.2 Questions and Answers

A Complete an interview with a city planner. Use the present perfect progressive form of the verbs in parentheses in the questions. Write *for* or *since* in the answers.

Bay City News Talks to . . . Lisa Daniel

By Pedro Martin

Lisa Daniel is the chairperson of the Bay City Planning Committee. Bay City News spoke to her about her job and the future of the city.

Q Lisa, how long __*have*__ you __*been working*__ (work) as a city planner?
　　　　　　　　　(1)　　　　　　　(1)

A I've been doing this __*since*__ 2003.
　　　　　　　　　　　　(2)

Q And _____ you _____ (work) on the city's planning
　　　　　(3)　　　　　　　　　　　(3)
　committee for Bay City long?

A Not really. I've been working as a Bay City planner _____ three years.
　　　　　　　　　　　　　　　　　　　　　　　　　　　(4)

Q What _____ the planning committee _____ (focus)
　　　　　(5)　　　　　　　　　　　　　　　　　　(5)
　on lately?

A Well, we've been looking at environmentally friendly design _____ last year.
　　　　　　　　　　　　　　　　　　　　　　　　　　　　(6)

Q That sounds interesting. _____ the planning committee
　　　　　　　　　　　　　(7)
　_____ (develop) new green belts in our city?
　　　(7)

A Yes. We've been increasing green belts around the city _____ 2005. For example,
　　　　　　　　　　　　　　　　　　　　　　　　　　(8)
　we've been tearing down old, unused warehouses and turning the land into parks.

Q _____ you _____ (address) some of the
　　(9)　　　　　　　　　　(9)
　environmental issues that all cities are facing?

A Yes. We've been traveling to other cities _____ the past two years and studying
　　　　　　　　　　　　　　　　　　　(10)
　environmental projects.

Q Where are there some interesting environmental projects these days?

A Well, Berlin, for example.

Q What _____ (happen) there?
　　　　(11)

A Berlin has been doing some very interesting work adding trees and plants to the tops of buildings in the
　last few years.

Q Is Bay City growing like other big cities?

A Absolutely. Bay City's population has been increasing _____ 1990. It has caused
　　　　　　　　　　　　　　　　　　　　　　　　　　(12)
　some problems, but we have been keeping housing costs low _____ the city
　　　　　　　　　　　　　　　　　　　　　　　　　　　　　(13)
　passed the new rent laws.

B Pair Work Make a list of some of the problems in your town or city. Then, with a partner, write five questions about the problems to ask a member of your town or city planning committee.

- *high housing costs*
- *crowded public transportation*
- *pollution*

Has the city been growing a lot recently?
What improvements have you been talking about?

3 Present Perfect Progressive or Present Perfect?

Grammar Presentation

The present perfect progressive focuses on an ongoing action or event, which may or may not be finished. The present perfect often suggests that the action or event is complete.

*Planners **have been reclaiming** green belts all over the city.* (They may still be doing this.)
*Planners **have reclaimed** green belts all over the city.* (They are not doing this anymore.)

3.1 Present Perfect Progressive or Present Perfect?

A Use the present perfect progressive for an action or event that started in the past and may or may not be finished yet.	*Urban planners **have been creating** green belts in cities.* (They aren't finished. They may still be doing this.)
You can use the present perfect for an action or event that is finished.	*Urban planners **have created** green belts in cities.* (They have finished. The green belts are done.)
B Use the present perfect progressive to focus more on the *activity* of the action or event.	*I've **been writing** a paper on city planning.* (focus on the activity of writing)
Use the present perfect to focus on the *results* of the action or event.	*I've **written** a paper on city planning.* (focus on the completed paper)
C Use the present perfect progressive for situations that are new or temporary (only for a short time).	*It takes time to find housing in the city, so I've **been staying** with my aunt and uncle.* (I am doing this for a short time only.)
Use the present perfect for situations that are permanent (last for a long time).	*He's **lived** in the same house for 30 years.* (This is a permanent situation.)
D Use the present perfect, not progressive, when you say how much or how many times something has happened.	*The planners **have visited** Berlin three times.* *They **have built** three green apartments in Brooklyn.*
E With *get, go, increase, live, study,* and *work,* you can often use either form. The progressive suggests the action or event is new or temporary.	*We **have lived** here for 20 years.* *We **have been living** here for two months.*

3.1 Present Perfect Progressive or Present Perfect? *(continued)*

F Do not use the progressive form with stative verbs such as *be*, *believe*, *hate*, *know*, *like*, and *understand*.	They *have known* about the problem for many years. They have ~~been knowing~~ about the problem for many years.

📊 Data from the Real World

The present perfect is much more common than the present perfect progressive, especially in writing. When you have a choice of forms in writing, use the present perfect if you need to sound more formal.

Present perfect ▬▬▬▬▬▬▬▬▬▬▬▬
Present perfect progressive ▬

Less formal: *I've been living* here since 2008.
More formal: *I have lived* here since 2008.

🖥 Grammar Application

Exercise 3.1 Present Perfect Progressive or Present Perfect?

A Check (✓) the sentences that you can rewrite in the present perfect progressive. Then do B with a partner.

1 Environmental problems in our city have increased. ☑

   _____

2 For example, air pollution has been a big problem. ☐

   _____

3 We have known about the causes of air pollution for many years. ☐

   _____

4 Studies have shown that green belts reduce air pollution. ☐

   _____

5 Planners have talked about creating more green belts in our city. ☐

   _____

6 They have studied the effects of green belts in other cities for the past year. ☐

   _____

7 For example, planners have reclaimed two green belts in New York City. ☐

   _____

8 As a result, air quality has improved by 10 percent. ☐

   _____

B Pair Work Compare your answers in A with a partner. Discuss the reason for each of your answers. Then rewrite the sentences you checked. Use the present perfect progressive.

A *You can rewrite number 1 in the present perfect progressive. "Environmental problems have been increasing."*

B *Right. But you can't rewrite number 2 because be is . . .*

A Complete the paragraphs about a student's description of her neighborhood. Write the form of the verbs in parentheses – either the present perfect or the present perfect progressive.

There have been a lot of changes in my neighborhood in the last year. Some changes ___*have been*___ (be) good. For example,
(1)

four new restaurants _____
(2)

(open). The city _____ (build) a
(3)

new children's playground, and it should be

ready next month. They _____
(4)

also _____ (build) some green
(4)

apartments – they finished them six months

ago. A lot of new people _____ (move) in already.
(5)

Unfortunately, some things _____ (get) worse. About six stores
(6)

_____ (close) down, just on my street. Two of my favorite stores
(7)

_____ (go) out of business. Also, crime _____ (increase).
(8)   (9)

Thieves_____ (break) into the deli on my street twice in the last
(10)

six months. I guess both good and bad things can happen at the same time.

B Now listen and check your answers. You can use both present perfect progressive and the present perfect for two of the verbs in A. Which ones?

C Pair Work Compare your neighborhood with the one in A. Talk with a partner about the good changes and the bad ones. Use the present perfect or the present perfect progressive.

A *We've had some good changes in my neighborhood. For example, the city has built a new park. How about you?*

B *The city has started a farmers' market right in my neighborhood. We've been getting great fresh fruit and vegetables straight from the farm right down the street.*

4 Avoid Common Mistakes ⚠

1 **Use *have* when forming the present perfect progressive.**

have
They ‸ been creating green belts in cities.

2 **Use *has* with singular third-person subjects (*he, she, it*). Use *have* with other subjects.**

has
This city ~~have~~ been getting more expensive in the last few years.

3 **Use the present perfect with stative verbs. Do not use the present perfect progressive.**

known
Experts have ~~been knowing~~ about the problem for many years.

4 **Use the present perfect progressive, not the present progressive, with *for* and *since*.**

have been
Environmental problems ~~are~~ getting worse here for many years.

Editing Task

Find and correct eight more mistakes in this interview with a green architect.

Kyle Jones	Urban planners and architects *have* ‸ been remodeling city buildings to make them more energy efficient. This been making life in our city kinder to the environment. It have also been making life healthier for city residents. Today, we are asking the architect Vinh Hu about his work. Mr. Hu, how long you been designing green buildings?
5 Vinh Hu	Oh, a long time. We're designing these buildings for almost 20 years. We've been believing for a long time that green buildings are an important way to improve city life. We've also been knowing for a long time that most people prefer green apartments. In the future, no one will want to live in a building that isn't environmentally friendly.
10 Kyle Jones	What you been working on lately?
Vinh Hu	We've been building two new apartments on Murray Street.
Kyle Jones	Yes, I am watching those apartments go up for a while. What makes them green?
Vinh Hu	They use solar energy for heat.
Kyle Jones	Very interesting! Thank you, Mr. Hu.

Adjectives

A Good Workplace

1 Grammar in the Real World

A What makes a good workplace? Read the poster about workplace rights. What are some rights that workers have?

B Comprehension Check Answer the questions.

1 Why is it important to know your rights on the job?
2 What are two fair treatment rights that workers have?
3 What are two safety rights that workers have?
4 Who do you report unsafe conditions to?

C Notice Find the sentences in the poster and complete them.

1 _____ employers follow the laws.

2 You have a right to _____ treatment on the job.

3 You also have a right to a workplace that is not _____ .

4 You have the right not to feel _____ or _____ at work.

Look at the words you wrote. Which words do they describe?

KNOW YOUR RIGHTS ON THE JOB

In the United States, you have **legal** rights to **fair** treatment in the workplace. You also have rights to safe conditions at work. **Ethical**[1] employers follow the laws, but some employers do not, so you should know what your rights are on the job.

FAIRNESS

5   You have a right to **fair** treatment on the job. Women, men, **young** people, and **old** people all have **equal** rights. Discrimination is **illegal**. For example, women and men have the right to **equal** pay for the **same** job.

You also have a right to a workplace that is not **hostile**.[2] If your co-workers treat you badly because of your race or the place you come from, this is **illegal**.
10   You have the right not to feel **embarrassed** or **humiliated**[3] at work.

Report **hostile** behavior at work to the Equal Employment Opportunity Commission (EEOC). It is your **legal** right.

SAFETY

Workers have the right to a **safe** workplace. These are some examples of
15   **unsafe** or **unhealthy** conditions.

- working near **toxic**[4] chemicals
- working with **dangerous** machines
- **slippery** floors
- **sharp** objects
- loud **noise**

You have the right to **free training** courses on the **safety** issues in your
20   workplace. For example, you have the right to get training on how to use **dangerous** machines.

If you see **dangerous** or **unsafe** conditions at work, report them to your supervisor or the Occupational Safety and Heath Administration (OSHA). Your company cannot fire you for reporting problems. Everyone has the right
25   to a **safe**, **fair** workplace.

[1]**ethical:** good, correct, moral
[2]**hostile:** unfriendly, showing strong dislike
[3]**humiliate:** make you feel ashamed, lose respect for yourself
[4]**toxic:** poisonous

A Good Workplace   **131**

2 Adjectives

Grammar Presentation

<table>
<tr>
<td>Adjectives describe nouns – people, places, things, and ideas.</td>
<td>Ethical employers follow the laws.
(Ethical describes employers.)
Discrimination is illegal.
(Illegal describes discrimination.)</td>
</tr>
</table>

2.1 Using Adjectives

<table>
<tr>
<td>A Adjectives usually go before nouns, not after.</td>
<td>Women and men have the right to equal pay.
Women and men have the right to <s>pay equal</s>.
Workers have legal rights to fair treatment.
Workers have <s>rights legal</s> to <s>treatment fair</s>.</td>
</tr>
<tr>
<td>B However, adjectives can go after be or after linking verbs like become, look, feel, sound, smell, taste, seem, and appear.</td>
<td>My company is an ethical employer.
That job looks safe.
The boss seems nice.</td>
</tr>
<tr>
<td>C Adjectives do not have plural forms. Do not add -s.</td>
<td>This is your legal right. These are your legal rights.
These are your <s>legals</s> rights.
Ethical employers create an ethical workplace.
<s>Ethicals</s> employers create an ethical workplace.</td>
</tr>
<tr>
<td>D Use an (not a) before an adjective that starts with a vowel sound with a singular count noun.</td>
<td>An ethical employer means an ethical workplace.
<s>A</s> ethical employer means . . .
Don't use an unsafe machine without training.
Don't use <s>a</s> unsafe machine . . .</td>
</tr>
</table>

2.2 Using Nouns as Adjectives

<table>
<tr>
<td>A You can use some nouns as adjectives before other nouns.

Do not make these plural.</td>
<td>Workers have safety rights. They also have health rights. They also have <s>healths rights</s>.</td>
</tr>
<tr>
<td>B To describe the age or duration of a noun, you can use expressions like 15-year-old or six-month as adjectives before the noun. Notice that the age and time nouns (e.g., year) are always singular, never plural.</td>
<td>Fifteen-year-old teenagers work in some restaurants.
<s>Fifteen years old</s> teenagers work in some restaurants.
I want to take a six-month course in green office design.
I want to take a <s>six months course</s>.</td>
</tr>
</table>

2.3 Using More Than One Adjective

Opinion	Size	Quality	Age	Shape	Color	Origin	Material	Type
beautiful nice	big long	free safe	old young	round square	blue red	Canadian Thai	cotton leather	evening training

When you use two or more adjectives before a noun, use the order in the chart above, from left to right.	
	She drives an *old* (AGE) *Japanese* (ORIGIN) *car* (NOUN) to work.
	He wears *black* (COLOR) *leather* (MATERIAL) *boots* (NOUN) to work.
	There's an *interesting* (OPINION) *new* (AGE) *safety* (TYPE) *course* (NOUN) at work.

Adjectives: Order Before Nouns: See page A9.

Grammar Application

Exercise 2.1 Word Order

A Rewrite these sentences. Use *be* + adjective.

1 Some factories have unhappy workers. Some workers ___are unhappy___ .

2 They earn low wages. Their wages _____ .

3 They have bad working conditions. Their working conditions _____ .

4 They work long hours. Their hours _____ .

B Rewrite these sentences. Put the adjective before the noun. Use *a* or *an* where needed.

1 The workers' pay at this company is equal. At this company, the workers get ___equal pay___ .

2 The bosses are ethical. They are _____ .

3 The training courses are free. They are _____ .

4 Our work day is eight hours. We have _____ .

Exercise 2.2 Using Adjectives

A Listen to Annie telling Nick about her new job. Then complete the conversation with the words in the box.

beige	cotton	great	leather	new	sport
black	fantastic	interesting	long	running	ugly

Nick I hear you have a ___*new*___ job.
(1)

Annie Yes. I'm a technician at PC Emporium.

Nick That's great. What are your hours?

Annie We work 40 hours a week.

Nick And do you get a vacation?

Annie Yes. Even new employees get a

_____ vacation – two weeks.
(2)

Nick That sounds _____ ! Do they
(3)
train you?

Annie Sure. I'm taking an _____ training
(4)
course right now. It goes for three days.

Nick Everything sounds _____ !
(5)

Annie Not everything. We have to wear an _____ uniform. I wear
(6)
_____ pants and a _____ shirt. The pants are
(7)   (8)
_____ and the shirt is _____ . Oh, and black shoes.
(9)   (10)

Nick _____ shoes?
(11)

Annie No! _____ shoes.
(12)

B Listen again and complete the paragraph about the conversation. Sometimes, more than one answer is possible.

Annie has a ___*40-hour*___ work week. She gets a _____ vacation
(1)   (2)
each year. Right now, she's taking a _____ training course. She
(3)
wears _____ _____ pants, a _____
(4)   (4)   (5)
_____ shirt, and _____ _____ shoes to work.
(5)   (6)   (6)

Exercise 2.3 Adjective Endings

📊 Data from the Real World

Here are some common adjective endings with the most common adjectives that use them.

-able	-ful	-ial	-ic	-ical	-ive	-ous
comfortable	wonderful	social	public	medical	expensive	serious
available	beautiful	special	basic	political	positive	ridiculous
reasonable	awful	financial	economic	physical	active	dangerous

134 Unit 13 Adjectives

A Write the correct adjective endings in the opinion column about working conditions.

On average, American workers get only

two weeks of paid vacation. I think that is ridicu l_ous_ .
(1)

There are many beauti_____ places in the United States,
(2)

but no one has time to see them. Vacation time is more

reason_____ in a lot of other countries. For example, the French get about 37 paid
(3)

vacation days, and the Koreans get about 25. American companies give short

vacations for econom_____ reasons. It is expens_____ for the company to pay
(4)   (5)

workers for time off, but short vacations don't help give

employees a posit_____ attitude about their workplaces.
(6)

The working hours in the United States are another

problem. Some Americans have a 50-hour work week. Some

say they do not have time for a soc_____ life. A long work
(7)

week can also be danger_____ . If you work all the time, you
(8)

can have med_____ problems. This is a seri_____ issue.
(9)   (10)

B Pair Work Imagine you are working in your ideal job.
Tell your partner about:

- what you can wear
- the hours you work
- how much vacation you have
- what your co-workers are like

In my ideal job, I don't wear a uniform. I wear casual clothes, like my favorite black running shoes and a sweatshirt. I have a 40-hour work week with no overtime, and I get a four-week vacation every year.

3 More About Adjectives

Grammar Presentation

3.1 Adjectives Ending in -ed and -ing

A Use -ed adjectives to describe how a person feels.	I'm *interested* in workers' rights. I get *bored* when I work by myself.
B Use -ing adjectives to say what something or someone is like.	My new job is *interesting.* Working in an office is *boring*.

3.2 Adjective Patterns

A You usually need a noun or pronoun after an adjective.	*I have a black shirt and a beige* shirt */ a beige* one. *I have a black shirt* ~~and a beige~~. *I wear nice clothes to work, but I don't wear expensive* clothes */ expensive* ones. ~~I don't wear expensive~~.
B Adjectives follow a measurement noun (*years, feet,* etc.).	*There are* eighteen-year-old *workers in some of the factories.* *That ladder is over ten* feet high.
C Adjectives can follow the pronouns *something, anything,* and *nothing.*	*I want to wear* something special *for my first day at work.* *Are you doing* anything interesting *this weekend?*
D Adjectives can follow the verb *make* + an object.	OBJECT ADJECTIVE *My boss* makes *me* nervous. OBJECT ADJECTIVE *Chemicals* make *some people* sick.
E Do not use these adjectives before a noun: *afraid, alike, alive, alone, asleep, awake, aware.* They usually come after the verb *be.*	*The workers were all still* alive *after the factory explosion.* *He's not* asleep. *He's* awake. *I'm* afraid *of heights.*

📊 Data from the Real World

Research shows that these are some of the most common pairs of adjectives ending in *-ing* and *-ed*.

amazing	amazed		exciting	excited
annoying	annoyed		frustrating	frustrated
boring	bored		interesting	interested
confusing	confused		relaxing	relaxed
depressing	depressed		surprising	surprised
embarrassing	embarrassed		worrying	worried

Grammar Application

Exercise 3.1 -ed or -ing?

A Complete the conversations. Choose the correct word.

1 A Have you ever felt __(embarrassed)/ embarrassing__ by a joke that someone told at work or at school?

  B Yes, I have. Someone joked about my accent. That was __annoyed / annoying__ .

2 A Are you __interested / interesting__ in workers' rights? Or do you think it's a __bored / boring__ issue?

  B No, it's a __fascinated / fascinating__ subject. I'm not __bored / boring__ by it at all.

3 A Are you __annoyed / annoying__ by different kinds of discrimination at work?

  B Yes, of course. I'm __surprised / surprising__ that it still happens. It's a __depressed / depressing__ situation.

4 A Is your job ever __relaxed / relaxing__ ?

  B No, but I don't think work is supposed to be __relaxed / relaxing__ . My job is sometimes __excited / exciting__ , and I like that.

5 A Did you ever wear an __embarrassing / embarrassed__ uniform to school or to work?

  B No. I wore a uniform, but it wasn't __embarrassed / embarrassing__ because I liked it.

B Pair Work Practice the conversations with a partner. Then practice them again. This time, give your own answers.

Exercise 3.2 Adjective Patterns

Complete the conversations with *one/ones* and the words in parentheses.

1 A Which pants should I wear, the blue pants or the ___*brown ones*___ ?
      (brown)

  B The brown pants look better.

2 A How's your job?

  B It's OK. There are some nice co-workers and some _____ .
                                                          (less friendly)

3 A Joe has such an interesting job! He always has funny stories to tell.

  B That's true. We only have _____ .
                                   (boring)

4 A Who goes to your restaurant?

  B Most of the customers are young professionals, but there are _____ , too.
                                                                      (older)

5 A I work for an ethical employer.

  B You're lucky. I work for an _____ .
                                      (unfair)

A Correct the mistakes in these sentences. You may need to add or change words.

1 Many ~~aware~~ people are ∧ of gender, race, and ethnic
   aware
   discrimination in the workplace.

2 However, many aware people are not of size and age
   discrimination in the workplace.

3 For example, if a thin woman and an overweight woman
   apply for the same job, the thin often gets the job.

4 If a tall man and a short man try to get a promotion, the
   tall often gets the promotion.

5 A recent survey showed that the average Chief Executive
   Officer (CEO) in the United States is 6 tall feet.

6 Another survey showed that only 3 percent of CEOs in the
   United States are less than tall 5 feet, 7 inches.

7 Many older afraid workers are of age discrimination.

8 An older employee with a lot of experience can make nervous a young boss.

9 Some laws make illegal age discrimination.

10 For example, after you are 40 years, a law called the Age Discrimination Employment Act
   protects you.

B Pair Work Have you heard about someone who experienced discrimination?
Tell a partner about it.

A Add adjectives to the questions below.

1 Do you want a job where you do something _____ every day?

2 In your job, do you ever do anything _____ ?

3 Have you met anyone _____ at work recently?

4 Did anything _____ happen at your job recently?

B Group Work Ask and answer your questions in A. Give extra information in your answer.

A *Do you want a job where you do something exciting every day?*

B *No, actually, I don't. I don't have the energy for that. I want a quiet job where
   I don't do anything exciting or dangerous.*

Exercise 3.5 Using *Make* + Object + Adjective

A Answer the questions about work or school. Use the words in the box or your own ideas to help you answer the questions.

chemicals	early mornings	interesting work	long vacations
dangerous machines	an ethical boss	late nights	loud noise
discrimination	friendly co-workers	long hours	uncomfortable chairs

1 What makes you happy in the workplace?

_____

2 What things about your job make you unhappy?

_____

3 What workplace situations make you worried?

_____

4 Has anything in your workplace ever made you sick?

_____

B Pair Work Discuss your ideas in A with a partner.

4 Avoid Common Mistakes ⚠

1 **Notice the correct spelling of adjectives ending in *-ful* (not *-full*).**
stressful
She has a ~~stressfull~~ job.

2 **Don't confuse these common verbs and adjectives: *interest ≠ interested, relax ≠ relaxed, stress ≠ stressed, worry ≠ worried*.**
worried
I'm ~~worry~~ about my job.

3 **Be careful with adjectives that describe ages and length of time before a noun.**
Fifteen-year-old
~~Fifteen-years-old~~ teenagers work in some restaurants.

4 **Remember to put opinion adjectives before others in a list before a noun.**
wonderful little
We work at a ~~little wonderful~~ shop on the weekends.

Editing Task

Find and correct eight more mistakes in this blog on work–life balance.

Balancing Work Life and Personal Life

interested
I have a very busy life. I have a fun job, and I am ~~interest~~ in my work. My boss is fair, and I work for an ethical company. I have friends. My life sounds perfect, right? However, I work a 60-hours week. I can't get all my work done during the day, so I take it home. I do not spend much time with my husband and our little beautiful four-years-old daughter. I also do not see my wonderfull friends. This makes me feel very stress. I am never relax. I know my friends
5   and family are worry about me.

I think I have a problem. I need some balance between my work life and my personal life. I know there are usefull articles with tips for balancing your life. The problem is, I do not have the time to read them!

Adverbs of Manner and Degree

1 Grammar in the Real World

A Is language learning easy or hard for you? Read the online article about language learning strategies. What are some ways to learn a language, both inside and outside the classroom?

B Comprehension Check **Answer the questions.**

1 What is a learning strategy?
2 What are two strategies that help you do well in class?
3 Why is it a good idea to get a good night's sleep before a test?
4 What are two strategies that help you communicate?

C Notice **Find the sentences in the article and complete them.**

1 In class, listen _____ and take notes.

2 Make a list of new words and study the list _____ .

3 Also, do not stay up _____ the night before a test.

4 If you do not understand a word or phrase, _____ ask the person to explain.

Do the words in your answers describe people, or do they describe how an action happens?

Learn to Learn a **LANGUAGE**

¹**style:** way of doing something that is typical of a person, group, place, or time

²**technique:** a specific way of doing a skillful activity

Everyone has his or her own style¹ of learning a new language. Some students listen **quietly** in class. Others ask lots of questions. Some students study **alone**, and others study in groups. However, one thing is true for all learners. You can become a better language
5 learner by using learning strategies. Language learning strategies are techniques² that help you learn. There are strategies that help you do **well** in your class, and there are strategies that help you use the language with others.

There are many study strategies for your classes. For example, in
10 class, listen **carefully** and take notes. The first time you read something, skim it. This means you read the material **quickly** and only look for the main points. Then read again and take notes on your reading. Make a list of new words and study the list **regularly**. Do not study for a test at the last minute. Also, do not stay up **late** the night before a test.
15 Instead, get lots of sleep. A good night's sleep helps you think **clearly**.

Strategies also help you communicate with people in a new language. Talking to people is a good way to improve listening and speaking. However, some people speak very **quickly**, and they do not speak **clearly**. **Politely** ask a person to speak **slowly** and **clearly.** This is a useful
20 strategy. It is also a good idea to ask the person to repeat things. If you do not understand a word or phrase, **politely** ask the person to explain.

Learning strategies are good both for your classes and for communication outside of class. They help you to learn a new language **quickly** and **easily**.

2 Adverbs of Manner

Grammar Presentation

Adverbs of manner describe how an action happens.	I read *quietly* in the library. The teacher says the answers *quickly*.

2.1 Forming Adverbs of Manner

A Add *-ly* to most adjectives to form adverbs of manner.	quick → quickly She *quickly* memorized the words. careful → carefully Nick read the chapter *carefully*.
B Some adverbs have the same form as adjectives: *alone, early, fast, hard, high, late, low, right, wrong*.	He studied *alone*. (adverb; describes how he studied) The boy is *alone*. (adjective; describes the boy)
These adverbs usually go after the verb.	He ~~alone~~ studied. He studied *alone*.
C The adverb form of *good* is *well*.	Tom did *well* on the test. Tom did ~~good~~ on the test. She speaks English *well*. She speaks English ~~good~~.
Well only goes after the verb.	We communicate *well*. We ~~well~~ communicate.
D Some adjectives end in *-ly*. They are not adverbs. Examples: *friendly, lively, lovely, silly, ugly*.	Sara is *friendly*. (adjective; describes Sara) She makes *silly* faces in class. (adjective; describes faces)

2.2 Using Adverbs of Manner

A Most adverbs of manner come after the verb or after the verb + the object. Do not put an adverb between a verb and the object.	He spells *terribly*. She always writes her essays very *carefully*. They take ~~carefully~~ tests.
B Many adverbs of manner can also come before the verb for emphasis.	She *nervously* looked at the test.

2.2 Using Adverbs of Manner (continued)

C	Adverbs of manner usually come between the auxiliary verb (*be*, *have*) or modal verb (*can*, *should*) and the main verb.	They are *quietly* waiting for the test results. He has *suddenly* left the room. You can *politely* ask a question.
D	Do not use adverbs after *be* or linking verbs (*appear*, *look*, *feel*, *sound*, *seem*, *smell*, *taste*). Use an adjective instead.	The test *sounds* easy. The test sounds ~~easily~~.

Grammar Application

Exercise 2.1 Forming Adverbs

Complete the sentences with the correct adverb forms.

The Learners' Blog

What learning strategies do YOU use? Here's what our readers are using!

Marc J. I have a lot of reading assignments. I read _____*quickly*_____ (quick) through a
(1)
whole chapter. Then I read it _____ (careful) a second time.
(2)

Lisa L. I'm studying Chinese. I make flash cards for new words, and I study them
_____ (regular). It works! I always do _____
(3)   (4)
(good) on tests.

Roberto R. I don't like to study _____ (alone), so I joined a study group.
(5)
We study _____ (hard), but we have a good time, too!
(6)

Danielle F. I always go to bed _____ (early) before a big test.
(7)
The next day, I think _____ (clear) and do
(8)
_____ (good).
(9)

Nick B. When I read a textbook chapter, I skim the headings and _____
(10)
(quick) read the first sentence of each paragraph.

Jin P. There are a lot of hard words in textbooks! If I don't know a word, I read the
sentence _____ (slow) and try to figure out the meaning.
(11)

Read a student's blog entry about memory tricks. Decide if each word in **bold** is an adverb or an adjective. Circle the adverbs. Underline the adjectives.

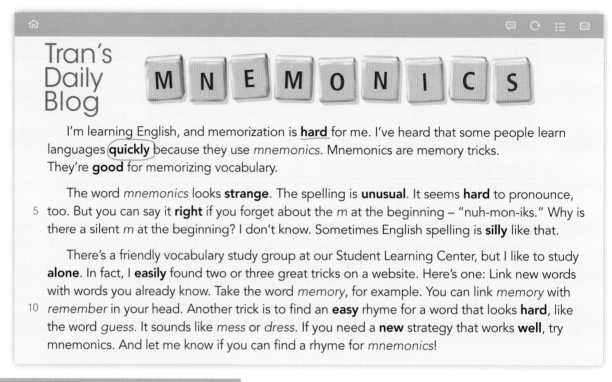

Tran's Daily Blog

MNEMONICS

I'm learning English, and memorization is **hard** for me. I've heard that some people learn languages (quickly) because they use *mnemonics*. Mnemonics are memory tricks. They're **good** for memorizing vocabulary.

The word *mnemonics* looks **strange**. The spelling is **unusual**. It seems **hard** to pronounce, too. But you can say it **right** if you forget about the *m* at the beginning – "nuh-mon-iks." Why is there a silent *m* at the beginning? I don't know. Sometimes English spelling is **silly** like that.

There's a friendly vocabulary study group at our Student Learning Center, but I like to study **alone**. In fact, I **easily** found two or three great tricks on a website. Here's one: Link new words with words you already know. Take the word *memory*, for example. You can link *memory* with *remember* in your head. Another trick is to find an **easy** rhyme for a word that looks **hard**, like the word *guess*. It sounds like *mess* or *dress*. If you need a **new** strategy that works **well**, try mnemonics. And let me know if you can find a rhyme for *mnemonics*!

Complete the sentences about preparing for tests. Circle the correct words.

1 Studies show that students who do not sleep (well)/ good do <u>poor</u>/<u>poorly</u> on tests.

2 Try to get a <u>good</u>/<u>well</u> night's sleep before a test.

3 Do not stay up <u>late</u>/<u>lately</u> the night before a test.

4 It is common to feel <u>nervously</u>/<u>nervous</u> the night before a big test, so try to relax.

5 Review everything <u>carefully</u>/<u>careful</u> two nights before a test; that way, you will sleep <u>sound</u>/<u>soundly</u> the night before the test.

6 The evening before a test, spend your time <u>peaceful</u>/<u>peacefully</u>: listen to music or take a warm bath.

7 On the morning of the test, eat <u>proper</u>/<u>properly</u>. For example, some experts recommend a high-protein breakfast like eggs.

8 Drink water <u>frequently</u>/<u>frequent</u> throughout the day.

Exercise 2.4 Word Order

A Rewrite the sentences. Change the adjectives into adverbs, and put them in the correct place. Sometimes more than one answer is correct.

1 I got up for my 8:00 a.m. class. (early)   *I got up early for my 8:00 a.m. class.*

2 Max is taking notes. (neat)   _____

3 Tim always studies. (alone)   _____

4 She asks questions in class. (polite)   _____

5 My teacher pronounces new words. (clear)   _____

6 I study hard, so I pass all my tests! (easy)   _____

7 Ana has learned some mnemonics. (quick)   _____

8 I proofread my paper. (careful)   _____

B Over to You   Make a list of the strategies you have seen in this unit so far. Check (✓) the ones you use now and the ones you are going to try to use. Add your own strategies to the list if you want. Then compare lists with a partner. Use adverbs of manner.

    A *What strategies do you use?*

    B *I make flash cards and study them regularly. How about you?*

3 Adverbs of Degree

Grammar Presentation

Adverbs of degree make other adverbs or adjectives stronger or weaker.

The reading was quite confusing.
The teacher speaks kind of softly.

3.1 Adverbs of Degree

			somewhat
more formal	quite extremely very	rather fairly	
stronger ←——————————————————→ **weaker**			
less formal	really so	pretty	kind of sort of

A Adverbs of degree can be used with adjectives or adverbs to make them stronger or weaker.	ADVERB ADVERB *The teacher speaks extremely softly.* ADVERB ADJECTIVE *The reading was extremely difficult.* ADVERB ADJECTIVE *I had a really wonderful day!*
B Do not use the weaker adverbs of degree in negative statements.	*Tim did not study very hard for the test.* *Tim did not study ~~fairly~~ hard for the test.* *Ana did not ask ~~somewhat~~ politely.*
C Use these adverbs of degree with adjectives or adverbs to give opinions: *amazingly, dangerously, horribly, incredibly, seriously, terribly, wonderfully.*	*She did amazingly well on the test.* *We worked incredibly hard on our class project.* *Your paper is wonderfully creative.*
D Use *enough* after an adverb or an adjective to show whether an amount is acceptable.	*I studied hard enough.* (an acceptable amount) *Your essay seems long enough.* (an acceptable amount) *I did not study hard enough.* (an unacceptable amount) *Your essay doesn't seem long enough.* (an unacceptable amount)
E Use *too* before an adverb or an adjective to show whether an amount is more than necessary.	*We studied too hard!* (more than necessary) *Your essay is too long.* (more than necessary) *We did not study too hard.* (not more than necessary) *Your essay is not too long.* (not more than necessary)

Grammar Application

Exercise 3.1 Adverbs of Degree

A Complete the sentences. Circle the adverb of degree that matches the type in parentheses: either weak, strong, or in the middle.

1 My English class is (sort of)/ pretty fun. (weak)

2 The teacher is **really** / **pretty** nice. (strong)

3 My teacher speaks **very/kind of** quickly. (weak)

4 I listen **really/pretty** hard, but I don't understand everything. (in the middle)

5 My math class is **extremely/somewhat** difficult. (weak)

6 I do the assignments **pretty/very** carefully. (strong)

7 We have a **very/rather** difficult quiz every Friday. (strong)

8 I study **so/fairly** hard every night. (strong)

9 I get **fairly/quite** nervous before every quiz. (in the middle)

10 I'm **pretty/really** sure I'm going to get a good grade. (in the middle)

B Over to You Write six sentences about your teachers, your classes, and your schoolwork. Then discuss your sentences with a partner. Use adverbs of degree that are weak, strong, and in the middle.

A *I'm pretty sure I'm going to get a good grade in English.*

B *Why?*

A *I study very hard before every test.*

Exercise 3.2 Using *Too* and *Enough*

A Match the statement on the left with the correct response on the right. Complete the responses with *too* or *enough* and the adjectives or adverbs in parentheses.

1 I didn't do as well as I expected on the test. ___f___

2 I have to rewrite my essay. _____

3 I have a big test tomorrow. _____

4 Is my homework OK? It's due soon. _____

5 The group meets at 8:00 a.m. Can you come? _____

6 We have only two days to write a paper. _____

7 The teacher didn't hear my questions. _____

8 We've studied all day. I'm tired! _____

a Yes, we've studied _____ .
  (long)
  Let's go to bed.

b Two days doesn't seem _____ !
  (long)

c Sure. That's not _____ for me.
  (early)

d Then don't stay up _____
  (late)
  tonight!

e Maybe you didn't speak _____ .
  (loudly)

f Maybe you didn't study *hard enough* .
  (hard)

g Maybe it was _____ .
  (short)

h Sure. It looks _____ . You
  (good)
  can turn it in.

B Pair Work Practice the statements and responses in A with a partner.

Data from the Real World

Research shows that the formal adverbs of degree are more common in class papers, presentations, and other formal situations.	The questions were *extremely* difficult. (more formal)
Use the less formal adverbs of degree in conversations with friends, in e-mails, and in other informal situations.	The questions were *really* difficult. (less formal)

Read a formal letter that a student wrote to a professor. Choose the correct adverbs of degree.

Dear Dr. Green,

I am in your Math 101 class. I am really / (quite) worried about my grades for this class. I am
(1)

pretty / fairly sure that I am not doing very / so well. The work for this class is so / extremely difficult
(2)   (3)   (4)

for me. I do the assignments pretty / rather carefully, but I do not understand everything. I study
(5)

quite / so hard for every test. However, I did not study extremely / sort of hard for the last test, and I
(6)   (7)

know I did not do so / very well.
(8)

Can you give me some advice? I am very / really eager to improve in your class.
(9)

Thank you.

Sincerely,

Matthew Yee

Exercise 3.4 Listening for Adverbs of Degree

A Listen to a group of students. They are working on a flier about study skills. Complete their conversation with the adverbs of degree that you hear. Then compare your answers with a partner.

Alison	So, what are some tips for studying and getting good grades?
Dinh	Well, it's important to study _____*really*_____ hard.
	(1)
Alison	Right. It's also _____ important to do all of your
	(2)
	homework. What do you think, Carlos?
Carlos	Um, my vocabulary notebook is _____ helpful to me!
	(3)
Alison	How does that help?
Carlos	When I want to use a new word, my notebook has sentences to help me
	remember how to use it.
Dinh	Hmm, I don't know . . .
Carlos	Oh, it works _____ well, in my opinion.
	(4)
Dinh	OK. So, a vocabulary notebook is a _____ good idea.
	(5)

Alison Yes. So we have three tips. Study, do your homework, and keep a vocabulary notebook. What else?

Dinh Asking questions. Ask questions in class. That's _____ important.

(6)

Carlos Here's another one: I think it's a _____ good idea to have a study

(7)
group. It's _____ important to have people to study with and to

(8)
talk about class with, in my opinion.

Dinh I agree. Studying together is _____ helpful!

(9)

B Group Work Brainstorm ideas for a group about study skills. Use the ideas from the conversation and your own ideas. Then make a flier on a piece of paper. Use formal adverbs in your flier, not the informal ones that the students used.

4 Avoid Common Mistakes ⚠

1 **Use an adverb, not an adjective, to describe how something happened.**

carefully
She studied very ~~careful~~.

2 **Well is the adverb for good.**

well
He did ~~good~~ on the test.

3 **Do not put an adverb between the verb and the object.**

the questions loudly
They answered ~~loudly the questions~~.

4 **In negative statements, only use strong adverbs.**

very
They did not study ~~fairly~~ hard.

5 **Remember that some adverbs have the same form as adjectives.**

hard
He is working ~~hardly~~ at his new job.

Editing Task

Find and correct seven more mistakes in this conversation about studying.

Marisa I didn't do ~~good~~ on the test today!

well

Sam Did you study hardly last night?

Marisa I tried, but it was so loud in the library. How about you?

Sam I didn't do good, either. I studied, but I didn't sleep pretty well.

5 **Marisa** And the test seemed easy.

Sam But it wasn't. It was too hard!

Marisa Well, what happened? We took carefully notes.

Sam And we listened good in class.

Marisa Maybe we didn't study careful enough.

10 **Sam** I'm suddenly getting nervous!

Marisa Why?

Sam Well, we don't have a pretty long time before the next test!

Prepositions

Food on the Table

1 Grammar in the Real World

A Where did the food you ate today come from? Read the article about how food is produced and sometimes wasted. Where are three places that food goes before it reaches our plates?

B Comprehension Check **Answer the questions.**

1 How much food did Americans throw away in 2018? Is this food safe to eat?

2 According to the article, why do farmers throw away food?

3 Why do processing plants throw away food?

4 What are food banks?

5 Why is it better to buy food from local farmers?

C Notice **Find the sentences in the article and complete them.**

1 _____ 2016, 41.2 million people _____ the United States could not afford to eat every day.

2 Our food has often traveled hundreds of miles _____ farms _____ our plates.

3 _____ the farm, food usually goes _____ a processing plant.

4 Trucks take it _____ the country to warehouses, distribution centers, and supermarkets.

Look at the words you wrote in the blanks. Which words show time? Which show place? Which show movement?

From **Plow** to **Plate**

(and Sometimes to the Trash)

[1]**processing:** the preparation, change, or treatment of food with chemicals to make it last longer

[2]**warehouse, distribution center:** large building used for storing goods

In 2016, 41.2 million people in the United States struggled with hunger. **In** 2018, a study found that Americans throw out 150,000 tons of food a day, or about a pound per person. Most of the wasted food is fruit, vegetables, dairy, and meat. Most of this food is perfectly good and safe to eat. Why do we waste this food? How can we waste less of it?

Our food has often traveled hundreds of miles **from** farms **to** our plates. **At** every step of this journey, people throw away food. **On** farms, farmers throw away food that is the wrong size, shape, or color. **From** the farm, food usually goes to a processing[1] plant. **At** the processing plant, workers clean it, package it, and sometimes cook it or add chemicals. They also throw away food they cannot transport or sell. Then food leaves the plant. Trucks take it **across** the country to warehouses, distribution centers,[2] and supermarkets. All of these places throw away food that people do not buy.

After this long process, we buy the food and store it **in** our refrigerators. Sometimes we forget it, or we buy too much. Then we throw it away, too. Restaurants also throw away food that we do not order or eat.

We can waste less food. Supermarkets and restaurants can give unused food to food banks – groups that distribute food to poor and hungry people. **At** the supermarket, we can ask ourselves, "Do I really need to buy this? Will I use this food right away?" We can also buy food **from** local farmers. This food does not go **through** processing plants, so there is less waste.

2 Prepositions of Place and Time

Grammar Presentation

Prepositions can show place and time.	People often have too much food *on* the table. *In* 2018, a study found that Americans throw out 150,000 tons of food a day, or about a pound per person.

2.1 Prepositions of Place

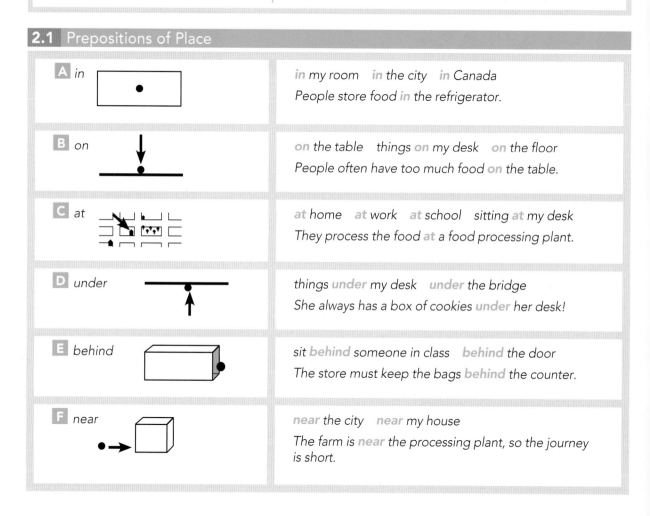

A *in*	*in* my room *in* the city *in* Canada People store food *in* the refrigerator.
B *on*	*on* the table things *on* my desk *on* the floor People often have too much food *on* the table.
C *at*	*at* home *at* work *at* school sitting *at* my desk They process the food *at* a food processing plant.
D *under*	things *under* my desk *under* the bridge She always has a box of cookies *under* her desk!
E *behind*	sit *behind* someone in class *behind* the door The store must keep the bags *behind* the counter.
F *near*	*near* the city *near* my house The farm is *near* the processing plant, so the journey is short.

2.2 Prepositions of Time

A Use prepositions of time to say when events happen.

Use *at* for clock times and with *night*.	The trucks arrive *at* noon every day with fresh food. We often go out *at* night.
Use *in* for parts of the day (except *night*), months, seasons, and years.	*In* the spring, the farmers plant new crops. The trucks arrive at the plant *in* the morning.
Use *on* for dates and special days.	People often have barbecues and picnics *on* July 4.

B In sentences that include two different times . . .
use *before* to refer to the earlier time.

I need to go grocery shopping *before* dinner. (First is grocery shopping, then dinner.)

use *after* to refer to the later time.

After breakfast, we do the dishes. (First is breakfast, then the dishes.)

C Use *during* to refer to the time that something is in progress.

The food loses freshness *during* its journey to supermarkets.

food loses freshness

journey

D Use *for* to say how long something takes or lasts.

The food stays at the distribution center *for* three days.

Day 1   Day 2   Day 3

Use *since* to refer to the time from a point in the past up to now.

Since June, the farm has sold 120 tons of fruit.

June   now

2.3 Prepositional Phrases

A prepositional phrase is a preposition followed by an object of a preposition. The object must be a noun phrase or a verb in the *-ing* form.

PREP.   OBJECT OF PREP.
They put the food *in the refrigerator*.

PREP.   OBJECT OF PREP.
The fruit is *on the counter*.

PREP. OBJECT OF PREP.
We need fresh water *for drinking*.

Exercise 2.1 Prepositions of Place and Time

A Complete the magazine article. Circle the correct prepositions.

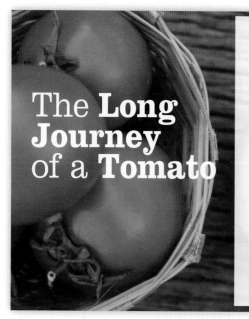

The Long Journey of a Tomato

__On / At__ Monday, July 13, Jeff Green picked the tomatoes at his farm
(1)
in Florida. The next day, a truck arrived. It took the tomatoes to a processing
plant __near / in__ Jeff's farm. The plant was about five miles away.
(2)
The tomatoes were there for three days. __At / During__ that time, workers
(3)
checked them, washed them, and put them __at / in__ plastic containers.
(4)
__In / On__ July 17, the tomatoes went on trucks. The trucks took them to a
(5)
distribution center 300 miles away. __After / Before__ that, the tomatoes
(6)
went to a supermarket in New Jersey. Ana Luz bought them, took them home,
and put them in her refrigerator. __After / Before__ that, the tomatoes sat
(7)
__in / on__ the supermarket shelf __for / since__ two days. It was Friday,
(8)   (9)
July 24. Ana did not know that her "fresh" tomatoes were 11 days old.

B Pair Work Write answers to the questions below. Use prepositions. Then ask and answer
the questions with a partner.

1 **A** When did Jeff Green pick tomatoes on his farm?

  B *On Monday, July 13.*

2 **A** Where did a truck take the tomatoes?

  B _____

3 **A** Where was the processing plant?

  B _____

4 **A** How long were the tomatoes at the processing plant?

  B _____

5 **A** Where did the processing plant workers put the tomatoes?

  B _____

6 **A** Where did the tomatoes sit for two days?

  B _____

Exercise 2.2 Prepositions of Place

A Look at the picture and complete the answers. Use the prepositions in the box. You will use some prepositions more than once.

at	behind	in	on	under

1 A Where is the box of oranges?   **B** It's ___*on*___ the floor.

2 A Where are the paper bags?   **B** They're _____ the checkout stand.

3 A Where are the cartons of milk?   **B** They're _____ the checkout stand.

4 A Where are the cartons of juice?   **B** They're _____ the refrigerator case.

5 A Where are the bananas?   **B** They're _____ the melons.

6 A Where is the cashier standing?   **B** She's _____ the checkout stand.

7 A Where is the water?   **B** It's _____ the shelf _____ the refrigerator case.

8 A Where are the tomatoes?   **B** They're _____ a box _____ the floor.

9 A Where are the apples?   **B** They're _____ the bananas.

B Over to You Answer these questions in complete sentences. Use a preposition from the box in A. Then compare your answers with a partner.

1 Where are you right now?

_____

2 Who is sitting behind you right now?

_____

3 Who is sitting near you?

_____

4 What is on your desk?

_____

3 Prepositions of Direction and Manner

Grammar Presentation

Prepositions can show direction and manner (a way of doing something).	*The food goes from the processing plant to the supermarket.* (direction: from X → Y) *She prepares the food with fresh ingredients.* (manner: how she prepares the food)

3.1 Prepositions of Direction and Movement

Use these prepositions to show how people and things move.

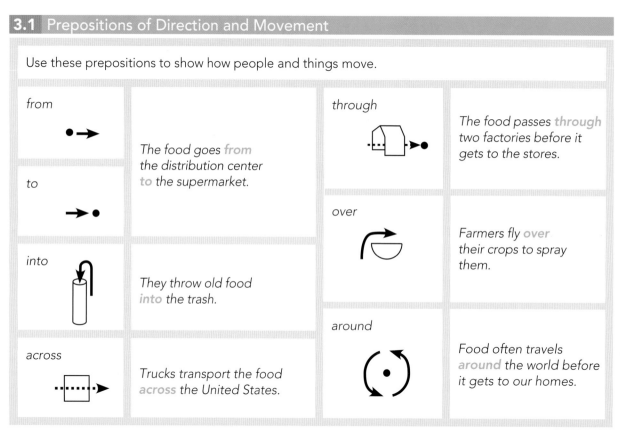

from

The food goes from the distribution center to the supermarket.

to

into

They throw old food into the trash.

across

Trucks transport the food across the United States.

through

The food passes through two factories before it gets to the stores.

over

Farmers fly over their crops to spray them.

around

Food often travels around the world before it gets to our homes.

3.2 Prepositions of Manner and Logical Relationships

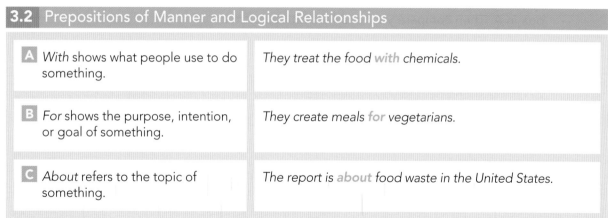

A With shows what people use to do something.	*They treat the food with chemicals.*
B For shows the purpose, intention, or goal of something.	*They create meals for vegetarians.*
C About refers to the topic of something.	*The report is about food waste in the United States.*

3.2 Prepositions of Manner and Logical Relationships *(continued)*

D *As* refers to the role or job of a person or thing.	*He works as a truck driver for a food processing company.*
E *Of* shows a close relationship, such as possession, identity, or being a part of something.	*People in the United States waste about a pound of food each per day.* *Most of this food is perfectly good to eat.*
F *Between* refers to the space that separates two people, things, or numbers.	*Families waste between 25 percent and 33 percent of the food that they buy.*

3.3 Using Prepositions with Noun Phrases and Pronouns

A You can use prepositions before noun phrases and pronouns. Use the object form of personal pronouns (*me, him, us*).	*On my birthday, I had a special meal.* *Some friends cooked it for me.*
B You can use prepositions with *Wh-* questions (questions that start with *who, what, which,* etc.).	*Who do I send this fruit basket to?*

📊 Data from the Real World

Research shows that the 20 most common prepositions in writing and speaking are:

about	around	at	between	during	from	into	on	since	to
after	as	before	by	for	in	of	over	through	with

Exercise 3.1 Prepositions of Direction and Movement

A A teacher is taking a group of students on a tour of a local supermarket. Complete the conversation. Use the prepositions in the box.

| across | around | from | into | over | through | ~~to~~ | to |

Ms. Ross OK, everyone, let's go _to_ the fruit and vegetable
(1)
section. Now, can anyone tell me: Where do these
peaches come _____ ?
(2)

Claire Let's see. Georgia.

Ms. Ross Right. And we're in Oregon. They came a long way.
They traveled right _____ the United
(3)
States, from the South to the Northwest.

Rob But peaches from Georgia are the best. I flew
_____ Georgia once and saw some
(4)
fruit farms from the air. Do you think these peaches
came _____ Oregon by air?
(5)

Ms. Ross They probably came by truck. Workers put them
_____ boxes and put the boxes into
(6)
refrigerated trucks. Then they probably passed _____ a couple of
(7)
factories and warehouses, too. Now, let's look at these beans. Where are they from?

Julia Kenya.

Ms. Ross Correct. A lot of these fruits and vegetables probably traveled _____
(8)
the world before they got here.

Exercise 3.2 Pronunciation Focus

Some common prepositions have two
pronunciations: a strong form and a weak form.

	Strong Form	Weak Form
at	/æt/	/ət/
for	/fɔːr/	/fər/
from	/frʌm/ (or /frɑm/)	/frəm/
of	/ʌv/ (or /ɑv/)	/əv/
to	/tuː/	/tə/

Use the weak form in informal conversation, when you speak quickly and naturally.

Let's go to the supermarket.
These tomatoes are from Florida.

Use the strong form:
• when you speak formally, slowly, and carefully
• when you need to stress the preposition
• when the preposition is at the end of the sentence
• with *to* when the next sound is a vowel sound

Welcome to this presentation of my work.
I was driving to the store, not from the store.
Where do these peaches come from?
Let's go to a farmers' market.

A Listen to the questions and answers and repeat them.

1 **A** Are they from California?   **B** No.

2 **A** So, where are they from?   **B** From Georgia.

3 **A** Is that a box of apples?   **B** No, it's a box of tomatoes.

4 **A** I'll see you at the restaurant.   **B** No, let's go to the cafeteria.

5 **A** Who is this peach for?   **B** It's for you. Enjoy!

6 **A** Are you going to the supermarket today?   **B** No, we're going to a farmers' market.

B Pair Work Now practice asking and answering the questions in A with a partner.

Exercise 3.3 Prepositions of Place, Manner, and Logical Relationships

A Listen to the presentation and complete it with the prepositions that you hear.

Good morning. My talk today is __*about*__ merchandising. Supermarkets position
(1)

items carefully. They place things _____ refrigerator
(2)

cases, _____ shelves, and even _____
(3)   (4)

the checkout stand. This is called *merchandising.*

Merchandising helps supermarkets sell more items to people

in the store. For example, they put candy _____ other
(5)

food items, so children ask for the candy when their parents are

buying other things. Supermarkets also place certain items near the

floor. They put them _____ a place that children can see easily. For
(6)

example, they put items children want _____ the lower shelves. And
(7)

have you ever noticed kitchen gadgets _____ the food items on the
(8)

shelves? This is another example of merchandising.

Supermarkets also place items like magazines at the checkout stands. People

see them when they are waiting in line and put them _____ their carts.
(9)

In addition, research shows that people buy more cold items, for example juice or

cheese, when the refrigerated shelves are open. That's because they can see what is

_____ them.
(10)

So, next time you're waiting in line _____ the checkout stand, ask
(11)

yourself, "Why did I buy this? Was it because I needed it, or just because I saw it?"

Even _____ careful shoppers, we all sometimes put things we don't
(12)

need in our carts.

B Pair Work When you go to a supermarket, what do you notice?
Discuss your ideas with a partner. Talk about these things:

- the prices of things

- information about ingredients, or what is in things

- information about where food comes from

- any other things that you notice or look for

A *The first things I notice are the products at the ends of the aisles. What about you?*
B *I usually look for what's on sale.*

4 Phrasal Prepositions and Prepositions After Adjectives

Grammar Presentation

Some prepositions consist of more than one word. These are called *phrasal prepositions*. Many adjectives have particular prepositions that follow them.	*Wei was standing in front of me at the checkout stand.* *Are you good at shopping for the best prices?*

4.1 Using Phrasal Prepositions

You can use phrasal prepositions just like one-word prepositions, before noun phrases and pronouns. Use the object form of personal pronouns (*me, him, us*).	*The organic food store is next to <u>the bank</u> on Ginsberg Street.* *My teacher was standing in front of <u>me</u> at the supermarket checkout yesterday.*

▦ Data from the Real World

Research shows that these are the most common phrasal prepositions in speaking and writing.

Phrasal Prepositions	Meaning	
as well as	means "and" or "also"	Restaurants, *as well as* supermarkets, throw away tons of food every year.
because of	tells you the reason	The food loses its freshness *because of* the long journey from the plow to the plate.
close to	means "near"	I live *close to* a small store.
in front of		At the checkout stand, do you look at what the person *in front of* you is buying?
instead of	means "A, not B"	Nowadays, I shop at a farmers' market *instead of* a big supermarket. (I shop at farmers' markets, not big supermarkets.)
next to		The tea is *next to* the coffee on the supermarket shelf.
out of		When the food comes *out of* the processing plant, it goes to a distribution center.
outside of		Do you buy food that is produced *outside of* the United States?
such as	means "for example"	The supermarket places products *such as* candy and toys on the lower shelves.
up to		Take the elevator *up to* the second floor, and you will see the books about food and nutrition.

4.2 Using Adjectives with Prepositions

A You can use adjectives with prepositions before nouns, noun phrases, and pronouns. Use the object form of personal pronouns (*me, him, us*).

The cafeteria was *full of* <u>students</u>.

Junk food is *bad for* <u>people's health</u>.

I was *surprised by* <u>the article about wasted food</u>.

Frozen food is *separate from* <u>the fresh fruit</u> in the supermarket.

I'm *worried about* <u>the chemicals used in food</u>.

Fresh vegetables are *good for* <u>us</u>.

He looks sick. Is anything *wrong with* <u>him</u>?

B You can use adjectives with prepositions without a noun or pronoun in sentences with a *Wh-* word (*who, what, which,* etc.).

<u>What</u> are the high food prices *due to*?
<u>Which</u> games are the kids *excited about*?
<u>Who</u> is the supermarket manager *responsible for*?

Data from the Real World

These are the most common adjectives used with prepositions.

Adjectives	Preposition	
aware full	of	Many people are not *aware of* the cost of transporting food. Farmers' markets are *full of* fresh, local produce.
different separate	from	The tomatoes from my friend's garden were *different from* the supermarket tomatoes. Restaurants keep produce *separate from* meat and poultry.
due similar	to	High food prices this year are *due to* bad weather. The price of local fruit is sometimes *similar to* the price of imported fruit.
familiar wrong	with	Are you *familiar with* this type of merchandising? There's something *wrong with* these peaches. They're hard and dry.
good surprised	at	Are you *good at* math? Can you add up these prices? I was *surprised at* the amount of food we waste.
interested	in	I'm not *interested in* the quality of the food. I just want to eat.
responsible good	for	Who is *responsible for* the quality of food in the student cafeteria? Cooking at home is *good for* you.
worried excited	about	I'm *worried about* all the chemicals that they use to treat food. We're *excited about* the new restaurant in town.

🖥 Grammar Application

Exercise 4.1 Phrasal Prepositions

Complete the sentences. Use the words in the box.

because	close	instead	~~outside~~	outside	such	well	well

1 Many types of food come from places <u>***outside***</u> of our own country or region.

2 Items _____ as exotic fruits often travel across continents to supermarkets.

3 Transportation costs, as _____ as production costs, are very high.

4 Buying food from farms _____ of our own country or region means food travels farther.

5 _____ of these factors, food prices are high.

6 Nowadays, many people prefer to buy local food _____ of food from other countries.

7 They prefer to buy food from farms that are in or _____ to their own region or state.

8 If you go to a local store or market _____ of a store that is a long way from your home, you are saving gas, as _____ as helping your neighborhood economy.

Exercise 4.2 More Phrasal Prepositions

Look at the pictures. Complete the statements. Use the words in the box.

as well as	close to	~~next to~~	out of
because of	in front of	next to	outside of

1 In picture 1, Lisa is sitting **_next to_** Diego.

2 Ali is sitting _____ Blanca.

3 Chelsea is sitting _____ Anne.

4 Anne isn't sitting _____ Blanca.

5 In picture 2, the traffic is going slowly _____ the snow.

6 There are trucks _____ cars on the highway.

7 The traffic is going _____ the city.

8 The highway is _____ the city.

A Complete the questionnaire about shopping. Write the missing prepositions.

Shopping Behavior

1 When you are in a supermarket, are you aware ___*of*___ different package sizes? Are you more likely to buy a larger package than a smaller package of something?

2 At a supermarket, what do you get excited _____ ?

3 Are you ever surprised _____ how much your grocery bill is at the checkout?

4 Do you only buy things that are good _____ you?

5 Is your supermarket cart often full _____ things you don't really need?

6 Do you buy books, clothes, and food all in one store, or do you prefer bookstores and clothing stores that are separate _____ supermarkets?

7 When you spend too much at the supermarket, do you think it is due _____ your choices, or is it the fault of the supermarket?

8 Do you think there is anything wrong _____ the way people shop in supermarkets? If yes, what?

B Pair Work Make your own questionnaire about shopping. Choose five questions from A. Then add three questions of your own.

Shopping Behavior

1 _____

2 _____

3 _____

4 _____

5 _____

6 _____

7 _____

8 _____

9 _____

10 _____

C Pair Work Take turns asking and answering your questions.

D Group work Discuss your questions with other classmates.

Tell the class anything interesting you learn.

Ana, Luis, Roberto and I never buy things we don't really need. We all make a shopping list and only buy the things on it.

5 Avoid Common Mistakes ⚠

1 **Use *in*, not *at*, with large areas such as cities, states, and countries.**

There are thousands of farmers' markets ~~at~~ *in* the United States.

2 **Use *on*, not *at* or *in*, for days and dates.**

I always do my grocery shopping ~~in~~ *on* Saturdays.

3 **Use *for*, not *during* or *since*, to refer to how long something takes or lasts.**

The food stays at the processing plant ~~since~~ *for* two or three days.

4 **Use the correct preposition after an adjective.**

I am interested ~~on~~ *in* ways to save money on food.

Editing Task

Find and correct six more mistakes in this article about the problem of wasting food.

       Meg Handford lives ~~at~~ *in* a small town in Oregon. She read about food processing and distribution. She was worried on the amount of gas people use to transport food from farms to supermarkets and from supermarkets to homes. She thought it was bad to the environment, so she decided to do something about it.

5   Meg wanted to make things better. She thought, "Maybe people can share shopping trips." So in July 2014, Meg set up Food Pool.

       Food Pool is like a car pool. In a car pool, neighbors and colleagues travel to work together in one car instead of two or three. With Food Pool, neighbors go to the supermarket or a farmers' market together. They do this in Saturdays or other free days.

10   Meg started a website. She was surprised at the number of interested people. Soon her inbox was full in e-mails. Now there are more than 50 families at her area that share the trip to the supermarket. Food Pool has been running since five years and is growing every year.

Life Lists

1 Grammar in the Real World

A What exciting things do you want to do someday? Read the blog about a "life list." What does the writer hope to do someday?

B Comprehension Check **Answer the questions.**

1 What is a life list?

2 What is one reason to create a life list?

3 What are two tips to help you create a life list?

C Notice **Find the sentences in the article and complete them.**

1 I _____ ride in a hot-air balloon.

2 I _____ travel to all 50 states in the United States.

3 _____ you _____ create a life list, too?

4 Understand that it _____ take time to accomplish the things on your list.

Are the sentences about the present or the future?

My LIFE LIST

September 23

posted by: Lisa Sanchez

Welcome to a new feature of my blog – my life list. What is a life list? It's a list of things that you **are going to do** before you die, if you can.

5 Here are some things on my life list:

- I**'m going to ride** in a hot-air balloon.
- I**'m going to live** in Spain.
- I**'m going to write** a poem.
- I**'m going to travel** to all 50 states in the United States.

10 Psychologists[1] agree that life lists are motivating. They encourage people to try new things. However, to achieve the goals on your list, you need to be realistic[2] and have a plan. For example, I**'m not visiting** all 50 states this year. I don't have the money! First, I**'m going to make** a plan to save money for each trip, and I**'m going to do** research on the

15 places I want to visit. That is the point of a life list. It motivates you to work toward your goals. I**'m going to have to** work to accomplish my life list!

Are you **going to create** a life list, too? Here are some tips:

1 Make a list that reflects the direction you want for your life. For example, I want to understand more about the world, so

20 travel is a big part of my life list.

2 Understand that it **is going to take** time to accomplish the things on your list – maybe a lifetime!

If you follow these simple steps, you **aren't going to be** disappointed. Your life **is going to be** full of new adventures and

25 new accomplishments.

[1]**psychologist:** someone who studies the mind and emotions and their relationship to behavior

[2]**realistic:** showing an understanding of how things really are

2 Be Going To, Present Progressive, and Simple Present for Future Events

Grammar Presentation

Be going to describes future plans, predictions, and expectations. The present progressive and the simple present can also refer to the future.

I'm going to ride in a hot-air balloon.
I'm moving to Spain next month.
My flight leaves at 7:00 tomorrow morning.

2.1 Be Going To: Statements

STATEMENTS

Subject	Be	(Not) going to	Base Form of Verb	
I	am			
You We They	are	(not) going to	live	in Spain.
He She It	is			

CONTRACTIONS

Affirmative	Negative	
I'm	I'm not	
You're We're They're	You're not We're not They're not	You aren't We aren't They aren't
He's She's It's	He's not She's not It's not	He isn't She isn't It isn't

2.2 Be Going To: Yes/No Questions and Short Answers

Be	Subject	Going to	Base Form of Verb
Am	I		
Are	you we they	going to	visit Spain?
Is	he/she/it		

Short Answers

Yes, I **am**.	No, I'm **not**.
Yes, you **are**. Yes, we **are**. Yes, they **are**.	No, you **aren't**. No, we **aren't**. No, they **aren't**.
Yes, he/she/it **is**.	No, he/she/it **isn't**.

2.3 *Be Going To*: Information Questions

Wh- Word	Be	Subject	Going to	Base Form of Verb
What	**am**	I		see?
Where **When**	**are**	you we they	**going to**	go?
	is	he / she / it		

Wh- Word	Be	Going to	Base Form of Verb
Who **What**	**is**	**going to**	visit Spain? happen?

2.4 Using *Be Going To*, Present Progressive, and Simple Present

A	Use *be going to* when future plans are *not* specific or definite.	*I'm going to visit* Spain someday. (I don't know when exactly.) *I'm going to have* a baby before I'm 35. (This is my plan, but I'm not pregnant yet.)
B	Use the present progressive when future plans are specific or definite.	*I'm visiting* Spain next week. (I have plane tickets and my plan is definite.) *I'm having* a baby in June. (I'm pregnant and I know when the baby will be born.)
C	Use *be going to* to talk about predictions, expectations, or guesses.	*You're going to have* fun in Miami next week.
D	Use *be going to* when a future event is certain to happen because there is evidence for it. Do not use the present progressive.	Look at those clouds. It's *going to rain* soon. Look at those clouds. It ~~is raining~~ soon.
E	Use the simple present, not *be going to*, for scheduled events in the future, such as class schedules, timetables, and itineraries. Some common verbs for this meaning are *arrive, be, begin, finish,* and *leave.*	My flight *is* tomorrow. I *leave* at 7:00 a.m.

Grammar Application

Complete the sentences with the correct form of *be going to* and the verbs in parentheses.

1 Lisa's blog _is going to motivate_ (motivate) people to create life lists.
2 Jessica _____ (create) a life list on her blog. Here are two of the goals she wants to put on her list.
3 She _____ (not miss) the family reunion this year.
4 Jessica and her twin sister Kelly _____ _____ (attend) a twins convention someday.
5 Sam _____ (not achieve) any of his goals this year, but someday he will.
6 Here are some things that I _____ (do) someday.
7 I _____ (take) a trip to New York.
8 I _____ (learn) martial arts someday.
9 My mother and I _____ (ride) in a hot-air balloon for her birthday.
10 Remember, you _____ (not do) everything in one year!

Exercise 2.2 *Be Going To*: Questions

A Complete the conversation with the correct form of *be going to* and the verbs in parentheses.

Marco Hey, Julio. What _are_ you _going to do_ (do) now?
        (1)   (1)
Julio   I'm going to start a new job.
Marco   Where ___are___ you _going to work_ (work)?
              (2)   (2)
Julio   At the Central Café.
Marco   Nice! What ___are___ you _going to do_ (do) there?
                    (3)   (3)
Julio   I'm going to cook! I always wanted to be a chef – it's number 10 on my life list.
Marco   That's great! ___Are___ you _going to get_ (get) some training?
                       (4)   (4)
Julio   Yes. I'm going to learn a lot on the job! And I'm also going to take a class at Briteway Community College.
Marco   What ___are___ you _going to take_ (take)?
              (5)   (5)
Julio   I'm going to take a class on food safety.
Marco   That's great. ___Is___ it _going to_ (be) hard?
                       (6)   (6)
Julio   No, I don't think so.
Marco   What _is going to happen_ (happen) with the rest of your life list?
                        (7)
Julio   Oh, the trip to China?
Marco   Yes. When _is going to_ that _happen_ (happen)?
                   (8)   (8)
Julio   Well, first I'm going to earn a good salary at the Central Café. I'm going to save a lot of money, and then I'm going to go to China.
Marco   That sounds like a plan!

B Write questions about Julio for the answers below. Use *be going to*.

1 _What is he going to do?_
He's going to start a new job.

2 _Where is he going to work?_
He's going to work at the Central Café.

3 _What is he going to do?_
He's going to cook.

4 _Is he going to learn a lot on the job?_
Yes, he's going to learn a lot on the job.

5 _Is he going to take a class?_
Yes, he's going to take a class at the community college.

6 _What is he going to take a class?_
He's going to take a class on food safety.

7 _Does he think the class is going to be hard?_
No, he doesn't think the class is going to be hard.

Exercise 2.3 *Be Going To*, Present Progressive, or Simple Present?

A Listen and complete the conversation with the form of the verbs that you hear: *be going to*, present progressive, or simple present.

| Anne | So, Jin, what **are** you **going to do** (do) this weekend? |

Jin: I'm finally _going to accomplish_ (accomplish) one of my big goals: (1)
I _'m going to ride_ (ride) in a hot-air balloon. (2) (3)

Anne: Wow! Did you already make a reservation?

Jin: Yes. I _'m going to take_ (take) the flight that goes over the ocean. (4)

Anne: The ocean! You _are going to have_ (have) a great time. (5)

Jin: Yeah, and I heard the weather report. It _is going to be_ (be) great (6)
this weekend. Do you want to come?

Anne: When _are_ you _going to go_ (go)? (7) (7)

Jin: We _are going to meet_ (meet) in the park at noon on Sunday, and (8)
the flight _is going to leave_ (leave) at 1:00 p.m. (9)

Anne: I'd love to come, but I have other plans.

Jin: What _are_ you _going to do_ (do)? (10) (10)

Anne: I _'m going to go_ (go) to the airport on Sunday (11)
afternoon. I _'m going to pick up_ (pick up) an old friend. She (12)
is going to stay (stay) with me for a week, and her flight (13)
is going to arrive (arrive) right at noon. (14)

Jin: Well, it sounds like you _'re going to have_ (have) a good time, too! (15)

B Listen again and check your answers.

A Complete another entry from Lisa's blog. Use *be going to*, the present progressive, or the simple present and the verb in parentheses. Use contractions where possible.

⌂   💬 ⟳ ☰ ✉

Achieving #7 on My Life List

January 15
posted by: Lisa Sanchez

Finally! I **'m going to achieve** (achieve) goal number seven on my life
                    (1)
list! I've bought my ticket, so it's definite now. I ~~'m going to~~ moving
                                                        (2)
(move) to Spain! I 'm going to leave (leave) on Friday, February 3.
                    (3)
I got a job, too! I 'm going to work (work) as a tour guide for a hotel
                    (4)
in Barcelona. I 'm going to start (start) on March 3, so I planned a
                (5)
little trip. I 'm going to travel (travel) around the country for three
              (6)
weeks. I already bought a rail pass.

I've checked the weather, too. It is going to be (be) great.
                                    (7)
It 's going to be ~~nice~~ (be) nice the entire time. Any advice?
      (8)

2 Responses   leave one

Robert: Lisa, you were having (have) a fantastic time!
                            (9)
            But watch out – I've been to Spain many times in the winter. It ~~was~~ going to raining
                                                                                            (10)
            (rain). You ~~needed~~ 're going to need (need) an umbrella.
                        (11)
Amy: Hey Lisa, I ~~was~~ 'm traveling (travel) in Spain at the same time!
                        (12)
            I bought a rail pass, too! I ~~was arriving~~ 'm arriving (arrive) in Catalonia
                                        (13)
            on February 11. I ~~was~~ staying (stay) at the youth hostel.
                            (14)
            I made a reservation for three days. There's a big festival in Catalonia in February. I've heard
            a lot about it. It 's going to be (be) fun. Do you want to meet up?
                            (15)

B Pair Work Compare your answers with a partner. For each answer, explain the reason for the verb form you chose.

A On a separate piece of paper write six things for your life list. Begin with *I'm going to . . .*

I'm going to ride a horse on the beach.

B Pair Work Ask questions with *be going to* about your partner's list. Then write down the six things your partner wants to do.

A *What are you going to do?*
B *I'm going to ride a horse on the beach.*
A *Where are you going to do that?*

3 Avoid Common Mistakes ⚠

1 **Use *be* with *going to* to describe future plans.**

　　　is
She∧going to write a poem someday.

2 **Use the correct form of *be* with *going to*.**

　　　　　are
Jared and Jason is going to go to a twins convention next year.

3 **Use *be* before the subject in *Wh-* questions with *be going to*.**

　　　are you
What ~~you are~~ going to do?

Editing Task

Find and correct eight more mistakes in this web interview about life lists.

Life Lists

The following is the second in a series by Alex Wu of interviews with people about their life lists.

	are
Alex	So, Heather, what∧you and your husband ~~are~~ going to put on your life lists?
Heather	We going to put a lot of things on our list. We going to do some things together and some
5	things separately.
Alex	What Tom is going to do?
Heather	Well, Tom is a twin. He and his brother is going to attend the International Twins Convention.
Alex	I've heard of that. That's right here in Ohio.
Heather	Right. In fact, the convention is this weekend. They going to drive there on Saturday.
10 Alex	That's usually an outdoor event, right?
Heather	Yes, and unfortunately, it going to rain this Saturday.
Alex	Too bad. What they are going to do?
Heather	The event is going to be inside at a hotel now.
Alex	That's good. I bet they is going to have a great time this weekend.

1 Grammar in the Real World

A What do you think it's like to be 100 years old? Read the magazine article about centenarians. What are some of the effects of people living longer?

B Comprehension Check Answer the questions.

1 What will happen to the population by the end of the twenty-first century, according to the U.S. Census Bureau?
2 What are two negative effects of a large number of centenarians?
3 What is one positive effect of aging?
4 Why do older people tend to be happier?

C Notice Find the sentences in the article and complete them.

1 There _____ be several million centenarians in the United States by the end of the twenty-first century.

2 What changes _____ we see with so many people over 100?

3 For example, more people _____ have illnesses such as cancer and heart conditions.

4 Many older people _____ possibly not have enough money to support themselves for a longer period of time.

Do we use *will* to talk about the future, the present, or the past?

In 2000, there were 50,281 people over the age of 100 in the United States. In 2014, there were 72,197. This number **will** grow, and as a result, many more people **will** live to see their

5 100th birthday. In fact, there **will** be several million centenarians[1] in the United States by the end of the twenty-first century. This is according to the U.S. Census Bureau. What changes **will** we see with so many people over 100?

10 The United States **will** see many changes because of this. For example, more people **will** have illnesses such as cancer and heart conditions. According to a study by the University of Albany in New York, we **will** probably not have enough

15 doctors to take care of them. In addition, these

changes **will** affect government services. This means that there **will** be less money for programs such as Social Security[2] and Medicare.[3] Many older people **will** possibly not have enough

20 money to support themselves for a longer period of time. As a result, many **will** need to work in their 70s and even in their 80s.

On the other hand, there are some very positive aspects of aging. One is increased

25 happiness. A study by Stanford University in California found that older people tend to be happier than younger people. Why? As people age, they change their goals. They know they have less time ahead of them, and as a result, they

30 focus on the present. They spend more time on their relationships and know themselves better. This leads to increased happiness.

As people live longer, there **will** be more of us in the world. With more people who are happier,

35 though, perhaps the world **will** be a happier place.

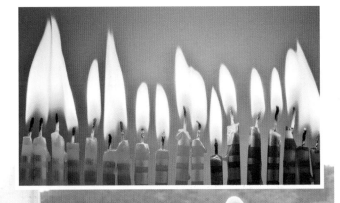

---

[1]**centenarians:** people aged 100 or older

[2]**Social Security:** a U.S. government program that gives financial help to people who are old, people whose husbands or wives have died, and people who cannot work

[3]**Medicare:** a U.S. government program that pays part of the medical expenses of people 65 or older

Centenarians[1]

2 Future with *Will*

Grammar Presentation

Will describes events that take place in the future.	*There will be several million centenarians in the United States by the end of the twenty-first century.*

2.1 Statements

Subject	Will (Not)	Base Form of Verb
I You He / She / It We They	**will** **will not** **won't**	help people.

2.2 Yes / No Questions and Short Answers

Will	Subject	Base Form of Verb
Will	I you he / she / it we they	help?

Short Answers			
Yes, I **will**.	No, I **won't**.		
Yes, you **will**.	No, you **won't**.		
Yes, he / she / it **will**.	No, he /she / it **won't**.		
Yes, we **will**.	No, we **won't**.		
Yes, they **will**.	No, they **won't**.		

2.3 Information Questions

Wh- Word	Will	Subject	Base Form of Verb
How **Where** **When**	will	we they	solve the problem?

Wh- Word	Will	Base Form of Verb
What	will	happen?

2.4 Using *Will*

A Use *will* to make predictions. Predictions are things that people believe about the future.	*Many people will live to 110.* *There will be several million centenarians by the end of the twenty-first century.*
B You can use *likely, possibly, probably, certainly, definitely,* and *undoubtedly* after *will* and before the main verb to show different degrees of certainty. In negative statements, these adverbs can usually go between *will* and *not* or before *won't*.	*Humans will possibly live to 200 in the distant future.* *Technology will undoubtedly change the world.* *They will probably not do much physical work.* *They definitely won't do much physical work.*

2.4 Using *Will* (continued)

Maybe and *perhaps* start a sentence. **less certain** ◄─────────► **more certain** maybe certainly possibly likely definitely perhaps probably undoubtedly	*Maybe older people will not have enough money.* *Perhaps the world will be a happier place.*
C Use the full forms (*will*, *will not*) in formal writing.	*Increased population will lead to crowding.* *People will not need to work so hard in the future.*
Use the contracted forms (*'ll*, *won't*) in informal situations.	*I'll live in a little house near the ocean.* *We won't have to work very hard.*

📊 Data from the Real World

Research shows that the normal position for adverbs of certainty is after *will*.	*Many older people will possibly not have enough money to support themselves.*
You can also put the adverb before *will* to add emphasis, but this is less common.	*My parents didn't have to work in their 70s, but I probably will.*

🖥 Grammar Application

Exercise 2.1 *Will:* Statements

Complete the statements with *will*. Use the verbs in parentheses.

1 People *will live* (live) longer in the future.

2 In fact, many people _will see_ (see) their 100th birthday.

3 This means that there _will be_ (be) a lot more healthy older people.

4 These healthy older people _will need_ (need) something productive to do. (won't)

5 Therefore, many people _will not retire_ (not retire) at the age of 60 or 65.

6 They _will work_ (work) in their 70s.

7 However, they _will not do_ (not do) as much physical work.

8 This _will help_ (help) the economy, as it _will not cause_ (not cause) problems for government programs such as Social Security and Medicare.

A Complete the questions in an online interview with an expert on aging. Use *will* and the correct form of the words in parentheses.

⌂

Chris Zurawski's **Future Blog**

I recently interviewed Dr. Sam Young. Dr. Young is an expert on aging and how it will change the government and the economy. Following is our discussion.

Q Dr. Young, _will people live_ (people/live) longer in the future?
(1)

A Yes. People will live longer. Life expectancy will increase in most countries.

Q _____ (why/people/have) longer lives?
(2)

A Well, they'll have better medical care, and that will mean a healthier life.

Q _____ (people/live) longer everywhere in
(3)
the world?

A I think so. A lot of countries will have more centenarians. There will be
millions in countries such as the United States and Japan.

Q So, _____ (everyone/be) healthy?
(4)

A Well, no, not everyone. People will live longer, but they'll have more
long-term illnesses such as cancer and diabetes.

Q I'm only 24. I'm worried about Social Security. _____
(5)
(what/happen) to Social Security?

A Social Security will begin to have serious problems in the future. Something
will need to change.

Q But let's say it doesn't change. _____
(6)
(what/happen)?

A In that case, Social Security payments will be very low, or they won't be
available at all.

Q So, _____ (how/people
(7)
like me/support) ourselves?

A Even today, Social Security provides only about one-third of the average
person's income. So, just like now, most people will need other sources of
income as they age.

Q _____ (what other
(8)
sources of income/people/have)?

A A lot of people your age will work longer. You'll keep your jobs. Some will
work part-time, but many will continue to work full-time for many years.

In the future, people will live longer – and work longer.

B Add adverbs to some of Dr. Young's statements. Use the cues in parentheses to choose an adverb with the appropriate degree of certainty. Sometimes more than one answer is correct.

certainly	likely	perhaps	probably
definitely	maybe	possibly	undoubtedly

probably
1 Life expectancy will increase in most countries. (in the middle)

definitely
2 Better medical care will mean a healthier life. (more certain)

likely
3 A lot of countries will have more centenarians. (in the middle)

maybe
4 People will have more long-term illnesses such as cancer and diabetes. (less certain)

probably
5 Social Security will begin to have serious problems in the future. (in the middle)

possibly
6 Social Security payments will be very low. (in the middle)

undoubtedly
7 Most people will need other sources of income as they age. (more certain)

perhaps
8 A lot of people your age will work longer. (less certain)

Certainly
9 Many will continue to work full-time for many years. (more certain)

Exercise 2.3 *Will*: Questions, Answers, and Adverbs

A Listen to an informal conversation about the future. Complete the summary of Sara's ideas. Circle the correct words.

Sara thinks she probably <u>will/will not</u> live to be 100. She thinks
        (1)
she <u>will probably/will probably not</u> have problems with money in old age.
   (2)

B Listen again. Circle the correct adverb.

1 Sara will (probably)/certainly live to be about 85 or 90.

2 Sara will <u>perhaps/undoubtedly</u> work in her 80s.

3 At 80, Sara will <u>probably/definitely</u> have the same job she has now.

4 After retirement, Sara will <u>possibly/definitely</u> travel or garden.

5 Sara will <u>perhaps/very likely</u> not have enough money to travel.

6 Sara thinks she <u>possibly/certainly</u> won't get Social Security.

7 Sara thinks the government will <u>probably/undoubtedly</u> not have any money left in the future.

Listen again and check your answers.

C Group Work Use *will* and adverbs of certainty to talk about your future. Discuss these questions and give your own ideas.

- How long do you think you'll live? Why do you think that?

- How long will you work? What kind of job will you have at age _____ ?

- What will you do after you retire?

A *How long do you think you'll live?*
B *I'll probably live to be about 100.*
C *Perhaps I'll live to be 90. I hope so.*

3 Future with *Will, Be Going To,* and Present Progressive

Grammar Presentation

Will, be going to, and the present progressive can describe future events.	Life expectancy *will increase.* *I'm going to* look for a new job. *She's starting* a retirement account next week.

3.1 Using *Will, Be Going To,* and Present Progressive for the Future

A Use *will* or *be going to* to talk about plans in the future. Use the present progressive for arranged events.	*I'll open* a retirement account soon. *I'm going to open* a retirement account soon. (This is my intention, what I want to do.) *I'm opening* a retirement account next week. (I have an appointment at the bank at a specific time next week. It's scheduled.)
B Use *will* or *be going to* to make predictions, expectations, or guesses about the future.	*More people will live* longer in the future. *More people are going to live* longer in the future.
C Use *be going to* when a future event is certain to happen because there is evidence for it.	*Look at those dark clouds. It's going to rain.* *We have a lot of work to do. We are not going to finish* until 6:30.
D Use *will* for immediate decisions.	*I have to go. I'll call you later.* (= I just decided to call you.) *I have to go. I'm going to call you later.* *I have to go. I'm calling you later.*

3.1 Using *Will, Be Going To,* and Present Progressive for the Future *(continued)*

E Use *be going to* for intentions: things you hope or intend to do in the future.

I am healthy. I'm going to live to be 100 years old!

I'm not going to retire and sit at home.

Do not use *will* or the present progressive with intentions.

I am healthy. I will live to be 100 years old!

I am healthy. I'm living to be 100 years old!

F Use *will* and *be going to* with adverbs to show different degrees of certainty about future events.

You can use *likely, possibly, probably, certainly, definitely,* and *undoubtedly* after *be* and before *going to* when you want to show different degrees of certainty. For negative statements, put the adverb immediately after *be.*

He definitely won't retire this year.

He hasn't studied. He is probably going to fail the exam.

People are certainly going to work longer in the future.

They are probably not going to take any English courses next year.

Maybe and *perhaps* can start sentences with *be going to.*

Perhaps the government is going to fix Social Security.

less certain		more certain
maybe		certainly
possibly	likely	definitely
perhaps	probably	undoubtedly

📊 Data from the Real World

Research shows that *will* is 20 times more common in academic writing than *be going to.*

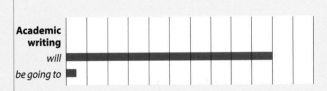

Write: *People **will be** happier in the future.*

Research shows that *be going to* is three times more common in speaking than *will.*

Say: *"Everyone's **going to work** to age 70 in the future."*

Grammar Application

Complete this university press release. Circle *will* or the present progressive. If both are possible, circle both.

For Immediate Release

New Program at Bay City University for Senior Citizens

Bay City, September 5

Life expectancy <u>is increasing</u> / (will increase) in the future.
(1)
This means that the population of Bay City (will grow) / is growing
(2)
as well, and the number of Bay City students over the age
of 60 (will increase) / is increasing someday. Already, the
(3)
number of people over 60 who want to study is growing, and
it <u>is probably doubling</u> / (will probably double) in the next 20 years.
(4)
As a result, Bay University <u>is needing</u> / (will need) more programs and
(5)
more courses for older students.

Therefore, Bay City University (will announce) / is announcing plans
(6)
later this week for a new department for students over 60 called Lifelong
Learning. The department (will open) / is opening officially next year.
(7)
However, Lifelong Learning <u>is holding</u> / (will hold) an orientation event
(8)
this Friday afternoon to introduce the department. Interested students
can talk to instructors from the department about the courses they
<u>are teaching</u> / (will teach) next year.
(9)

A Complete the conversation with *will* or *be going to* and the words in parentheses. Sometimes, both are correct.

Lisa   What _*are you going to do*_ (do) in your old age?
(1)

Zack   Well, I've thought about this. I ʼ*m not going to retire* (not retire) early.
(2)
Maybe I'll retire in my 70s, but not before. Anyway, after retirement, I
ʼ*m going to travel* (travel).
(3)

Lisa That's expensive. You _will not have_ (not have) the money!
(4)

Zack You know, you're right. I _'m going to start_ (start) a savings account right
(5)
away. How about you? What _are_ you _going to do_ (do) in your old age?
(6)   (6)

Lisa Well, I _'m going to go_ (go) back to school.
(7)

Zack But you don't like school now. You _are not going to like_ (not like) it later.
(8)

Lisa I _'m going to change_ (change) my attitude. In fact, I _'ll change_
(9)   (10)
(change) it right now! Let's go to the library and study.

Zack That's a great idea! I _'m going to drive_ (drive).
(11)

B Pair Work **Compare your answers with a partner. Discuss the reason for your choices.**

Exercise 3.3 Adverbs

A What will life be like when you are old? Read some predictions about the future. Add an
adverb that matches the degree of certainty in parentheses.

certainly	~~maybe~~	~~probably~~
definitely	perhaps	~~undoubtedly~~
~~likely~~	~~possibly~~	

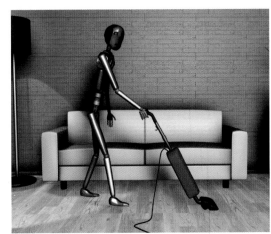

likely
1 Robots will ∧ do all of our housework. (in the middle)
   probably
2 Computers won't ∧ have keyboards. (in the middle)
   maybe
   We are ∧ going to use our voices to communicate
   with them. (less certain)
   undoubtedly
3 There will ∧ be no ice in the Arctic. (more certain)
   perhaps
4 People are ∧ not going to drive their own cars. (less certain)
   possibly
   Satellites or computers will ∧ control them. (less certain)
   definitely
5 Space flight is ∧ going to be available to anyone. (more certain)
   certainly
   People will ∧ take vacations in space. (more certain)

B Pair Work Do you agree or disagree?

A *I agree with number 1. Robots will definitely do all of our housework.*
B *Why do you think that?*
A *We already have this type of robot today. People use robots to build cars . . .*

C Over to You Make predictions about your life in the future. Use *will, be going to,* and adverbs. Compare your predictions with a partner.

A *What will your life be like in the future?*
B *I'm going to make a lot of money. I'm definitely going to retire early. How about you?*

4 Avoid Common Mistakes ⚠

1	**Use *will* before the main verb in statements about the future.**
	will In the future, people∧live to 110.
2	**Use *will* for predictions, not *would*.**
	will Perhaps, a few years from now, I ~~would~~ have a job with a good salary.
3	**Use *be* with *going to* for the future.**
	am I take good care of myself. I∧going to live to be 100 years old!
4	**Use the base form of the verb after *will*.**
	live People will to ~~live~~ longer in the future. He will ~~lives~~ longer.

Editing Task

Find and correct eight more mistakes in this interview with an actor.

For Immediate Release

Pablo Percy   A lot of women actors quit around the age of 40 or 50. They say there aren't good parts for older women.
What ~~would~~ *will* you do in your later years?

5   **Melanie Hinton**   Well, I won't retire and sit at home. I work until I'm 90!

Pablo Percy   But there aren't many good parts for older women. How would you find work?

Melanie Hinton   The entertainment business is changing. In the future, there be

10   a lot more older people making movies *and* watching movies. That means there would definitely be more parts for older people, including older women, in the future.

Pablo Percy   Are you sure?

Melanie Hinton   Absolutely. In fact, I wouldn't wait for these parts. I will to write

15   my own scripts. I going to have a script ready next year.

Pablo Percy   What is it going to be about?

Melanie Hinton   I going to write a love story about two 80-year-olds.

Pablo Percy   Sounds wonderful!

Future Time Clauses and Future Conditionals

Learning to Communicate

1 Grammar in the Real World

A What do you know about learning a language? Read the passage from a textbook. How do humans learn to communicate?

B Comprehension Check Answer the questions.

1 According to the textbook excerpt, how many words does a typical two-year-old child know?
2 What do children talk about before ages four or five?
3 What happens after children learn to read?
4 Two things make it possible for humans to learn language. What are they?

C Notice Find the sentences in the textbook passage and complete them.

1 _____ he is six, he _____ learn to form
   (a)   (b)
correct grammatical sentences.

2 _____ he starts school, he _____ begin to
   (a)   (b)
read and write.

3 _____ he starts to read, he _____ learn to
   (a)   (b)
speak about things that are not happening right around him.

4 _____ he is literate, Jake _____ learn about
   (a)   (b)
a thousand words every year.

Do the words in the a blanks refer to place or time?
Do the verbs in the b blanks talk about the present or the future?

CHILDREN and LANGUAGE LEARNING

¹**literate:** able to read and write
²**genetic feature:** a characteristic of living things passed on from parents to children

Jake is two years old, and he is a typical American child. He plays, laughs, and cries. He also talks. He can understand about 200 English words. He uses fixed phrases. For example, he says "all gone" when he finishes his food. **Until he is about four or five, Jake will talk** mostly
5 about things around him — where he is and what he is doing at the moment. **When he is five years old, he will understand** thousands of words and will speak normally. **Before he is six, he will learn** to form correct grammatical sentences.

When he starts school, he will begin to read and write.
10 **After he starts to read, he will learn** to speak about things that are not happening right around him — the past, the future, and faraway people and places. **Once he is literate,¹ Jake will learn** about a thousand words every year. **When he is 18, he will be** ready for college. He will have all the language and world knowledge he needs for his classes.
15 Then, for the rest of his life, he will continue to learn.

Was Jake born with the ability to learn to speak, read, and write? Many experts say yes. Animals often live close to human beings, but they do not learn human language. Therefore, Jake must have a natural ability to learn his language. However, he speaks English only because
20 his parents and the people around him use English.

Learning how to communicate is a combination of natural, genetic features² and our social environment. We need both things to be "human."

2 Future Time Clauses

Grammar Presentation

Future time clauses show the time and order (first or second) of a future event.

FIRST EVENT   SECOND EVENT
Once he is literate, *he will learn about a thousand words every year.*

FIRST EVENT   SECOND EVENT
After he starts to read, *he will learn to speak about things that are not happening around him.*

2.1 Future Time Clauses

FUTURE TIME CLAUSE				MAIN CLAUSE			
Time Word	Subject	Simple Present		Subject	*Will*	Base Form of Verb	
Before **After** **When**	he	starts	school,	he	will	learn	to read.

MAIN CLAUSE				FUTURE TIME CLAUSE			
Subject	*Will*	Base Form of Verb		Time Word	Subject	Simple Present	
He	will	learn	to read	**before** **after** **when**	he	starts	school.

2.2 Using Future Time Clauses

A Use future time clauses to say when the event in the main clause happens.	learns to read
	starts school
	FIRST EVENT SECOND EVENT
Use *after* when the event in the time clause happens first.	*After she starts school, she will learn* to read.
Use *when* when two events happen at or around the same time.	*When he graduates from high school, he will go to college.*
Use *as soon as* or *once* when the event in the main clause happens immediately after the event in the time clause.	leaves college gets a job
	FIRST EVENT SECOND EVENT
	As soon as he leaves college, he will get a job.
	Once he is literate, he will learn thousands of new words.
Use *before* when the event in the main clause happens first.	SECOND EVENT FIRST EVENT
	Before Anne starts school, she will learn hundreds of words.
Use *until* to show when the event in the main clause will stop or change.	*talks about* immediate environment
	four or five years old
	Until he is about four or five, Jake will talk mostly about his immediate environment.
	(Jake will stop doing this when he is four or five.)
B The time clause can come before or after the main clause. Remember to use a comma when the time clause comes first.	*As soon as he leaves college,* he will get a job.
	He will get a job as soon as he leaves college.
C Even though the verb in the time clause is in the simple present, it refers to a future event.	*He will learn more English* before he visits California next year.
	I will stay in school until I graduate two years from now.

◤ Grammar Application

Circle the correct verb.

1 Larisa is a typical three-year-old Russian girl. Before she
will start /(starts) school at age 5, she **learns / will learn** to print her
name in the Cyrillic alphabet: Лариса.

2 Her parents **will teach / teach** her to read simple words like *cat* (Кот)
before she **will start / starts** school, too.

3 When she **goes / will go** to kindergarten, Larisa **starts / will start** to
learn to read and write more simple words.

4 She **will learn / learns** even more words as soon as she
starts / will start primary school.

5 Once Larisa **gets / will get** to the first grade, she
learns / will learn to use handwriting instead of printing.

6 When she **is / will be** about nine years old, she
will recognize / recognizes thousands of words.

7 She **reads / will read** some of her textbooks in English
when she **goes / will go** to college.

8 After she **will finish / finishes** college, she **knows / will know** tens of thousands of words.

А	Б	В	Г	Д	Е	Ё
Ж	З	И	Й	К	Л	М
Н	О	П	Р	С	Т	У
Ф	Х	Ц	Ч	Ш	Щ	Ъ
Ы	Ь	Э	Ю	Я		

Complete the description of a class in American Sign Language (ASL). Circle the correct
time word.

ASL 101: Thursday, 7:00–9:00 p.m.   Room 203, Davidson Hall

(Before)/ Until the course begins, you will receive a questionnaire about why you are
(1)
interested in studying American Sign Language. This information will help us plan the course.
Until / Once the course begins, we will not speak in class. **As soon as / Until** classes start, we
(2)   (3)
will communicate only in sign language.

When / Before the course begins, we will learn the basic signs for greeting new people:
(4)
Hello, My name is . . . , I live in . . . , etc. This is a good place to start. We will practice these signs
as soon as / until you can use them automatically.
(5)

Until / When you begin studying sign language, it will be quite difficult. But **after / until**
(6)   (7)
you know the basics, it will become much easier. **Until / Before** the course ends, you will learn
(8)
to use a lot of sign language and have a lot of fun!

Exercise 2.3 More Future Time Clauses

A Dave is going to take all four levels of Spanish at Bay City College. Read the information about how many words a typical student in the program knows at each level. Complete the statements about Dave. Use the verbs in parentheses and the numbers in the chart.

	Starting Vocabulary	Ending Vocabulary
Level 1 student	about 500 words	about 1,500 words
Level 2 student	about 1,500 words	about 2,500 words
Level 3 student	about 2,500 words	about 3,500 words
Level 4 student	about 3,500 words	about 5,000 words

1 When he starts Level 1, Dave _will know_ (know) about _500_ words.

2 When he finishes Level 1, Dave _____ (know) about _____ words.

3 Dave will try to learn 1,000 more words before he _____ (finish) Level 2.

4 Dave will not start Level 3 until he _____ (know) about _____ words.

5 Once he _____ (reach) Level 4, Dave _____ (know) more

than _____ words.

6 Once Dave _____ (read) and _____ (write) Spanish fluently,

he _____ (apply) for a job in Spain.

B Pair Work Complete each sentence in a way that is true for you. Then discuss your answers with a partner.

1 I _will continue_ (continue) to study English until I _speak the language well_ .

2 When I _____ (finish) this English course, I _____ .

3 I _____ (get) a job as soon as I _____ .

4 Before I _____ (complete) this course, I _____ .

A *I'll continue to study English until I speak it well. How about you?*

B *I'll continue to study English until I read and write it well.*

A *I'll get a job as soon as I finish all the classes in this program. How about you?*

B *I'll get a job as soon as I finish my job training course.*

C Group Work Tell a group member about your partner's answers in B. Compare your answers.

A *Mei will get a job as soon as she finishes all the courses in this program.*

B *Rob will get a job as soon as he finishes the program, too.*

3 Future Conditionals; Questions with Time Clauses and Conditional Clauses

Grammar Presentation

Future conditional sentences describe possible situations in the future.	*If I pass all my exams,* I will go to college. *If Dave learns to read and write Spanish well,* *will he get* a job in Spain?

3.1 Future Conditionals: Statements

FUTURE CONDITION				MAIN CLAUSE			
If	Subject	Simple Present		Subject	*Will*	Base Form of Verb	
If	he	passes	his exams,	he	will	go	to college.

MAIN CLAUSE				FUTURE CONDITION			
Subject	*Will*	Base Form of Verb		*If*	Subject	Simple Present	
He	will	go	to college	**if**	he	passes	his exams.

3.2 Yes/No Questions

FUTURE CONDITION OR FUTURE TIME CLAUSE				MAIN CLAUSE			
If/Time Word	Subject	Simple Present		*Will*	Subject	Base Form of Verb	
If **After** **When**	she	learns	Spanish,	will	she	get	a job in Spain?

MAIN CLAUSE				FUTURE CONDITION OR FUTURE TIME CLAUSE			
Will	Subject	Base Form of Verb		*If*/Time Word	Subject	Simple Present	
Will	she	get	a job in Spain	**if** **after** **when**	she	learns	Spanish?

3.3 Information Questions

FUTURE CONDITION OR FUTURE TIME CLAUSE				MAIN CLAUSE			
If/Time Word	Subject	Simple Present		Wh- Word	Will	Subject	Base Form of Verb
If After When	you	finish	this class,	what	will	you	do?

MAIN CLAUSE				FUTURE CONDITION OR FUTURE TIME CLAUSE			
Wh- Word	Will	Subject	Base Form of Verb	If/Time Word	Subject	Simple Present	
What	will	you	do	if after when	you	finish	this class?

3.4 Using Future Conditional Clauses and Future Time Clauses

A	Use *if* to refer to a situation that is possible in the future but that we cannot be certain about.	*If he finishes the program, he will get a job.* (We don't know if he will finish the program.)
B	Use *when* to refer to a situation at a point in the future that is expected or likely to happen.	*When he finishes the program, he will get a job.* (We expect him to finish the program.)
C	Use a main verb in the simple present in the conditional clause.	*If she gets a better job, she will be very happy.* *If she will get a better job, she will be very happy.*
D	Use a comma in writing when the conditional clause or time clause comes first.	*If she arrives late, she will miss the lecture.* *When they finish their work, they will leave.*

Data from the Real World

Research shows that in conversation, people often use time clauses and conditional clauses alone in answers.

A *When will you start Level 3 of your course?*
B *As soon as I finish Level 2.*

A *Will you take another English course next year?*
B *Yes, if I have time.*

Grammar Application

Exercise 3.1 Future Conditionals

Listen to an interview with a scientist about Edna the ape. After you listen, write the verbs in the correct form.

Bob Diaz Edna is a mature female ape. Researchers are going to try to find out if they can teach Edna to communicate. We asked Dr. Sheila Viss, one of the researchers, about the study. Dr. Viss, if you _**teach**_ (teach) Edna, _**will**_
(1)   (2)
she _**learn**_ (learn) human language?
(2)

Dr. Viss That is what we hope to find out. First, if we _____ (use) American
(3)
Sign Language, Edna _____ (learn) the meaning of some signs.
(4)
For example, we think Edna _____ (use) the sign for "more" if she
(5)
_____ (want) more food.
(6)

Bob Diaz If Edna _____ (learn) a sign that works in one situation, _____
(7)   (8)
she _____ (use) the same sign in a different situation?
(8)

Dr. Viss Yes. For example, we think Edna _____ (make) the sign for a toy
(9)
when she _____ (want) a different toy.
(10)

Bob Diaz So, if she _____ (want) something special, _____ she
(11)   (12)
_____ (combine) the signs?
(12)

Dr. Viss We think she will. If she _____ (do) this, Edna _____
(13)   (14)
(make) simple sentences. For example, when she _____ (want)
(15)
food quickly, she _____ (make) the signs for "give-food-hurry."
(16)

Bob Diaz When she _____ (learn) to communicate, _____ she
(17)   (18)
_____ (learn) quickly?
(18)

Dr. Viss Well, probably not. Edna will learn slowly compared to a human child.

Exercise 3.2 More Future Conditionals

A Pair Work New words and expressions come into English every day. Match these new words with their definitions. They appear in most new dictionaries. Discuss with a partner how you think these expressions became popular.

1 blowback (noun) _____

2 to friend (verb) _____

3 a screenager (noun) _____

a a young person who spends a lot of time in front of a computer

b a bad result of a political action

c to add someone to your list of friends on a social networking site

e

f

g

friend² /'**frend**/ **verb** to connect with someone on a social website so that you can share information, pictures, etc.: *A lot of people from my old job have friended me.*

B Read the sentences about how a new word or expression enters the language. Combine the sentences to make future conditional sentences. If the conditional clause is first, use a comma.

1 People use new words and expressions every day. The new words survive.

If people use new words and expressions every day, the new words will survive.

2 You have a new development in technology. You get a new word that describes it.

_____

3 New words also enter the language. There is a big world event such as a war.

_____

4 Someone uses the new word on the Internet. People copy it.

_____

5 For example, you use the word. Your social networking friends use it, too.

_____

6 A new word or expression becomes popular. A lot of people use it.

_____

7 A person on a TV news show says the new word. It sounds important.

_____

8 A new word appears in the dictionary. A lot of people use it in speaking and in writing.

_____

9 People stop using the new word or expression. It dies.

_____

C Pair Work Ask and answer conditional questions about the information in B.

A *If people use a new word or expression every day, will it survive?*
B *Yes, it will.*

Exercise 3.3 Time Clauses and Future Conditionals

A Listen to a campus radio interview with Jawad, a student. Complete the sentences about his plans.

1 Jawad will be successful if he _____ .

2 Jawad will get a good job if he _____ .

3 If he does well in his English classes, Jawad _____

_____ .

4 Jawad will apply for a job when _____ .

5 When he graduates and gets his certificate, Jawad _____ .

B Pair Work Discuss your plans with a partner. Ask questions like the ones in the interview. Use time clauses and future conditional clauses where appropriate.

■ Why are you here at [your school]?

■ What are your plans?

■ After you finish the program, what will you do?

■ How will you feel when . . . ?

A *Why are you here at the community college?*
B *Well, I'm here for my career. If my English improves, I'll probably find a better job.*

4 Avoid Common Mistakes ⚠

1 **Use the simple present in the conditional clause, not *will*.**

If I ~~will~~ get good grades, I will go to college next year.

2 **Use *will* in the main clause, not the simple present.**

                    will know
If she learns 1,000 words every year, she ~~knows~~ 3,000 words in three years.

3 **Use the simple present in the time clause, not *will*.**

     finishes
When he ~~will finish~~ this course, he will take a vacation.

4 **Use *if* for something that is possible. Use *when* for something that you are certain will happen.**

If
~~When~~ I become rich, I will help poor people.

Editing Task

Find and correct nine more mistakes in this web article about how birds can learn.

Intelligent Crows

A team of scientists is doing experiments with crows to test their intelligence. This is what the scientists think will happen:

-     *are*
  When the crows ~~will be~~ thirsty, they will look for water.

5 - As soon as they will fi nd water, they drink it.

- If there is no water, the crows search for it.
- If they don't get the water easily, the crows think of ways to get it.

For example, if the water will be in a narrow tube, it will be difficult to

10 reach it. However, the scientists think that the crows will learn the following:

- If they will drop a stone into the tube, the water level will rise.
- If they will drop more stones, the level will rise more.
- The crows drop stones into the tube until the crows reach the water.
- When the experiment is successful, the scientists will prove that crows

15   are intelligent birds.

Amazing Science

1 Grammar in the Real World

A Can you think of three recent medical inventions? Read the article from a science magazine. Which invention do you think is the most interesting?

B Comprehension Check Match the technology with what it does.

1 The "ishoe" _b_
2 The Rocket-Powered Arm _c_

3 The Autonomous Wheelchair _d_
4 The Smart Pill _d_

a understands the human voice.
b tells NASA scientists if you have problems with balance.
c helps you pick things up.
d gives doctors information about their patients' health.

C Notice Look at the verbs in **bold** in the article. Underline the verbs that are about the past. Circle the verbs that are about the future.

Medical BREAKTHROUGHS

Some medical problems need engineers, not doctors. Technology **can** often solve problems when doctors alone **can't** help. Here are some examples of medical breakthroughs[1] from the world of engineering.

The "ishoe"

Often when astronauts return from space, they **are not able to** balance.[2] MIT student Erez Lieberman invented the "ishoe" to deal with
5　this problem. The ishoe is a pad that goes inside a shoe and uses sensors[3] to send information about balance to a computer or cell phone. NASA scientists use this information to help the astronauts recover their balance. Lieberman
10　**could** see that his invention had other uses, for example, diagnosing[4] balance problems in elderly people.

The Autonomous Wheelchair

In the future, people **will be able to** tell
15　their wheelchairs where they want to go. The Autonomous Wheelchair **can** learn to recognize its environment by listening to its user's instructions. In addition, it uses Wi-Fi[5] to build a map of the person's home.

20　## The Smart Pill

The doctor **can't** always be sure if some people are taking their medication. Now a "smart" pill **can** tell a doctor when a patient last took his or her medication and report on the
25　state of the person's health at the time.

The Rocket-Powered Arm

Another invention from space research is the Rocket-Powered Arm. Until recently, people with artificial arms **were not able to** lift heavy
30　objects. Now there is a new kind of power for artificial arms – rocket fuel. With rocket-powered arms, people **will be able to** lift objects up to 20 pounds.

These are just some of the amazing
35　technological advances that will help improve people's lives. Who knows what other inventions they will come up with?

---

[1]**breakthrough:** an important discovery or development that helps to solve a problem

[2]**balance:** have weight equally divided so something or someone can stay in one position

[3]**sensor:** a device that discovers and reacts to changes in things such as movement, heat, and light

[4]**diagnose:** recognize the exact disease or condition a person has

[5]**Wi-Fi:** a method of connecting to the Internet without using wires

2 Ability with *Can* and *Could*

Grammar Presentation

Can and *could* describe ability and possibility.	Technology *can* often solve problems when doctors alone *can't* help. Lieberman *could* see that his invention had other uses.

2.1 Statements

Subject	Modal Verb	Base Form of Verb
I You He / She / It We They	**can** **can't** **cannot** **could** **couldn't** **could not**	help people.

2.2 Yes / No Questions and Answers

Modal Verb	Subject	Base Form of Verb		Short Answers		
Can **Could**	I you he / she / it we they	help?	Yes, No,	I you he / she / it we they	**can.** **can't.** **could.** **couldn't.**	

2.3 Information Questions

Wh- Word	Modal Verb	Subject	Base Form of Verb	
How **Where** **When**	can could can	we they you	solve	the problem?

Wh- Word	Modal Verb	Subject	Base Form of Verb
What **Who**	can could	we they you	help?

Modal Verbs and Modal-like Expressions: See page A7.

2.4 Using Can and Could

A You can use *can* / *can't* to talk about general ability and what people know how to do.	My grandfather *can* swim, but he *can't* walk very well. Engineers *can* solve problems when doctors *can't*.
B You can use *can* / *can't* to talk about people's senses and mental abilities.	*Can* you *see* that tall building on the left? Some patients *can't remember* if they took their medication.
C You can use *can* / *can't* to talk about what is or is not possible and about known facts.	Elderly people *can* have serious health problems after a fall. Technology *can't* solve every problem.
D Use *could* / *couldn't* for the past.	Lieberman *could* see other uses for his product. In the past, people with artificial arms *couldn't* lift heavy objects.

Grammar Application

Exercise 2.1 *Can* and *Can't*: Statements

Complete the article about how a computer is helping a man. Use *can* or *can't* and the verbs in the box.

breathe ~~move~~ ~~move~~ ~~move~~ ~~send~~ speak talk ~~use~~

Connecting with ERICA

When he was younger, Steve Nichols was very fit. However, in 2016 he learned he had ALS, a disease that causes loss of muscle control. Now Nichols _can't move_ (1) most of his body. For example, he _can breathe move_ (2) his tongue. Because of this, he _can't speak_ (3). He also has trouble breathing. He _can't move breathe_ (4) without a machine.

However, Nichols _can move_ (5) _(5)_ his eyes. His computer, ERICA, has software that changes text to speech, so he _can talk_ (6) to his wife and family. When Nichols looks at a letter on the keyboard on his computer screen, the computer types that letter. With ERICA, he _can send_ (7) e-mails. In addition, he _can use_ (8) the Internet. ERICA keeps Nichols connected to the rest of the world.

A Engineers in Japan have created nurse robots to help care for patients. Unscramble the words to write questions about these robots. Use *can*.

1 what / do / these robots / ?

   What can these robots do?

2 speak / they / ?

   Can they speak?

3 understand / how many languages / they / ?

   How many languages can they understand?

4 they / patients / lift / ?

   Can they lift patients?

5 one robot / how much weight / lift / ?

   How much weight can one robot lift.

6 a robot / recognize / people / ?

   Can a robot recognize people.

7 they / give medicine / to people / ?

   Can they give medicine to people?

8 make / what kinds of decisions / they / ?

   What kinds of decisions can they make?

B Listen to an expert answer the questions in A. Write the answers.
Write things the nurse robots *can* do.

1 _They can do a lot of things._

2 _Yes, they can speak._

3 _8 language they can speak 8 language_

4 _They can move patients from bed._

5 _They can lift 134 pld._

6 _They can recognize peoples._

7 _They can call a doctor and emagency_

8 _So far they can make very simple decisions._

C Notice Listen again. Write three things nurse robots *can't* do.

1 _They can't do everything change beds_

2 _They can't change the medicines._

3 _They can't lift heavy weight patient._

Exercise 2.3 *Can, Can't, Could, or Couldn't?*

A Complete the paragraphs with *can, can't, could,* or *couldn't.*

Do You Use This Technology?

Before the invention of smartphones, you _____*could*_____ easily contact
(1)

family and friends away from their homes or offices. Now you _____
(2)

talk to them anywhere you like and however you like! You _____ send
(3)

instant messages through an app or do a video call. You _____ text,
(4)

talk, email, or send a picture or just an emoji. It's up to you. There's only one thing

you _____ do yet and that's send yourself! Do you remember when
(5)

we didn't have these devices? Back then, we _____ watch TV shows on
(6)

the subway and we _____ surf the Internet on the train. It seems pretty
(7)

strange now that we _____ do all these things. Many people don't even
(8)

need to know where things are anymore because we have map apps on our phones.

_____/ you still read a paper map? If you_____ , don't
(9)   (10)

worry. Just tap on your app, tell it where you want to go, and follow the directions.

You _____ do that 20 years ago!
(11)

B Group Work **Make your own list of four important inventions in everyday life.
Then compare your lists in a group and discuss the questions. Use inventions in these
areas or your own ideas.**

Inventions in . . .

- medicine
- travel
- communication
- home appliances
- entertainment

1 Can you remember (or imagine) life without these inventions?
What was it like?

2 What can people do now that they couldn't do before these inventions?

3 As a group, choose the three most important inventions. What are they?
Why are they the most important?

On my desert island,
I'll have knife, wifi and smartphone

3 Be Able To

Grammar Presentation

> You can use *be able to* to talk about ability and possibility.
>
> *Some astronauts are not able to balance after a space flight. People will be able to talk to their wheelchairs.*

3.1 Statements About the Present, Past, and Future

PRESENT AND PAST

Subject	*Be*	*(Not) Able To*		Base Form of Verb	
I	am / 'm was				
You We They	are / 're were	(not) able to	use		a computer.
He / She / It	is / 's was				

FUTURE

Subject	*Will (Not)*	*Be Able To*	Base Form of Verb	
I You We They He / She / It	will / 'll will not won't	be able to	use	a computer.

3.2 Yes/No Questions and Short Answers About the Present and Past

Be	Subject	*Able To*	Base Form of Verb	
Are	you	**able to**	lift	heavy objects?
Were				

Short Answers			
Yes, I **am.**	No, **I'm not.**
Yes, I **was.**	No, **I wasn't.**

3.3 Yes/No Questions and Short Answers About the Future

Will	Subject	*Be Able To*	Base Form of Verb	
Will	you	**be able to**	lift	heavy objects?

Short Answers	
Yes, I **will.**	No, I **won't.**

3.4 Information Questions About the Present, Past, and Future

PRESENT AND PAST

Wh- Word	Be	Subject	Able To	Base Form of Verb
When How How often	are were	you	able to	go?

Wh- Word	Be	Able To	Base Form of Verb
Who	is / 's was	able to	go?

FUTURE

Wh- Word	Will	Subject	Be + Able To	Base Form of Verb
When How How often	will	you	be able to	go?

FUTURE

Wh- Word	Will	Be + Able To	Base Form of Verb
Who	will / 'll	be able to	go?

3.5 Using Be Able To

A You can use *be able to* to talk and write about ability in the present, past, or future.	Sometimes astronauts *are not able to* balance after a space flight. In the past, artificial arms *weren't able to* lift heavy objects. In the future, people *will be able to* tell their wheelchairs where to go.
B You can use *be able to* to talk and write about possibility.	People *will be able to* talk to their wheelchairs in the future.

3.5 Using *Be Able To* (continued)

C In affirmative statements, you can use *was / were able to* for a specific event or a specific action that someone completed successfully in the past. Do not use *could*.	*Lieberman was able to design a special shoe a few years ago.* *Lieberman ~~could design~~ a special shoe a few years ago.*
Both forms are correct in negative statements.	*In the past, they weren't able to lift heavy objects.* *In the past, they couldn't lift heavy objects.*
D You can use *be able to* after *going to, want to, would like to, need to,* and *have to.*	*In the future, people are going to be able to use these inventions.* *Many people would like to be able to use these inventions now.*
Do not use *can (can't)* or *could (couldn't)* after these verbs.	*Scientists want to be able to invent new technologies.* *~~Scientists want to can invent new technologies.~~*
📊 *Can* and *could* are more common than *be able to* in everyday conversation, especially in present time. Use *be able to* if you need to sound more formal.	*Can your phone open your front door?* *The most advanced robots are now able to make facial expressions.*

📊 Data from the Real World

People sometimes use *be unable to* instead of *be not able to*. This is more common in formal writing or speaking.

Formal: *When many astronauts return from space, they are unable to balance.*

Informal: *When many astronauts return from space, they are not able to balance.*

Be Unable To
in formal writing
in formal speaking
in conversation

Grammar Application

Exercise 3.1 Questions and Answers

A Complete the article from a magazine. Use a form of *be able to* and the verbs in parentheses. Then, on a separate piece of paper, write what numbers can use *could* instead of *was able to*.

Seeing Through You

___Are___ brain scanners ___able to see___ (see) your thoughts? _____Are_____
(1)   (1)
they _able to read_ (read) your mind?
(2)
_____Are_____ they _able to see_ (see) your
(2)   (3)
memories? Yes, according to some scientists. At a conference
in 2017, researchers _were able to prove_ (prove)
(3)   (4)
this. One researcher watched a movie, and the brain scanning
software _showed / was able to show_ (show) the basic pictures that he
(5)
was looking at.

How _could will / be able to use_ scientists _use / be able to use_ (use) this technology in the
(6)   (6)
future? Some scientists say they are already using brain scan technology. They say that
brain scans _are / was able to tell_ (tell) if someone is lying.
(7)

Scientists are not the only ones who plan to use technology like this in the future.
Some companies think they _will able to use_ (use) brain scanners for
(8)
advertising as well. Advertisers hope they _are able to see_ (see) the way
(9)
people respond to their products. _will / able to use_
What do you think? How _can will_ we _use / able to use_ (use) these
(10)   (10)
technologies in the future?

B Pair Work What do you think about the article? Are brain scanners a good thing or a bad thing? Discuss with a partner.

A *I think brain scanners are good because police will be able to tell if someone is lying.*

B *Perhaps the police will be able to catch more criminals with brain scanners.*

⬛ Data from the Real World

The simple past forms (*was/were able to*) are more frequent than the simple present forms (*am/is/are able to*). However, *be able to* is most common after modal verbs like *will* and *should* and after verbs like *going to* and *want to*.

Be Able To

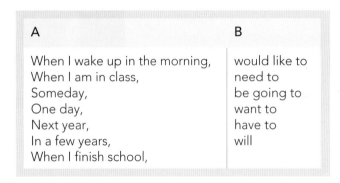

am/is/are able to

was/were able to

modal verb/verb + *be able to*

A Over to You Write five sentences about yourself. Write about work, school, technology, free time, or other ideas. For each sentence, choose one expression from Column A and one from Column B. Add *be able to*.

A	B
When I wake up in the morning,	would like to
When I am in class,	need to
Someday,	be going to
One day,	want to
Next year,	have to
In a few years,	will
When I finish school,	

Someday, I want to be able to buy a house.
When I finish school, I'm going to be able to get a better job.

1 When I wake up in the morning, I have to brush my teeth.

2 When I am in class, I need to listen to what teacher says.

3 Someday, I'm going to marry with beautiful woman.

4 One day, I would like to go to Hawaii.

5 Next year, I want to graduate ESL.

B Group Work Compare your sentences. Give more information. Who has similar experiences and dreams?

4 Avoid Common Mistakes ⚠

1 *Cannot* **is one word.**

        cannot

This technology ~~can not~~ do everything, but it can help.

2 **Don't forget the** *be* **or** *to* **in** *be able to.*

 wasn't   *to*

I not ∧able∧ understand the instructions for my new phone.

3 **In an affirmative sentence, use** *was/were able to* **for a specific action that someone completed successfully in the past. Do not use** *could*.

                                  was able to

My grandmother fell yesterday, but she ~~could~~ get up.

Editing Task

Find and correct 11 more mistakes in this online review of an electronic translator. Some sentences have more than one mistake.

TECHNOLOGY TUESDAY REVIEW:

The Instant Interpreter

                                    be

Will people really need to ∧able to speak other languages in the future? That is a question language students ask after they hear about the Instant Interpreter. This little machine translates for you when you visit a foreign country. It listens to what you say and is able translate your speech into eight world languages. It is also easy to

5 use. If you are able use a smart phone, you will able to use this.

      I tried the Instant Interpreter last week and I liked it. I able to order a cup of coffee in a restaurant. When the server asked me a question, the Interpreter gave me the translation, and I was able to answer. In the end, we were able to have a simple conversation. However, we not able understand everything we said to each other.

10   One problem with this machine is that it can not work quickly when your conversation becomes more complex. It needs time to able to learn your voice, too. I could solve the problem by talking to it a lot, so it learned my voice.

      If you need to be able get around in a foreign city, this is a good buy. You can not find a better translating machine on the market today.

Requests and Offers

Good Causes

1 Grammar in the Real World

A What kinds of volunteer work are common in your city or town? Read Lisa's e-mail about a volunteer project. What is she trying to do?

B Comprehension Check Match the person with his / her work assignment.

1 Professor Rodriguez __d__   **a** is going to bring plates.

2 Wei _____   **b** will do the vegetables.

3 Lara _____   **c** will pick up all the food.

4 Marcus _____   **d** is going to pick up the turkey.

5 Mohammed _____   **e** will make pumpkin pies.

C Notice Find the questions in the e-mail and complete them.

1 Professor Rodriguez, _____ please pick up the turkey on Wednesday evening?

2 Wei, _____ make the pumpkin pies on Wednesday?

3 Professor Rodriguez, _____ please contact your sister?

4 Mohammed, _____ get in touch with your roommate?

Which sentences ask permission to do something? Which sentences ask someone else to do something?

To Bay City Community College Student Volunteer Group

From Lisa Chen

Subject Subject: Volunteer Work Assignments for Thanksgiving

Hi Everyone!

Here are the volunteer work assignments for the Thanksgiving dinner at the Bay City Homeless Shelter. Please contact me if you have any questions.

5   Professor Rodriguez, **could** you please pick up the turkey on Wednesday evening? Then, **could** you take it to Ana's apartment?

Wei, **would** you make the pumpkin pies on Wednesday? That way, Ana can use the oven for the turkey.

Ana, **can** Eun give you a hand?[1]

10   Lara, **will** you do the vegetables? **Do you mind if** I help out? I make great sweet potatoes.

Marcus, you said you had plates and silverware. **Can** you please bring them? Let me know if you cannot.

Mohammed has offered to take all the food in his van. Mohammed, 15   **can** you go by Ana's around 11:00 on Thursday morning and pick everything up? **Can** I go with you? Then, Ana, **can** we go to the shelter together? **Do you mind if** we take your car?

I think that's everything. Let's all meet at the shelter and start serving at 1:00 p.m. Oh, wait! We really need a few more people to help 20   with serving. Professor Rodriguez, **may** I please contact your sister? Mohammed, **can** I get in touch with[2] your roommate?

Finally, would you like to get together at my apartment on Friday for a "thank-you" pizza party?

See you soon, and thanks! Enjoy the attached photo!

25   Lisa

[1]**give you a hand:** help with doing something

[2]**get in touch with:** communicate with

2 Permission

Grammar Presentation

You can use *can, could, may,* and *do you mind if* to ask permission to do something.	"*Could* I go with you to Ana's?" "Sure. No problem." "*Do you mind if* we take your car?" "No, not at all."

2.1 Can, Could, May: Yes/No Questions and Responses

Modal Verb	Subject	Base Form of Verb		Responses	
Can				Yes, you **can**.	No, you **can't**.
Could	I	go	in your car?	Yes, (of course).	No, (I'm afraid not).
May					

2.2 Do You Mind If: Yes/No Questions and Responses

Do you mind if	Subject	Verb	Responses	
Do you mind if	I	**drive**?	No, I don't. Not at all. Sure. No problem.	Well, actually, I prefer to drive.

2.3 Asking for Permission

A Less formal ↕ More formal

can	*Can* is very common in conversation and informal writing. Use *can* in most situations.	*Can* I get in touch with your roommate?
could	*Could* is more formal and more polite than *can*.	*Could* we ride to the shelter with you, please?
may	*May* is very formal and polite.	*May* I please contact your sister, Professor Rodriguez?

B Use the base form of the verb after modal verbs, including *can, could,* and *may.* Do not use other forms of the verb.

Can I be part of your volunteer group?
Can I ~~am~~ part of your volunteer group?
Can I ~~being~~ part of your volunteer group?

C Use *Do you mind if . . .* to be polite or when you think the request is inconvenient for the other person.

Do you mind if we take your car?

With *Do you mind if . . . ?*, the verb agrees with the subject.

Do you mind if Eun gives you a hand?

You can also use *Do you mind?* alone.

Can we go to the shelter together?
Do you mind?

2.3 Asking for Permission (continued)

D You can say *please* with requests for permission, especially in formal situations. Use it at the end of the sentence or after the subject.	*Could I drive your car, please?* *May I please drive your car?*

2.4 Answering Requests for Permission

A Use *can* and *may* in short answers to requests for permission. Do not use *could*.	*"Can I come with you in your car?"* *"Yes, you can."* *"Yes, you ~~could~~."* *"Could I call you later?"* *"Yes." / "Yes, you can."* *"Yes, you ~~could~~."*
May is more formal.	*"May I sit here, please?"* *"Yes, you may."*
B In conversation, you can use other expressions such as *Sure, no problem. / Certainly. / Of course.*	*"Could I use your cell phone?"* *"Sure, no problem."*
Use *Certainly* and *Of course* in formal situations.	*"May I contact your sister?"* *"Of course." /* *"Certainly."*
C You can soften negative responses with an apology and/or a reason.	*"Can I ride in your car?"* *"Sorry, I don't have room."* *"I'm afraid I don't have room."* *"~~I don't have room.~~"*
Be careful with negative responses. *No, you can't* and other direct negative responses often sound rude.	
D Say *No* or *No, not at all* to agree with requests with *Do you mind if.*	*"Do you mind if I borrow your cell phone?"* *"No, not at all. Here you are." / "Sure, no problem."* (*Yes* = Yes, I do mind. You can't use it.)
No means "No, I don't mind." You can also say *Sure* or *Sure, no problem.*	*"Do you mind if I call you this evening?"* *"No, not at all."* (*No* = It's OK to call.)
Notice: *No* in response to *Do you mind if* means the opposite of *No* in response to *can*, *could*, and *may*.	*"Can I call you this evening?"* *"No, I'm afraid I'm busy."* (*No* = It's not OK to call.)

🖱️ Grammar Application

Exercise 2.1 Asking and Answering Requests for Permission

Lisa's volunteers reply to her e-mail, and their plans change. Correct the mistake in each request.

1 Dear Lisa: Yes, I can make the pies on Wednesday. Could I ~~to~~ borrow a pie pan from you?

Thanks, Wei

2 Hi, Lisa: Do you mind if I picks up the turkey on Wednesday morning?
Thank you, Professor Rodriguez

3 Dear Lara: Ana's oven is not working. Do you mind if she cook the turkey at your house? Thanks! Lisa

4 Hello, Lisa: Can my roommate calls you about volunteering? Do you mind if I give him your number? Mohammed

5 Dear Ana: May please I call you early on Wednesday morning to arrange a time? Professor Rodriguez

6 Dear Lisa: Yes, I can bring plates. Can you helping me carry them? Thanks! Marcus

7 Dear Professor Rodriguez: Yes, may you call on Wednesday morning. I'm available after 8:00 a.m. Ana

8 Hi, Ana: My car is not working. Could I please to ride to the shelter with you? Eun

Exercise 2.2 Formal Requests for Permission

A Listen to a student asking a teacher for permission. Complete his requests in the chart on page 215.

B Listen again. Does the teacher agree to the student's requests? Check (✓) Yes or No.

		Yes	No
1	_Could I ask you_ _____ a question, please?	✓	☐
2	_____ class early on Wednesday?	☐	☐
3	_____ the computer room?	☐	☐
4	_____ your CD player?	☐	☐
5	_____ our homework on Friday, not Thursday?	☐	☐

C Pair Work Now compare your answers with a partner.

Exercise 2.3 Asking for Permission

A Write two requests for permission to each person. Use the ideas in the box or your own ideas.

You want to:

~~ask a question about ...~~   discuss an idea for ...   ~~get help with ...~~   ~~take a day off ...~~
~~borrow something~~   get a ride somewhere   ~~sit down~~   ~~talk after class about~~

Your Teacher	A Friend	A Stranger in the Cafeteria	Your Boss
1 *Could I please talk to you after class about my paper?*	3 Could I borrow pencil?	5 Could I get help with you?	7 Could I sit down here?
2 Could I ask you a question about Homework?	4 Could I ge a a ride somewhere?	6 Could I discuss an idea for atmosphere?	8 Could I take a day off on this Wednesday?

B Pair Work Choose three of your requests. Read them to a partner. Do not identify the person you wrote the request to. Can your partner guess?

   A *May I take a break now?*
   B *Are you asking your boss?*

C Pair Work Take turns. Practice conversations. Use the situations from A. Make requests and respond.
(To a stranger in the cafeteria)

   A *Do you mind if I sit down here?*
   B *No, not at all.*

3 Requests and Offers

Grammar Presentation

You can use *can*, *could*, *will*, and *would* to ask people to do things. You can use *can*, *could*, *may*, and *will* to make offers.	*"Could you give me a hand?"* *"Yes, of course."* *"I'll help you with that."* *"Thank you."*

3.1 Requests and Responses with *Can, Could, Will,* and *Would*

Modal Verb	Subject	Base Form of Verb	Responses	
Can **Could** **Will** **Would**	you	help?	Yes, I **can**. / Sure. No problem. Of course. / All right. / OK. Yes, I **will**. Yes, I'd be happy to. / I'd love to.	Sorry, I **can't**. I'm afraid I **can't**.

3.2 Asking People to Do Things with *Can, Could, Will,* and *Would*

A Less formal ↑ *can/will*	*Can* you stop by Ana's around noon? *Will* you help me make the vegetables?
More formal ↓ *could/would*	*Could* you take the turkey to Ana's apartment? *Would* you make the pies, please?

Could and *would* are more polite and less direct.

3.2 Asking People to Do Things with *Can, Could, Will,* and *Would* (continued)

B You can say *please* to ask people to do things, especially in formal situations. Use it at the end of the sentence or after the subject.	*Would you help prepare the dinner, please?* *Can you please arrive at the shelter by noon?*
C You can use *will* and *would* to ask if someone is willing to do something. *Would* is more polite than *will*. Use *would* in formal situations, and use *will* only with people you know well.	*Will you buy the vegetables?* *Would you help us, Professor Rodriguez?*

3.3 Answering Requests to Do Things

A Use *can* and *will* in short answers. Do not use *could* or *would*.	*"Could you drive me there?"* *"Yes, I can."*
	                                        "Yes, I ~~could~~."
	
	"Would you help?" *"Yes, I will."*
	                                "Yes, I ~~would~~."

B In conversation, you can use other expressions, such as *Sure, no problem. / Certainly. / Of course.*	*"Will you clean up after dinner, please?"* *"Sure, no problem."*
Certainly and *Of course* show emphasis. They can also sound more formal.	*"Would you please help me with this?" "Certainly."*
C You can soften negative responses with an apology and/or a reason.	*"Can you help?"* *"I'm sorry, I don't have time this week."*
Be careful with negative responses. *No, I won't* and other direct negative responses often sound rude.	*~~No, I won't,~~ I don't have time this week.*

3.4 Making Offers with *Can, Could, May,* and *Will*

A You can use questions with *can, could,* and *may* to make offers. Less formal ↑ *can* ↕ *could* More formal ↓ *may*	*Can I help you with dinner?* *Could I help you clean up after dinner?* *May I help you with that?*

3.4 Making Offers with *Can*, *Could*, *May*, and *Will* (continued)

B You can also use statements with *I'll*, *We'll*, *I can*, and *We can* to make offers.	*I'll cook* the turkey this year. *We'll make* dinner tonight. *I can drive* you to the shelter. *We can prepare* the vegetables.

3.5 Responding to Offers

A You can say *Thank you* or *No, thank you* to respond to an offer. *Thanks* and *No, thanks* are less formal.	"I can give you a ride." "Thank you." / "Thanks." "Could I help you with that?" "No, thank you."
You can also respond with *That would be great* or *OK*.	"I'll cook the turkey this year." "That would be great." / "OK, thank you."
B You can respond *Yes, please* or *That would be great* to an offer that is a question.	"Can I make the vegetables?" "Yes, please."

⌨ Grammar Application

Exercise 3.1 *Can*, *Could*, *Will*, and *Would*: Requests and Answers

A You need your co-workers' help to plan a charity raffle (an event where everyone who donates to the charity has a chance to win a prize). Use the words to write requests with *please*.

1 could / buy snacks and drinks <u>*Could you please buy snacks and drinks?* /</u>
  <u>*Could you buy snacks and drinks, please?*</u>

2 would / set up tables <u>Would you set up tables, please? /</u>
  <u>Would you please set up tables?</u>

3 can / sell raffle tickets <u>Can you please sell raffle tickets? /</u>
  <u>Can you sell raffle tickets, please?</u>

4 will / buy prizes for the raffle <u>Will you please buy prizes for the raffle? /</u>
  <u>Will you buy prizes for the raffle, please?</u>

5 would / decorate the room <u>Would you please decorate the room? /</u>
  <u>Would you decorate the room, please?</u>

6 could / serve snacks and drinks _Could you please serve snacks and drinks? / Could you serve snacks and drinks, please?_

7 will / give a speech about the charity _Will you please give a speech about the charity? / Will you give a speech about the charity, please?_

8 would / everyone / help clean up after the party _Would you please help clean up after the party everyone? / Would you help clean up after the party everyone, please?_

B Pair Work Take turns asking and answering the requests in A.

A *Could you please buy snacks and drinks?*
B *Yes, of course. / I'm sorry. I don't have time to do that, but I can …*

Exercise 3.2 Formal and Informal Offers and Responses

A It is the evening of the charity raffle. Listen. Complete the offers. Listen again. Complete the responses.

1 A Hi, Tony. _I'll drive_ to the raffle tonight. OK?

   B Oh, that would be great. Thanks.

2 A Sarah, _We can help you_ carry those bags.

   B _Okay, thanks_ . They're really heavy.

3 A _Could I help you_ move those tables, Mr. Lee?

   B _No thank you_ . I just finished.

4 A _Can I put_ the snacks and drinks out now?

   B _Yes, please. thanks._

5 A Jordy, _we'll have_ you take tickets.

   B _Okay, thank._

6 A Ms. Moncur, _May I help you_ with the decorations?

   B _Yes, please. thank you._

7 A Oh, no!

   B _I can clean it up._

   A _Thanks._

8 A _Can I finish_ that for you, Paula?

   B _Yes, thank you._

B Which two conversations are the most formal?

_____ / _____

Exercise 3.3 Requests and Offers

> ### 📊 Data from the Real World
>
> Research shows people also use *Do you want to* to make requests. These requests sound less direct.
>
> | *Do you want to help me with the dishes?* |
> | *Do you want to drive now?* |

A Pair Work You and a partner are organizing a project for a good cause. Choose one of the projects below or use your own idea. Make a list of six to eight things you need to do.

- clean up a local park
- organize a party at a children's hospital
- organize a party at a senior center
- raise money for charity

Clean Up Green Park

1. Put up fliers for volunteers: Tina, Cho, and Luis

2. Organize volunteer groups: Victoria

3. Plan jobs for each group: Tomás and Sophie

B Pair Work Take turns. Offer to do jobs on your list from A. Write your name or your partner's name under the jobs you each offer to do.

C Group Work Work with another pair. Take turns making and responding to requests for help with your project. Ask questions with *can*, *could*, and *Do you want to . . . ?*

4 Avoid Common Mistakes ⚠

1 **Use the base form of the verb after *can*, *could*, *may*, *will*, or *would*.**

Could Lin ~~to~~ ride with you tomorrow?

2 **Use *please* in a request at the end of the sentence or after the subject.**

　　　please　　　　　　　　　　　　　　　　　　　　　　　party, please
Can please I ride with you to the party?　**or**　Can ~~please~~ I ride with you to the party?

3 **Don't use *could* in short answers to requests for permission.**

　　　　　　　　　　　　　　　　　　　　　can
"Could I use your phone, please?"　"Yes, you ~~could~~."

4 **Don't use *could* or would to respond to requests to do things.**

　　　　　　　　　　　　　　　　　　will
"Would you carry this bag for me?"　"Yes, I ~~would~~."

Editing Task

Find and correct six more mistakes in the e-mail messages.

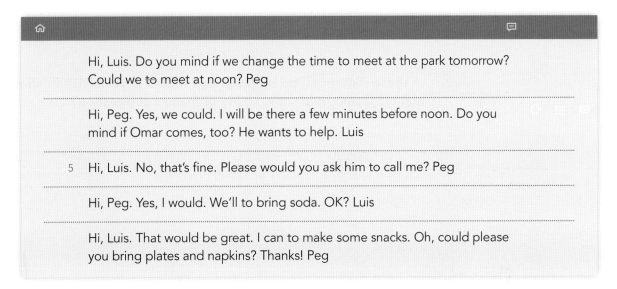

Hi, Luis. Do you mind if we change the time to meet at the park tomorrow? Could we ~~to~~ meet at noon? Peg

Hi, Peg. Yes, we could. I will be there a few minutes before noon. Do you mind if Omar comes, too? He wants to help. Luis

5　Hi, Luis. No, that's fine. Please would you ask him to call me? Peg

Hi, Peg. Yes, I would. We'll to bring soda. OK? Luis

Hi, Luis. That would be great. I can to make some snacks. Oh, could please you bring plates and napkins? Thanks! Peg

Advice and Suggestions

The Right Job

1 Grammar in the Real World

A What are some important things to think about when you plan your career or look for a job? Read the article on advice for people looking for jobs. Which suggestion do you think is the most useful?

B Comprehension Check Circle the correct words.

1 Everyone wants **the same things / different things** from a job.

2 Looking at your personal relationships **can / cannot** help you learn more about how you relate to co-workers.

3 It is **easy / difficult** to make changes after you have started a new job.

4 **Everyone / Not everyone** uses common sense when they look for a job.

C Notice Find the sentences in the article and complete them.

1 According to experts, you _____ think about these things.

2 You _____ ask yourself exactly what you want from a job.

3 You _____ also call the company.

In these sentences, do *ought* to and *should* show advice or show ability? Does *could* show ability or make a suggestion?

The Right Job for You

What are some important considerations[1] when you look for a new job? According to experts, you **ought to** think about these things:

First, know yourself! You **should** ask yourself exactly what you want from a job. Is it money, interesting work, nice co-workers, or something else?
5 Different people want different things from a job. Assess[2] yourself. Where[3] are you now, and where do you want to be?

You also **might want to** think about your personal relationships. Consider which relationships are going well, which ones are not, and, most importantly, why. This will help you understand how you relate to people you
10 work with.

Make changes! If you had problems in another job (maybe you were always late, or you did not finish projects), then you **should** make changes before you take a new job. It is too late when you are in the job.

Decide what you don't want! If you just want a nine-to-five[4] job, you **had**
15 **better not** work for a company that expects you to be on call 24-7.[5]

If you have an interview, prepare! You **should** find out about an employer's business before your interview. Study the company's website. You **could** also call the company. Ask to speak with someone about the job.

Of course, many of these ideas are common sense,[6] but a lot of people
20 just don't think about them. As a result, they are very unhappy in their jobs.

[1]**consideration:** something to think about when making decisions
[2]**assess:** judge or decide about
[3]**where:** in what situation
[4]**nine-to-five:** 9:00 a.m. to 5:00 p.m., a typical workday
[5]**24-7:** twenty-four hours a day, seven days a week, all the time
[6]**common sense:** the ability to use good judgment in making decisions and to live in a safe way

2 Advice

Grammar Presentation

Should, ought to, and *had better* are often used to give advice.	You **should** ask yourself exactly what you want from a job. You **had better** make changes before you take a new job.

2.1 Statements

Subject	Modal Verb / *Had Better (Not)*	Base Form of Verb	
I You He / She / It We They	**should shouldn't / should not ought to ought not to had better (not) 'd better (not)**	make	changes.

2.2 Yes / No Questions and Responses

Should	Subject	Base Form of Verb		Responses	
Should	I you he / she / it we they	take	a different job?	Yes, you **should**. Yes, she **should**.	No, you **shouldn't**. No, she **shouldn't**.

2.3 Information Questions

Wh- Word	*Should*	Subject	Base Form of Verb
When Who	**should**	I you he / she / it we they	call?

Wh- Word	*Should*	Base Form of Verb	
What Who	**should**	come	next?

2.4 Using *Should*, *Ought to*, and *Had Better* for Advice

A Use *should* and *ought to* for general advice.	You **should** assess yourself before you look for a job. She **ought to** look for a new job.
B Use *had better (not)* only for very strong advice and warnings. *Had better (not)* is much stronger than *should* or *ought to*. It suggests that something negative will happen if you don't take the advice. We usually only use it in speaking.	You **had better** finish this project, or you might lose your job!
C Use *should* in questions. *Ought to* and *had better* are not common in questions.	**Should** I ask about the salary at the interview?
D Use *maybe*, *perhaps*, or *I think* to soften advice. These expressions usually go at the beginning of the sentence.	**Maybe** you should be more careful when you write your résumé. **I think** he ought to look for a different job.
E You can also use *probably* to soften advice. It can go before or after *should*. It goes before *ought to*.	She **probably** should take the job. / She should **probably** take the job. She **probably** ought to take the job. She ~~ought to probably~~ take the job.
📊 *Should not* is much more common than *ought not to*. You can use *should not* in both speaking and writing.	

📊 Data from the Real World

Research shows that people often make advice stronger by adding *really*.

Really can go before or after *should/shouldn't*. When *really* goes before *should/shouldn't*, it is stronger.	You should **really** get advice from a career adviser. You **really** shouldn't quit your job before you've found another one.
Really goes before *ought to* and *had better*.	You **really** had better try to keep your current job. You **really** ought to update your résumé. You ~~ought to really~~ update your résumé.

Grammar Application

Exercise 2.1 Statements

Unscramble the words and add *you* to write sentences that give advice. Sometimes more than one answer is possible.

1 decide what you want from a job / should / really / .

   You really should decide what you want from a job. / You should really decide what you want from a job.

2 had better / think about the hours you prefer / really / .

   _____

3 ought to / decide if you want to be on call 24-7 / perhaps / .

   _____

4 maybe / look for job advertisements online / should / .

   _____

5 tell your family about your plans / ought to / probably / .

   _____

6 really / shouldn't / get discouraged / .

   _____

7 should / ask for advice from a career counselor / I think / .

   _____

8 really / take a job you don't like / had better not / !

   _____

Exercise 2.2 Asking for and Giving Advice

A Complete the requests for job advice from an online forum. Add *should*. Sometimes you also need to add a *Wh-* word.

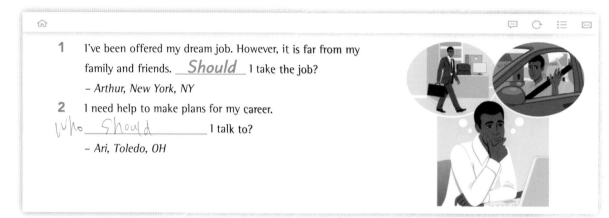

1 I've been offered my dream job. However, it is far from my family and friends. ___*Should*___ I take the job?

   – Arthur, New York, NY

2 I need help to make plans for my career.

   Who Should _____ I talk to?

   – Ari, Toledo, OH

3 I've been looking for a job for several months. I finally have an offer, but it's not the perfect job for me.
However, I really need money. ____Should____ I take the job?

– *Camilla, San Francisco, CA*   You should take the job.

4 I absolutely hate my job! I want to look for another one, but I have lots of student loans.
____What should____ I do?

– *Samuel, Miami, FL*

5 I would like to change careers, but I don't have experience in the career I like. My friend told me to
do volunteer work to get experience. ____Should____ I do this?

– *Eleni, Austin, TX*   Yes, you should.

6 I'm almost finished with school and I don't know what kind of job I want. ____What should____ I do?

– *Katya, Denver, CO*

7 My parents think money is the most important thing in a job. I want to look for a job that makes
me happy. ____Should____ I listen to my parents?

– *Helen, Seattle, WA*

B Pair Work **Discuss the situations in A with a partner. What do you think each person should do? Compare your answers.**

   A *I think Arthur ought to talk to his family about his decision.*

   B *I think he should just take the job. It's his dream job.*

C Listen to a career counselor give advice for each situation. Write the advice you hear.

1 Arthur *had better not take* the job and move.

2 Ari _____ to a career counselor.

3 _____ Camilla _____ the job.

4 _____ Samuel _____ for
another job.

5 Yes, Eleni _____ some
volunteer work.

6 Katya _____ talking to people.

7 _____ Terry _____ looking
for another job. It doesn't sound good, but he
_____ to his boss, too.

8 Helen _____ what makes her happy.

A Write two to four questions asking for advice about jobs / work or school.

B Pair Work Exchange your questions from A with a partner. Write responses to your partner's requests for advice. Then read and compare the advice. Do you agree with the advice? Why or why not?

A *I need to find a part-time job. Where should I look?*

B *I think you should ask at the school cafeteria. They often need help there.*

3 Suggestions

Grammar Presentation

Might (want to), could, why don't / doesn't, and *why not* are often used to make suggestions. Suggestions are not as strong as advice.	You *might want to* schedule your interview in the afternoon. *Why don't* you prepare questions for the interview?

3.1 Suggestions with *Might Want To* and *Could*

Subject	Modal Verb	Base Form of Verb	
I You He / She / It We They	**might want to** **might not want to** **could**	call	the company.

3.2 Suggestions with *Why Don't / Doesn't . . . ?*

Why Don't/Doesn't	Subject	Base Form of Verb
Why don't	I you we they	ask?
Why doesn't	he / she / it	

3.3 Suggestions with *Why Not . . . ?*

Why Not	Base Form of Verb	
Why not	buy	a new suit for the interview?

3.4 Making Suggestions

A Use *might (want to)* and *could* to make suggestions. They often express a choice of possible actions.	*You might schedule your interview in the morning, or you could wait until the afternoon.*
Might is often used with *want to*.	*You might want to think about volunteer work.* *You might not want to ask that question in an interview.*
Do not use *could not* in negative suggestions. Use *might not want to*.	*You ~~could not~~ ask that question in an interview.*
B *Why not* and *Why don't/doesn't* are both question forms and end with a question mark.	*Why don't you prepare questions for your interview?* *Why not prepare questions for your interview?*
Why don't/doesn't and *Why not* are very common in conversation. Do not use them in academic writing.	Say: *"Why don't you practice for your interview?"* Write: *Interviewees might want to practice for their interviews.*

Grammar Application

Exercise 3.1 Making Suggestions

Complete the conversations. Circle the correct words.

1 A I sent my résumé in for a job a few weeks ago, but I haven't had any response.

   B (You could)/ Why don't you call the company.

2 A I have an interview next week, and I'm worried about getting there on time. Traffic is so bad.

   B (You might)/ Why not schedule the interview for the middle of the day, when traffic isn't as bad?

3 A I can't find a job in my field. I really need some work, any work!

   B You why not /(might want to) look for temporary work. That's often easier to find.

4 A I have an interview tomorrow, but I don't know a lot about the company.

   B (You might want to)/ Why don't you do some research online. I'll help you.

5 A I'm nervous about my interview on Monday. I don't know what they'll ask me.

   B Well, (we could)/ why not practice together. I can ask you questions.

6 A I'm going to dress casually for my interview tomorrow. It's a very informal company.

   B You could not /(might not want to) dress too casually. It's still a job interview.

7 A I have to drive to my interview tomorrow, and I always get lost when I drive.

   B (You might want to)/ Why don't you print out directions or use a GPS.

8 A I just had a good interview, and I'm really interested in the job.

   B Why don't /(Why not) you follow up with a thank-you note? It's always a good idea.

Exercise 3.2 More Suggestions

A Pair Work Read about Alex. He has a job interview in a few days. Write three more suggestions for him. Then compare answers with a partner.

I always stay up late and wake up late in the morning.

My suit is pretty old.

I don't know what questions they'll ask me at the interview.

I don't have directions to the interview location.

I haven't had a haircut in a long time.

I talk too much when I'm nervous.

You could go to bed early.

B Pair Work Tell a partner what you worry about in job interviews. Give each other suggestions.

A *I worry about the questions they might ask.*
B *You might want to research the job and the company. Maybe that will help you.*

4 Avoid Common Mistakes ⚠

1 **Do not forget *had* or *'d* when you write *had better*.**

had
You ₌better start looking for another job.

2 **Use *had better (not)* only for very strong advice and warnings.**

should
At an interview, you ~~had better~~ speak clearly and look interested in the questions.

3 **Do not use *could not* in negative suggestions. Use *might not want to*.**

might not want to
You ~~could not~~ wear jeans for the interview.

4 **Do not use an *-ing* form or a *to-* infinitive after *Why not*.**

go
Why not ~~going~~ to a career adviser?
Why not ~~to~~ leave at 6:00 a.m.?

Editing Task

Find and correct five more mistakes in the conversation.

Jordan	There are a lot of changes happening at my company. I'm worried I might lose my job.

Isabela Well, you *had* ₌better probably start looking for something else.

Jordan I guess so.

5 Isabela At the same time, you better try to keep your current job. They say it's a lot harder to find a new job when you're unemployed.

Jordan Is there anything I can do?

Isabela Yes, there's a lot you can do. First, why not to talk to
10 your boss? You get along well, right? Why not asking for feedback on your work? Then, you probably ought to tell your boss you're working on those things. You might want to keep in touch with her by e-mail.

Jordan OK. What else?

15 Isabela Well, do extra work. You ought to take on extra tasks whenever you can. And you could not complain about anything.

Jordan That makes sense. Thanks, Isabela. I'd better ask you for advice more often!

UNIT 22

Necessity, Prohibition, and Preference

How to Sell It

1 Grammar in the Real World

A What are three different kinds of advertising you see every day?
Read the article about advertising companies. What are two difficulties
for advertisers?

B Comprehension Check Answer the questions.

1 How did people advertise in the past?
2 Why is it difficult for advertisers to appeal to consumers? *expensive*
3 How many advertisements do people see or hear each day? *3,000*
4 What must advertisers not do?

C Notice Find the sentences in the article and complete them.

1 Companies ___need to___ appeal to consumers so they buy their products.

2 Companies ___would rather___ not spend a lot of money on it.

3 They ___would prefer___ to save their money.

4 Each one ___has to___ be clever.

**Which of these sentences talk about something that is necessary?
Which talk about something that is preferred?**

232

The Challenges¹ of Advertising²

¹**challenge:** something that needs great mental or physical effort to be done well

²**advertising:** making something known generally in public, especially in order to sell it

³**persuade:** cause someone to do or believe something, especially by explaining why they should

⁴**appeal (to):** be attractive or interesting

⁵**clever:** showing quick intelligence in doing something

Advertising is not a new idea. Long ago, sellers called out to people on the street. They tried to persuade³ people to buy their products. Now advertising is everywhere. It is on the street, on the Internet, in magazines, and on phones.

5 Although there are now many ways to advertise, it is not an easy business. There are many challenges. Companies **need to** appeal⁴ to consumers so they buy their products. This can be quite difficult because people have so many choices these days. Each advertiser **must** make its choice seem better than all the others.

10 Advertising is also very expensive. Companies **would rather** not spend a lot of money on it. They **would prefer** to save their money. However, to sell their products, companies often **need to** spend large amounts of money on ads. Consumers see or hear up to 3,000 advertising messages each day. Each one **has to** be clever.⁵ This means 15 companies **have to** pay to show the ads on TV, online, or in other places, and they also **need to** pay creative people to make them.

There is another challenge for companies when they advertise. Today, there are numerous rules they **must** follow. For example, they **must not** lie. Companies also **need to** be careful when they try to sell 20 products to children.

Advertisers **must** do a number of different things at once. This is not easy, but it is also a big business with big rewards. Just one good advertisement can convince millions of people to buy a product.

2 Necessity and Prohibition

Grammar Presentation

Have to, have got to, need to, and *must (not)* are used to say what is necessary, not necessary, or prohibited.	An ad *has to* appeal to consumers. (necessary) They *do not need to* advertise abroad. (not necessary) Companies *must* follow rules when they create ads. (necessary) They *must not* lie in their advertising. (prohibited)

2.1 *Have To, Have Got To,* and *Need To*: Statements

Subject	Have To / Have Got To / Need To	Base Form of Verb	
I You We They	**have to / do not have to** **have got to** **need to / do not need to**	be buy	clever. advertising.
He / She / It	**has to / doesn't have to** **has got to** **needs to / doesn't need to**		

2.2 *Must*: Statements

Subject	Modal Verb	Base Form of Verb	
I You He / She / It We They	**must** **must not / mustn't**	be buy	clever. advertising.

2.3 *Have To* and *Need To*: Yes / No Questions

Do / Does	Subject	Have To / Need To	Base Form of Verb
Do	you	**have to** **need to**	advertise?
Does	he / she / it		

2.4 *Have To* and *Need To*: Information Questions

Wh- Word	Do / Does	Subject	Have To / Need To	Base Form of Verb
When **Why** **Where**	do	you	**have to** **need to**	advertise?
	does	he / she / it		

2.4 *Have To* and *Need To*: Information Questions (*continued*)

Wh- Word	Have To/Need To	Base Form of Verb
Who	**has to** **needs to**	advertise?

2.5 Expressing Necessity and Prohibition

A Use *have to* and *need to* to say something is necessary.	*Advertisers have to think about consumers.*
Have to is twice as common as *need to*.	*The company needs to be more creative.*
B You can also use *have got to* in affirmative statements. It is usually less formal. The contraction for *has* is *'s*.	*The ad has got to appeal to a lot of people.* *It's got to be interesting.*
Have got to is not usually used in negative sentences.	*The ad hasn't got to appeal to children.*
C *Must* is very strong and sounds formal or official. It is often used in writing to state rules or laws and is rare in speaking.	*Advertising companies must follow these rules.* *He must report this immediately.*
D You can use *don't have to* and *don't need to* to say something is not necessary.	*She doesn't need to finish that.*
However, use *must not/mustn't* to express strong prohibition or to forbid something.	*Companies must not lie in their advertising.*
Be careful: *have to* and *must* have a similar meaning in the affirmative, but they are very different in negative sentences.	*You must/have to use a pen.* (A pen is necessary.) *You don't have to use a pen.* (A pen is not necessary. You have a choice.) *You must not use a pen.* (A pen is prohibited. You have no choice.)
E Use *have to* and *need to* to ask about necessity. Use a form of *do* in the question and answer.	*"Do we have to follow this rule?"* *"Yes, we do."* *"Does this ad need to appeal to kids?"* *"No, it doesn't."*
📊 We often use *can't* instead of *must not* to express prohibition, especially in spoken English.	Say: *"You can't do that. It's against the rules."* Write: *Drivers must not exceed the speed limit.*

Pronunciation Focus: *Have To, Has To, Have Got To*

In informal conversation:	*have to* is often pronounced "hafta." *has to* is often pronounced "hasta." *got to* is often pronounced "gotta."

Grammar Application

Exercise 2.1 Statements

A Listen to an advertising manager discuss plans with his employees. Complete the sentences with the verbs you hear.

1 We _'ve got to_ do this quickly, so we really _have to_ work together.

2 Each team ___need to___ choose a leader.

3 The leader ___has to___ organize the team.

4 Then, you'll all ___need to___ work together to make a plan for the project.

5 I absolutely ___must___ have all plans by the end of the week.

6 You really ___must___ e-mail a report of your progress to me at the end of each week.

7 The report ___doesn't have to___ be long, but it ___need to___ explain your progress clearly.

8 You ___can't___ forget this because I ___need to___ report to the president every week.

9 We ___'ve got to___ create some really interesting ads.

10 But remember, we ___must___ be honest in all of the ads.

B Which sentence says that something is not necessary? Which sentence says that something is prohibited?

Exercise 2.2 Questions and Answers

Complete the e-mail messages with the correct form of the verbs in parentheses.

⌂   💬 ⟳ ☰ ✉

Hi team,   October 21, 10:00 a.m.

Remember, we are meeting tomorrow to discuss our plan. I _____*need to*_____ (need to) get
(1)
your ideas on it. I _____ (have to) hand the plan in on Friday. Let me know if you have
(2)
questions. – Nick

Nick,   October 21, 10:15 a.m.

_____ we _____ (have to) bring specific ideas for ads to the
(3)   (3)
meeting? – Blanca

Hi Blanca,   October 21, 10:30 a.m.

No, you _____ (not need to) have specific ideas. But, we _____
(4)   (5)
(must) start brainstorming soon. I _____ (have to) give Mr. Gomez an update on our
(6)
ideas next week. – Nick

Dear Nick,   October 21, 10:45 a.m.

I have specific ideas. Is it OK if I start to work on them?   – Jason

Hi Jason,   October 21, 11:00 a.m.

It's better to wait. Mr. Gomez _____ (have to) approve our ideas before we begin
(7)
work on them. He _____ (need to) put them all together. Bring them tomorrow, and
(8)
we can discuss them.   – Nick

Hi Nick,   October 21, 11:15 a.m.

When _____ Mr. Gomez _____ (need to) have the ideas? I will
(9)   (9)
be on vacation for a few days next week. _____ I _____ (have to)
(10)   (10)
finish them before I leave?   – Claire

Dear Claire,   October 21, 11:30 a.m.

Yes, I'm afraid so. We _____ (have got to) do them quickly.
(11)
He _____ (need to) have them sometime next week.   – Nick
(12)

Exercise 2.3 More Questions and Answers

A Over to You Write answers to the questions.

1 What is one thing you have to do every day?
   I have to study English every day.

2 What is something you need to do but haven't done yet?
   I need to ~~give~~ get the money of job, but haven't done yet.

3 What is something you do at work or school that you don't have to do?
   I don't have to talk about private.

4 What is something that you must do at work or school?
   I must ~~for~~ listen to teacher say.

5 What is something that you must not do at work or school?
   I must not look the smartphone.

B Pair Work Ask and answer the questions in A with a partner. Try to add extra information.

A *What is one thing you have to do every day?*

B *I have to take my children to school every day. Their school starts at 7:30,*
   so I have to get up at 6:15.

C Group Work Tell the class about your partner.

Raul has to take his children to school every day. Their school starts at 7:30, so he has to get up at 6:15.

3 Preference

Grammar Presentation

Would rather, would like to, and *would prefer* are used to express preferences.	*I would rather not watch those commercials.* *They would like to see some new and interesting ads.* *I'd prefer to turn the TV off.*

3.1 *Would Rather*: Statements

Subject	*Would Rather (Not)*	Base Form of Verb
I You He / She / It We They	**would rather (not)**	advertise.

3.2 *Would Like* and *Would Prefer*: Statements

Subject	*Would (Not) Like /* *Would Prefer (Not)*	Infinitive
I You He / She / It We They	**would (not) like** **would prefer (not)**	to advertise.

3.3 *Yes / No* Questions

Would	Subject		Infinitive
Would	you	**like** **prefer**	to advertise?

Would	Subject		Base Form of Verb
Would	you	**rather**	advertise?

3.4 Information Questions

Wh- Word	*Would*	Subject		Infinitive
What	would	you	**like** **prefer**	to advertise?

Wh- Word	*Would*		Infinitive
Who	would	**like** **prefer**	to buy this product?

3.4 Information Questions (*continued*)

Wh- Word	*Would*	Subject		Base Form of Verb
What	**would**	you	**rather**	advertise?

Wh- Word	*Would*		Base Form of Verb
Who	**would**	**rather**	buy this product?

3.5 Expressing Preferences

A You can use *would rather*, *would like*, and *would prefer* to express preference. *Would prefer* is more formal.	I would rather spend a little money on advertising. I would prefer to listen to the radio.
Use *would rather* with a base form of the verb. Use *would like* and *would prefer* with an infinitive. The contraction of *would* is *'d*.	I would rather see more interesting advertising. I would like / would prefer to see more interesting advertising. I'd like to see more interesting advertising.
B In negative sentences, *not* goes between *would* and *like*. It goes after *would prefer* and *would rather*.	He wouldn't like to work at that advertising company. He would prefer not to work at that advertising company. We'd rather not watch all the commercials.
C You can use the verb *prefer* without *would*. When used without *would*, *prefer* takes -s with *he / she / it*.	She would prefer to watch shorter commercials. She prefers to watch shorter commercials. She ~~prefer~~ to watch shorter commercials.
D *Would prefer* and *prefer* can be followed by a noun, an infinitive, or a verb + *-ing*.	He prefers / would prefer a TV channel without ads. He prefers / would prefer to watch TV without commercials. He prefers / would prefer watching TV without commercials.
E Use *or* in questions about preference to offer a choice. The verb after *or* is usually in the base form.	Would you like to go out or (to) stay home? Would you rather go out or stay home?
F You can use *I'd rather not* to respond to suggestions or requests.	**A** We could go out tonight. **B** I'd rather not. I'm tired.
G You can make a comparison with *would rather* and *than*. If there is a verb after *than*, it is also in the base form.	I'd rather see one long ad than a few short ones. I'd rather see ads on the Internet than watch them on TV.

Exercise 3.1 Questions and Answers

Complete the conversation between two colleagues at an advertising agency. Use the correct form and the correct order of the words in parentheses. Add words if necessary.

A Let's discuss the ad for the new music player. What do you think? What ___*would*___ (1)
consumers ___*like to see*___ (would like / see)?
(1)

B Well, we need to give some detail about the size, weight, memory – things like that. Not too
much, though. People _would rather not get_ (not / would rather / get)
(2)
all the details in an ad. I think a consumer usually ~~would~~ _prefers get_ (prefer / get) a general
(3) to
idea and then research it more if they're interested.

A OK, good point. _Would_ ~~rather~~ they _rather see_ (would rather / see) an
(4) (4)
ad that's more informative or one that's more fun?

B Well, I _would like not to see_ (not / would like / see) an ad that's just informative.
(5)
I _would rather see_ (would rather / see) one that's really fun than one that's really
(6)
informative. That seems a little boring.

A OK, but I think we need to do both – entertain and inform.

B True. Now, what do you think? _Would_ people _prefer to see_ (would
(7) (7)
prefer / see) a man or a woman in the ad?

A Let's include both.

B I _would rather not_ (not / would rather). It costs a lot to hire two actors.
(8)

A Both men and women buy music players.
I _would prefer to hire_ (would prefer / hire) both. I think it's worth the cost.
(9)

B Let's think about that. This is a good start. We can discuss all of this tomorrow.

Exercise 3.2 More Questions and Answers

Unscramble the words to make questions.

1 see a lot of ads on TV / would / rather / not / you / ?
  Would you rather not see a lot of ads on TV?

2 prefer / e-mail ads / you / advertising by mail / do / or / ?

  _____

3 a lot of ads before you buy things / to see / like / would / you / ?

  _____

4 you / to watch TV / prefer / without commercials / would / ?

  _____

5 not / have advertising / would / you / online / rather / ?

  _____

6 ads on the radio / you / ads on TV / do / prefer / or / ?

_____

7 more informative ads or more funny ads / you / like / to see / would / ?

_____

8 not / rather / would / any advertising at all / you / have / ?

_____

4 Avoid Common Mistakes ⚠

1 **Use *don't have to* or *don't need to* to say something is not necessary, not *must not*.**

    don't need to
You ~~must not~~ take notes. I'll give you a copy at the end of the meeting.

2 **Do not use an infinitive with *would rather*. Use an infinitive with *would like* and (would) prefer.**
We would rather ~~to~~ use this idea for the ad.

3 **Use *would* before *rather*.**
    would
I ∧ rather not start work at 7 o'clock.

Editing Task

Find and correct seven more mistakes in the e-mail messages.

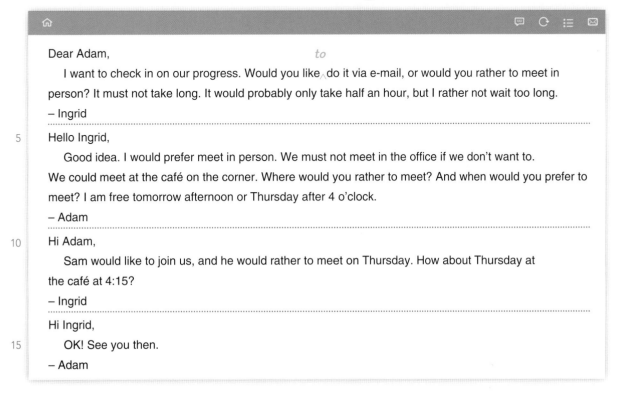

Dear Adam,

    I want to check in on our progress. Would you like ∧ *to* do it via e-mail, or would you rather to meet in person? It must not take long. It would probably only take half an hour, but I rather not wait too long.
– Ingrid

5   Hello Ingrid,

    Good idea. I would prefer meet in person. We must not meet in the office if we don't want to.
We could meet at the café on the corner. Where would you rather to meet? And when would you prefer to meet? I am free tomorrow afternoon or Thursday after 4 o'clock.
– Adam

10   Hi Adam,

    Sam would like to join us, and he would rather to meet on Thursday. How about Thursday at the café at 4:15?
– Ingrid

Hi Ingrid,

15   OK! See you then.
– Adam

Present and Future Probability

Life Today, Life Tomorrow

1 Grammar in the Real World

A What is one way you think society will be different in the future? Read the article about trends in the United States. What is happening in the United States now? What might happen in the future?

B Comprehension Check **Answer the questions.**

1 What are two possible reasons for the decline in the yearly birthrate?
2 How much does it cost to raise a child in the United States?
3 What is one possible positive result of the change in the birthrate?
4 What is one possible negative result of this change?

C Notice **Find the sentences in the article and complete them.**

1 The economy _might_ also affect birthrates.
2 Even small changes in the economy _could_ increase this cost.
3 For example, cities _could_ become less crowded.
4 There _might_ be fewer people in the workforce.

Do these sentences describe something that is certain or uncertain? Are *could* and *might* used to talk about the present, the future, or both?

Now

30 years from now

The UNITED STATES of TOMORROW

¹**trend:** direction of changes or developments

²**decline:** a decrease in amount or quality

³**yearly birthrate:** a measure of how many children are born each year

⁴**predict:** say that an event will happen in the future

Which current trends[1] are likely to affect us most? Which trends **might** be important for society in the future? One trend that **could** be important in the United States is a decline[2] in the yearly birthrate.[3]

5 The birthrate has been going down for several years. Why is this happening? According to experts, there **may** be more than one reason for this change. Women **might** be choosing to have fewer children because more women now have careers. The economy **might** also

10 affect birthrates. Today, it costs more than $300,000 to raise a child from birth to age 17. Even small changes in the economy **could** increase this cost. As a result, couples **may** worry about having children during unsure economic times.

15 How **could** a lower birthrate today affect U.S. society in the future? This is not completely clear. Some effects **could** be positive. For example, cities **could** become less crowded, and there **may** be less pollution. However, other effects **could** be negative. There **might** be fewer

20 people in the workforce. This **could** cause economic difficulties. In addition, as people age, there **could** be fewer doctors and other health professionals to care for them. This **could** cause a decline in the general health of the population.

25 No one can predict[4] exactly what society will be like in the future. However, when experts study trends like the yearly birthrate, they can learn important facts to help us plan for a better tomorrow.

2 Present Probability

Grammar Presentation

The modals *can't, cannot, could (not), may (not), might (not), must (not),* and *should (not)* talk about probability in the present. These modals express how certain you are that something is true.

This could be because more women now have careers.

The economy might also affect birthrates.

2.1 Affirmative Statements

Subject	Modal Verb	Base Form of Verb	
I You He/She/It We They	must should may might could	be	important.

2.2 Negative Statements

Subject	Modal Verb	Base Form of Verb	
I You He/She/It We They	must not/mustn't could not/couldn't cannot/can't should not/shouldn't may not might not	be	important.

2.3 Expressing Present Probability

Certain ↑ Almost Certain	**A** When you are **certain** that something is true in the present, you do not need a modal. Use a present form.	*The birthrate this year is not the same as last year.* *The birthrate is declining.*
	B Use *must (not)* to draw a conclusion about the present, often because you have evidence. You are **almost certain** about your conclusion.	*She must not live nearby. She never walks to work.*
	Do not use the contraction *mustn't* in this case.	*She mustn't live nearby. She never walks to work.*

2.3 Expressing Present Probability *(continued)*

C Use *could not*, *couldn't*, *cannot*, or *can't* when you are **almost certain** that something is impossible. These modals usually express strong disbelief or surprise. We usually use *can't* or *couldn't*.	The birthrate statistics *can't be* right. They look completely wrong. They *couldn't be* at home. They left for vacation yesterday.
D Use *should*, *should not*, or *shouldn't* when you are **fairly certain** that something is true, often because you have evidence. We often use *shouldn't*.	They *should be* at work. They usually are at this time of the day. They *shouldn't be* at work. It's Saturday.
E Use *may (not)*, *might (not)*, or *could* when you are **not certain** that something is true. You are uncertain, but you are making an "educated guess."	The economy *may (not) be* the reason for the declining birthrate. Experts are not sure.
Do not use *mightn't*. It is very rare.	The economy *might not be* the reason for the declining birthrate. The economy ~~mightn't~~ be the reason for the declining birthrate. Experts are not sure.
F *Can* is not usually used for present probability. Use *may*, *might*, or *could*.	They ~~can~~ be related. They look similar. They *might be* related. They look similar.

Fairly Certain

Not Certain

2.4 Answers to Questions About the Present

A You can use modals of present probability to answer questions about the present. Use them when you are not 100 percent sure about your answer.	"Where are they?" "They *might be* at home." "What does this information mean?" "It *could mean* society is changing."
B In short answers to *Yes/No* questions, you can use the modal alone.	"Do they know about this?" "They *must*."
C If *be* is the main verb in *Yes/No* questions, use the modal + *be* in short answers.	"Are they correct?" "They *must be*."

Grammar Application

Exercise 2.1 Present Probability

A Listen to the conversation about a trend for young adults. Complete the sentences you hear.

1 The economy _____ *must* _____ be part of the reason.
2 It _____ can't _____ be easy if you have a lot of debt and college loans.
3 And it _____ must _____ be hard for young people to find a good job these days.
4 Yes, but there _____ could _____ be other reasons, too.
5 They _____ may not _____ be able to afford an apartment.
6 It _____ might _____ be better financially for them to live at home.
7 It _____ can't _____ always be easy for them.
8 Maybe, but it _____ could _____ be nice, too.
9 Some parents _____ might _____ like to have their children around as they get older.
10 I guess it _____ could _____ depend on the family.
11 Of course. It _____ must _____ .

B Listen again. How certain are the speakers about each statement? Check (✓) the correct box.

	Not Certain	Almost Certain
1 The economy is part of the reason young adults move back home.	☐	✓
2 It isn't easy if you have a lot of debt and college loans.	☐	☐
3 It is hard for young people to find a good job these days.	☐	☐
4 There are other reasons students move home.	☐	☐
5 Students can't afford apartments.	☐	☐
6 It is better financially for them to live at home.	☐	☐
7 It isn't always easy for parents.	☐	☐
8 It is nice when children return home, too.	☐	☐
9 Some parents like to have their children around as they get older.	☐	☐
10 It depends on the family. (female speaker)	☐	☐
11 It depends on the family. (male speaker)	☐	☐

Exercise 2.2 Questions and Answers About Present Probability

Circle the correct words. Add *be* where necessary.

1 **A** Is this information correct?

   B It (**must**)/ could _____ *be* _____ . We checked it very carefully.

2 **A** Is the birthrate changing?

B It **must not / may** _____ . We'll know when we have all the statistics.

3 **A** Does he have children?

B He **shouldn't / must** _____ . I see him walking with a little boy every morning.

4 **A** Does she know him?

B She **should / can't** _____ . They work in the same office.

5 **A** Do they know about this?

B They **couldn't / might not** _____ . I'm not sure if anyone has discussed it.

6 **A** Is she away on vacation?

B She **might not / can't** _____ . I just saw her a few minutes ago.

7 **A** Does he live far away?

B He **might / can't** _____ . He's sometimes late for work.

8 **A** Does the birthrate affect society?

B It **may / must** _____ . It's hard to know.

Exercise 2.3 Using Modals of Present Probability

A Over to You **Write possible reasons for these trends. Use modals of present probability.**

1 More people are going to college.
This might be because there are fewer jobs.

2 More young adults live with their parents. _This may not grow up._

3 People have more credit card debt. _This must have because if you lost credit card, it's gonna be hard._

4 Fewer people have phones at home. _This should have because it is useful._

5 People are getting married later. _This could be because someone don't want to marry._

6 Couples are having children later. _This might be because it's gonna break up._

B Pair Work **Compare your reasons with a partner. Are they similar or different?**

3 Modals of Future Probability

Grammar Presentation

Cannot, could (not), may (not), might (not), and *should (not)* talk about future probability.	*Society might change a lot in the future.* *It shouldn't be difficult to see how things change.*

3.1 Affirmative Statements

Subject	Modal Verb	Base Form of Verb	
I You He / She / It We They	**will** **should** **may** **might** **could**	be	different in the future.

3.2 Negative Statements

Subject	Modal Verb	Base Form of Verb	
I You He / She / It We They	**will not / won't** **could not / couldn't** **cannot / can't** **should not / shouldn't** **may not** **might not**	be	different in the future.

3.3 Expressing Future Probability

Certain ↑	**A** Use a future form (*will* or *be going to*) when you are **certain** about the future.	*More people will live in cities in the future.* *A lot of cities are going to be bigger in the future.*
Almost Certain	**B** Use *cannot* or *can't* when you are **almost certain** that something is impossible in the future. They usually express strong disbelief or surprise. We usually use *can't*.	*The economy can't get any worse!*
Fairly Certain	**C** Use *should (not)* or *shouldn't* when you are **fairly certain** about the future, often because you have evidence. In the negative, we usually use *shouldn't*.	*The changes in society should be clear.* *It shouldn't be difficult to see the changes.*
Not Certain ↓	**D** Use *may (not)*, *might (not)*, or *could* when you are **not certain** about the future. You are uncertain, but you are making an "educated guess."	*More people may live with their families in the future.* *It could be more difficult to find affordable housing.*
	Do not contract **may not**. **Mayn't** is rare.	*There may not be any changes in the statistics next year.* *There ~~mayn't~~ be any changes in the statistics next year.*

3.3 Expressing Future Probability (continued)

	E Must, can, and couldn't are not usually used for future probability.	They ~~must~~ be tired tomorrow. They ~~can~~ be tired tomorrow. They ~~couldn't~~ be tired tomorrow.

3.4 Questions and Answers About Future Probability

A Should, may, might, and could are not usually used to ask questions about the future. Use a future form instead. You can use modals of future probability to answer questions about the future.	"*Are you going to* go to the lecture?" "Yes, but I *might be* late." "When *is* the lecture *going to* start?" "It *should start* in a few minutes." "How long *will* the economy have problems?" "It *could be* a long time."
B In short answers to Yes/No questions, you can use the modal alone.	"Will society change?" "It *should*."
C If be is the main verb in Yes/No questions, you can use the modal + be in short answers.	"Is the economy going to be different?" "It *should be*.

Grammar Application

Exercise 3.1 Future Probability

A Listen to an interview about what schools and education might be like in the future. Complete the sentences with the words you hear.

1. Schools and education _____*will*_____ be quite different.

2. There _____ be small changes.

3. There _____ be larger ones.

4. Technology _____ be the most important thing.

5. It _____ be necessary to have physical schools in the future.

6. For example, parents and schools _____ organize social activities in new places.

7. In some ways, we _____ need libraries.

8. There _____ always be some people who want to read real books.

B Listen again. How certain is Professor Li about each idea? Check (✓) the correct box.

	Not Certain	Certain
1 Schools and education will be quite different.	☐	☑
2 There will be small changes.	☐	☐
3 There will be larger changes.	☐	☐
4 Technology will be the most important thing.	☐	☐
5 There will not be physical schools in the future.	☐	☐
6 There will be new places to learn social skills.	☐	☐
7 There will not be libraries in the future.	☐	☐
8 Some people will want books in the future.	☐	☐

Exercise 3.2 Practicing Future Probability

Complete the online postings about future family trends. Circle the correct words.

Family Life in the Future: What Do You Think It Might Be Like?

Family life in the future will be more like it was in the past. Grandparents will live with their children and grandchildren. This **may** / **must** be for economic reasons, or it **may not** / **might** just be easier. Grandparents
(1)   (2)
could help raise the grandchildren. Also, it **might** / **should not** be nice for grandparents to have young people
(3)
in the same house.

Couples are having children later, when they are older. This **can't** / **may** cause problems. Older parents
(4)
could / **might not** find it difficult to deal with children, especially during their children's teenage years.
(5)
– Jake P.

Technology **couldn't** / **might** affect families in the future. We're all busy texting, talking on smartphones,
(6)
or using computers. We don't have time to just talk anymore. It shouldn't surprise us if families communicate
less in the future. This **could** / **can't** change family life a lot.
(7)
– Pete N.

Young adults are going to live at home longer. It **could** / **should not** be more difficult for them to find
(8)
jobs in the future, so they **should** / **may** need to live with their parents. This is not necessarily a bad thing. It
(9)
may / **may not** make families stronger over time.
(10)
– Darla B.

Exercise 3.3 Using Modals of Future Probability

A Over to You Write three predictions about the future. Use these topics or your own ideas.

- family life
- jobs and the workplace
- technology
- transportation
- living situations
- schools

I think family life could change a lot. More people may live in one house together.
We might have better public transportation in the future.

B Group Work Compare your predictions as a class or group. How similar or different are your ideas?

4 Avoid Common Mistakes ⚠

1 **Do not use *can* for present or future probability.**
   could
It's after 5 o'clock, but they ~~can~~ still be at work.

2 **Do not confuse *maybe* with *may be*.**
   may be   *Maybe*
The situation ~~maybe~~ different in the future. ~~May be~~ things will change.

3 **Do not use *couldn't* when you aren't certain. Use *may not*, *might not*, or *shouldn't*.**
   may not
She ~~couldn't~~ be in a meeting right now. I'll check and see.

4 **Do not use *must* or *must not* to talk about probability in the future.**
   will
The situation ~~must~~ be different next year. It always changes.

5 **Use the modal alone in short answers to *Yes/No* questions. Use the modal + *be* in short answers when *be* is the main verb in a *Yes/No* question.**
"Do they work together?"   "They might ~~work~~."
                              be
"Is the meeting at 11:00 a.m.?"   "It may∧."

Editing Task

Find and correct 11 more mistakes in the discussion about a class presentation.

Jim   OK. The trend we're going to discuss in our presentation is the increase in the number of people going to college. We have to start by discussing reasons.
                  might
Lucy   Well, it ~~can~~ be because a lot of people are unemployed. They can be getting a degree because they don't have work. They're in school.

5 Alex   Yes, that maybe the most important reason, but is it the only reason.

Lucy   No, it can't.

Alex   May be students are also preparing for a better job.

Lucy   Yes, that can be another reason.

Jim   OK, good. May be we'll add more reasons later. What about the future effects of this

10   trend, though? Will they be good or bad?

Alex   There must be a lot of good effects in the future I'm sure. because it must be good to have more educated people in the workplace in the future.

Lucy   Yes, but there can be some problems in the future, too. People could have a lot of debt when they finish school.

15 Jim   Hmm. Good point. I think So it couldn't be difficult to think of several more effects. We're doing very well so far. Let's summarize our ideas and see if we need any more information. We couldn't have enough, or we might have just what we need.

Transitive and Intransitive Verbs; Verbs and Prepositions

1 Grammar in the Real World

A How often do you read advice columns? Where do you read them: in newspapers, in magazines, or online? Read the advice column about problems in the workplace. What do you think is the best advice for getting along at work?

B Comprehension Check **Answer the questions.**

1 According to the advice column, why is it a bad idea to wear perfume in the workplace?

2 Why does Jorge think his co-worker is angry?

3 According to the advice column, why should people avoid telling jokes to people they don't know well?

4 Why does Mei Lee have a problem with her boss?

C Notice **Find the sentences in the advice column and complete them.**

1 A new employee _____ yesterday.

2 Something terrible _____ last week!

3 I _____ a joke at work.

4 I think I _____ him.

Which verbs are followed by a noun or pronoun?

252

Ask the EXPERT

Welcome to our advice column, where you can **ask an expert for** advice on all your workplace problems. Here are this week's questions and our expert's answers.

Dear Expert: A new employee **arrived** yesterday. She **wears too**
5 **much perfume**, and it **distracts**[1] **the other employees**. I'm her boss. What should I do? – Rosa M.

Dear Rosa: You should **discuss this with** your employee. You can tell her that most offices ask employees not to **use perfume** because some people are allergic[2] to it.

10 Dear Expert: Something terrible **happened** last week! I **told a joke** at work, and now a co-worker from China is angry with me. I think I **offended him**. – Jorge P.

Dear Jorge: **Apologize for** your behavior. Humor is very different in different cultures, so you probably shouldn't **tell jokes** to people you
15 don't know well. It's also not a good idea to **talk about** politics, religion, or how much money a person has.

Dear Expert: I have a very difficult boss. She constantly **makes outrageous**[3] **demands**. For example, she asked me to **get her suit** from the dry cleaners the other day. This is a personal task, not a work-
20 related task, and she shouldn't ask me to do this. How can I handle this? – Mei Lee W.

Dear Mei Lee: This is a difficult situation to **deal with**. It might help to **make a list** of things you are working on for your boss. When she asks you to run an errand,[4] **show the list** to her. Then she will know how
25 busy you already are.

---

[1]**distract:** take someone's attention away from what the person is doing

[2]**allergic:** having an illness from eating, touching, or breathing something specific

[3]**outrageous:** shocking and unacceptable

[4]**run an errand:** make a short trip to do something, such as buy groceries

2 Transitive and Intransitive Verbs

Grammar Presentation

A transitive verb needs an object. The object completes the meaning of the verb. An intransitive verb does not need an object.

VERB   OBJECT
The new employee *wears perfume*. (transitive)

VERB
The new employee *arrived*. (intransitive)

2.1 Transitive Verbs

Subject	Verb	Object
I You We They	**wear**	**perfume**.
He / She / It	**wears**	

2.2 Intransitive Verbs

Subject	Verb
I You We They	**arrived**.
He / She / It	**arrived**.

2.3 Using Transitive and Intransitive Verbs

A The object after a transitive verb is often a noun or an object pronoun.	She wears *perfume*. My boss doesn't like *me*.
B An intransitive verb does not have an object. However, it is often followed by an expression of time, place, or manner.	The flight arrived *at 5:30 p.m.* How many people work *at your office*? She resigned *unexpectedly*.
C Some verbs can be transitive or intransitive. Sometimes the meaning of the verb is the same.	TRANSITIVE He *drives a truck*. INTRANSITIVE He *drives* badly.
Sometimes the meaning of the verb is different.	TRANSITIVE She *runs a company* in Phoenix. (manages) TRANSITIVE She can *run* fast.

📊 Data from the Real World

Most English verbs are transitive.	
The most common intransitive verbs in speaking and writing are *come, die, fall, go, happen, live, remain, rise, stay,* and *work*.	*He died in 1998.* *Gas prices are rising.*
The most common verbs that can be transitive or intransitive are *begin, call, change, leave, move, open, run, start, stop,* and *study*.	OBJECT *Could you move your car, please?* (transitive) *We all sat very still. No one moved.* (intransitive)

🖥 Grammar Application

Exercise 2.1 Transitive or Intransitive?

Read the e-mail. Label each underlined verb *T* (transitive) or *I* (intransitive) according to how it is used in the e-mail. Circle each object.

Hi Emily,

Our new assistant started work yesterday. He seems great, except for one thing. He chews gum all the time. It distracts me and the other employees. We hear it all day long. Maybe I should explain my feelings, but I don't want to offend him. He works hard and
5 everyone likes him. I discussed the problem with my co-worker, Kyle, but he didn't care. He just laughed. When I arrived at work this morning, my manager and I spoke. She understood the problem. She's going to say something to the new assistant. Maybe that will help.

I hope your workday is going better than mine!

10 Yvette

Exercise 2.2 Questions and Answers

A Underline all of the transitive verbs in the questions. Circle all of the intransitive verbs.

1 What distracts you most when you are studying?

2 How often do you stay late at work (or school)?

3 What time do you usually leave for work (or school)?

4 What has changed in your work (or school) life recently?

5 What time do you usually begin your workday (or school day)?

6 What time does your workday (or school day) usually end?

B Pair Work Ask and answer the questions in A with a partner. Are your answers similar or different?

A *What distracts you most when you are studying?*

B *Nice weather really distracts me. I always want to go outdoors.*

3 Verb + Object + Preposition Combinations

Grammar Presentation

Some verbs are followed by an object and a prepositional phrase.	VERB OBJECT PREPOSITION She *discussed* *company policies* *with* the new employees. VERB OBJECT PREPOSITION He *borrowed* *a laptop* *from* his co-worker.

3.1 Some Verb + Object + Preposition Combinations

A Verb + object + *about* remind … about	We *reminded* them *about* the meeting at 3 o'clock.
B Verb + object + *for* ask … for thank … for	He *asked* me *for* advice. I *thanked* him *for* his help.
C Verb + object + *from* borrow … from get … from learn … from take … from	She *borrowed* the book *from* me. We *got* some good feedback *from* our manager. Have you *learned* a lot *from* her? They *took* the information *from* the new employees.
D Verb + object + *to* explain … to	She *explained* the problem *to* her boss.
E Verb + object + *with* discuss … with help … with spend … with	I *discussed* the project *with* my manager. He *helps* her *with* the mail. Does she *spend* a lot of time *with* him?

Grammar Application

Exercise 3.1 Verb + Object + Preposition Combinations

Listen to the conversation about a woman's day at work. Complete the sentences with the verbs and prepositions you hear.

1 I _explained_ company policies _to_ them.

2 I _spent_ some time _with_ them after the meeting.

3 I _discussed_ everything _with_ them one more time.

4 I couldn't fix them, so I _borrowed_ a laptop _from_ the technology department.

5 I _asked_ Robert _for_ some information.

6 I had to wait and _get_ it _from_ Carrie.

7 Carrie _reminded_ me _about_ a department meeting at 11:30.

8 Robert and Carrie both had time to _help_ me _with_ it then.

9 I _thanked_ Carrie and Robert _for_ their help.

Exercise 3.2 More Verb + Object + Preposition Combinations

A Over to You Write three sentences about things you have to do or have recently done at work or school. Choose from these topics.

- discuss something with someone
- explain something to someone
- get something from someone
- remind someone about something
- borrow something from someone
- help someone with something

I had to discuss a problem at work with my boss yesterday.

I have to borrow a textbook from my friend.
I had to explain about irregular verbs to my classmate.
I have to remind my classmate about our homework.

B Pair Work Read a partner's sentences. Tell the class about your partner.

Nuria borrowed some books from her teacher, and then she lost them.
She doesn't know what to do about this.

4 Verb + Preposition Combinations

Grammar Presentation

Some verbs are often followed by specific prepositions.	I always listen to my co-workers during meetings. Don't worry about the project. I'll help you.

4.1 Some Verb + Preposition Combinations

A Verb + about	
ask about	The new employees asked about company policies.
talk about	We talked about the problem at our meeting.
think about	I thought about it, and I don't think it's a good idea.
worry about	Do you worry about work problems?

B Verb + at	
laugh at	She is laughing at us.
look at	Could you look at this report and tell me what you think?

C Verb + for	
apologize for	I apologize for my behavior.
ask for	Did she ask for a raise?
look for	I'm looking for my boss. I have a question for him.
wait for	We've been waiting for you.

D Verb + on	
count on	You can count on me in a crisis.
depend on	A company's success depends on every employee's hard work.
rely on	He relies on me for help.

E Verb + to	
belong to	Does this belong to you?
happen to	What happened to Tom's boss? I haven't seen her lately.
listen to	We listened to the discussion.
talk to	Our boss talked to all the employees on Monday.

F Verb + with	
agree with	No one agrees with him.
argue with	It's not a good idea to argue with your co-workers.
deal with	I can't deal with her.

➤➤ Verb and Preposition Combinations: See page A5.

4.2 Using Verb + Preposition Combinations

A Verb + preposition combinations often include verbs for communication and verbs for thinking and feeling.	*You should ask about the new job.* (communication) *Don't worry about it.* (thinking and feeling)	
B The preposition can come at the end of an information question.	*"What did you talk about?"* *"We talked about work."* *"Who does this bag belong to?"* *"It belongs to me."*	
C Some verbs can combine with more than one preposition. The meaning may be different.	*I talked to him yesterday.* (had a conversation with) *We talked about our new project.* (discussed)	

Grammar Application

Exercise 4.1 Verb + Preposition Combination in Statements

Complete the text about company policies with the correct form of the verbs in parentheses and the correct preposition from the box.

about	about	for	to̶	to	with
about	at	to	to	with	

Yesterday, our boss ___*talked to*___ (talk) the new
(1)
employees on their first day. He _____
(2)
(talk) company policies. The employees
_____ (listen) him attentively. He said
(3)
everyone should _____ (think) the policies.
(4)
He told them to _____ (ask) anything that
(5)
was unclear.

One employee asked if it was acceptable to speak
his first language at work. The boss said, "We prefer
everyone to speak English, but we think it's important to _____ (look)
(6)
each situation. Sometimes it's acceptable to use your first language, for example, if
you're _____ (talk) a customer who speaks your language."
(7)
At the end of the meeting, he said, "We all _____ (belong) the
(8)
same organization and have the same goals. If you need help, please don't hesitate to
_____ (ask) it." It seemed like everyone _____ (agree) the
(9)   (10)
boss's views. Nobody _____ (argue) him.
(11)

A Use the words to write questions. Add the correct preposition.

1 Who / you / talk / most at work (or school) / ?

   Who do you talk to most at work?

2 What / you / usually talk / at work (or school) / ?

   _____

3 What / you / worry / at work (or school) / ?

   _____

4 Who / you / depend / for help / ?

   _____

5 Whose advice / you / listen / most / ?

   _____

6 Who / you / sometimes argue / ?

   _____

7 Who / you / usually agree / ?

   _____

8 What / clubs or professional organizations / you / belong / ?

   _____

B Pair Work Ask and answer the questions in A with a partner.

A *Who do you talk to most at work?*
B *I talk to my co-worker, Sandra.*

5 Avoid Common Mistakes ⚠

1 **A transitive verb needs an object. Don't forget the object.**

it

I went to see the movie, but I didn't like∧.

2 **Some verbs need a preposition. Don't forget the preposition.**

to

My co-workers often don't listen∧*me.*

3 **Use the correct preposition with verbs that need them.**

about

Don't worry ~~on~~ the presentation. I'll help you finish it.

4 **Don't use a preposition with verbs that don't need them.**

Let's discuss ~~about~~ the problem.

Editing Task

Find and correct eight more mistakes in this magazine article.

⌂   ☰ ✉

NOT APPRECIATED AT WORK?

Do these problems sound familiar to you? If so, you are not alone. These are the common problems our readers sent to us in our recent survey. Try our solutions! They could help you change your work life forever!

me

› Problem: Some people do not appreciate me, or even like∧.

Solution: Maybe you should talk your boss about the problem.

5 › Problem: My co-workers often argue me. I don't like it.

Solution: You could talk with the problem with your co-workers.

› Problem: Nobody listens me when I have a new idea.

Solution: Maybe you need to explain your ideas more clearly to them.

› Problem: I always thank my co-workers for their help, but they never thank.

10 Solution: You could discuss about the problem with them, but it may not change.

› Problem: My co-worker always asks me help. I don't mind helping him, but then
               I don't finish my own work.

Solution: Discuss this him. Tell him you want to help, but you must also do
               your work. I think he'll understand.

Phrasal Verbs

Money, Money, Money

1 Grammar in the Real World

A What are some good habits for managing money? What are some bad habits? Read the article about managing money. What two steps does the author's plan include?

B Comprehension Check Answer the questions.

1 Why should you write down your expenses?
2 According to the article, which expenses are the most important ones?
3 According to the article, what are some expenses that are not important?
4 What are two financial goals that the article mentions?

C Notice Find the sentences in the article and complete them with the missing verbs.

1 If this describes you, you might want to _____ your finances now, before bad habits _____ .

2 _____ with a notebook.

3 Over the next month, _____ all your monthly expenses.

How many words are there in each blank, one or two? Which words are followed by an object (transitive)? Which words are not followed by an object (intransitive)?

MONEY MATTERS

Does your money usually **run out** before the end of the month? Do you spend more money than you earn? Are you starting to **build up** credit card debt? Have you **taken out** a loan and can't **pay** it **off**? If this describes you, you might want to **sort out**[1] your finances now,

5 before bad habits **set in**.[2] Do not **put** it **off** until tomorrow. Here is a plan to help you get control of your money.

Step 1: **Figure out** your income and your spending habits. **Sit down** with a notebook and **write down** how much you make every month. Then **find out** where your money goes. Over the next

10 month, **write down** all your monthly expenses and **add** them **up**. Include everything you buy or spend money on. The purpose of this exercise is to get a clear picture of your usual spending habits. Do you **eat out** too much? What do you need to **give up**?

Step 2: **Set up** a budget. Use your notebook to **work out** what

15 you can spend. Then, prioritize[3] your expenses. Rent, food, electricity, and gas are the most important. These are high-priority[4] expenses. Movies and dinners out are not. You can allow yourself some treats, but remember to **put** money **away** for unexpected expenses, such as repairs when your car **breaks down**.

20 Once you are in control of your finances, you can set a goal like **paying off** your credit card or saving for a large purchase. You can also relax, enjoy life more, and worry less.

---

[1]**sort out:** organize something or solve a problem
[2]**set in:** begin and continue for a long time
[3]**prioritize:** put things in order of importance
[4]**high-priority:** important

2 Intransitive Phrasal Verbs

Grammar Presentation

Phrasal verbs are two-word verbs. They include a verb and a particle. A particle is a small word like *up, down, back, out, on, off,* or *in*.	VERB PARTICLE *Does your money usually run out before the end of the month?* VERB PARTICLE *Sit down with a notebook.*

2.1 Intransitive Phrasal Verbs

Subject	Verb	Particle
I You We They	sit sat	down.
He/She/It	sits sat	

2.2 Using Intransitive Phrasal Verbs

A Intransitive phrasal verbs do not need an object to complete their meaning.	*Sit down with a notebook.* *Do you eat out too much?*
B The particle comes after the verb.	*They came back from vacation today.*
Note: Do not put a word or phrase between the verb and the particle of an intransitive phrasal verb.	*They came ~~from vacation~~ back today.*
C The meaning of some phrasal verbs is easy to understand.	*I go out every night.* *Can you stand up for a moment?* *She went away for a month and then came back.*

2.2 Using Intransitive Phrasal Verbs *(continued)*

D	Some intransitive phrasal verbs have more than one meaning. The meaning of some phrasal verbs is not easy to understand.	*She walked into the room and then ran out.* (left) *Does your money run out?* (be completely used) *Her plane takes off at 12:00.* (leaves) *Debt counseling has taken off.* (grown; been successful) *My car broke down last week.* (stopped working) *He broke down in tears.* (started to cry) *We work out at a gym.* (exercise) *My job didn't work out.* (didn't go as planned)
E	Many everyday spoken commands use intransitive phrasal verbs.	*Hold on./Hang on.* (Wait.) *Go ahead!* (Do it!) *Come on.* (Hurry. Let's go.) *Go on.* (Continue.) *Look out!/Watch out!* (Be careful!) *Sit down.* (Sit.)

2.3 Some Intransitive Phrasal Verbs

break down (1. stop working 2. lose control)

come back (return)

come on (1. hurry 2. start)

eat out (eat in a restaurant)

get along (have a good relationship)

give up (stop)

go ahead (start or continue)

go away (leave; go to another place)

go on (continue)

go out (not stay home)

go up (rise; go higher)

grow up (become an adult)

hang on (1. wait 2. keep going)

hold on (1. wait 2. persist)

look out (be careful)

move in (1. take your things to a new home 2. begin living somewhere)

run out (1. leave 2. be completely used)

set in (begin and continue for a long time)

sit down (sit; take a seat)

stand up (stand; rise)

take off (1. leave on an airplane 2. grow; be successful)

watch out (be careful)

work out (1. exercise 2. go as planned)

▶▶ Phrasal Verbs: Transitive and Intransitive: See page A10.

📊 Data from the Real World

In general, phrasal verbs are less common in academic writing, but writers often use these verbs: *grow up, go on, go back, turn out, break down, come up, work out.*

Talks between the two countries have broken down.

One question came up in the discussion.

Grammar Application

Underline the phrasal verbs in the conversations. Circle the particles.

1 A Come on! We're going to be late.
  B Hold on. I'm coming.
2 A It's Friday night. Let's eat out somewhere.
  B I can't. My money's already run out, and I don't get paid until next week.
3 A I have some new neighbors. They moved in last week.
  B Are they nice? Do you think you'll get along?
4 A I want to go out now. Do you want to come?
  B No, go ahead. I'm tired. I'm going to stay home.

A Complete the story. Use the particles from the boxes.

along	away	back	in	up

Peter and Carlos grew __up__ in the same neighborhood.
(1)
They were good friends and got __along__ really well.
(2)
Carlos went __away__ to college when he was 18, but they
(3)
kept in touch. When Carlos came __back__ , they decided
(4)
to share an apartment. Peter found an apartment, and they
moved __in__ .
(5)

on	out	out	out	up

It all worked __out__ well for a while. They shared
(6)
the bills. They went __out__ for pizza or to see a movie
(7)
after work. Then Carlos got a great job in a bank and
wanted to eat __out__ more often and in more expensive
(8)
restaurants. Peter couldn't afford it, but he used his credit
card and tried not to worry. Life went __on__ as normal,
(9)
but Peter's spending was going __up__ every day.
(10)

down	down	on

One morning, Peter sat __down__ to have coffee and pay some bills online while
(11)
Carlos was at work. He saw his high credit card bill and broke __down__ . "I can't go
(12)
__on__ like this," he said. He called Carlos's voice mail and left a message. He said . . .
(13)

B Pair Work Study the story for two minutes. Tell it to your partner using the phrasal verbs.

Two boys grew up together. They were good friends and . . .

C Group Work **What do you think Peter said in his voice mail to Carlos? What do you think Carlos said to Peter in his response? Discuss in a group.**

I think Peter said, "Hi Carlos, it's Peter calling. I read my credit card bill this morning. It's very high. I can't go on like this . . ."

Exercise 2.3 Questions and Answers

A Complete the questions with the correct particle. Use Chart 2.3 on page 265 to help you.

1 Do you go _*out*_ on weekends very often?
2 Do you eat _____ for lunch, or do you bring your own lunch?
3 Do you exercise at home or work _____ at a gym?
4 Has your computer or car broken _____ lately and needed expensive repairs?
5 Have prices for anything been going _____ lately? If so, what has been getting more expensive?
6 After this course, would you like to go _____ and study more? If so, what would you study?
7 Do you make a budget? If so, does it usually work _____ ?

B Pair Work **Ask and answer the questions with a partner. How similar or different are your answers?**

3 Transitive Phrasal Verbs

Grammar Presentation

Transitive phrasal verbs need an object.	VERB PARTICLE OBJECT *Have you taken out a loan?* VERB OBJECT PARTICLE *Can you pay it back?*

3.1 Transitive Phrasal Verbs

Subject	Verb	Particle	Object (Noun)
I You We They	**figure** **figured**	**out**	the budget.
He / She / It	**figures** **figured**		

3.1 Transitive Phrasal Verbs (continued)

Subject	Verb	Object (Noun or Pronoun)	Particle
I You We They	**figure** **figured**	the budget it	**out.**
He/She/It	**figures** **figured**		

3.2 Using Intransitive Phrasal Verbs

A	Some phrasal verbs are transitive. They need an object to complete their meaning.	*He paid back the money he owed.* *She added up her expenses.*
B	Most transitive phrasal verbs are "separable." This means that noun objects can come **before** or **after** the particle.	VERB PARTICLE OBJECT *Write down your expenses.* VERB OBJECT PARTICLE *Write your expenses down.*
	Object pronouns come **before** the particle.	*Write them down.*
	Do not put an object pronoun after the particle.	*Write down ~~them~~.*
C	Indefinite pronoun objects (e.g., *something, nothing, someone, no one, everyone*) can come before or after the particle.	*She throws away everything.* *She throws everything away.*
D	Longer objects usually go after the particle.	*Is he setting up a new financial management company?* *Is he setting ~~a new financial management company~~ up?*
E	Some transitive phrasal verbs have more than one meaning.	*They are bringing up three children.* (raising a child) *I'd like to bring up the subject of money.* (introduce a topic) *Please turn down the radio. It's too loud.* (lower the volume) *I turned down the invitation to the party because I had to work.* (rejected)

3.2 Using Intransitive Phrasal Verbs (continued)

F Some phrasal verbs have one meaning when they are transitive. They have a different meaning when they are intransitive.	*I worked out a budget.* (transitive; solved or calculated something) *I work out at a gym every day.* (intransitive; exercise)

3.3 Some Transitive Phrasal Verbs

add up (add together; combine)

bring up (1. raise a child
2. introduce a topic)

build up (accumulate)

figure out (find an answer; understand)

find out (discover information; learn)

give up (quit)

pay back (repay money)

pay off (repay completely)

put away (1. save for the future
2. put in the correct place)

put off (delay, postpone)

set up (1. arrange 2. plan 3. build)

sort out (1. organize 2. solve)

take out (1. remove
2. obtain something officially)

throw away (get rid of something; discard)

turn down (1. lower the volume 2. reject)

work out (solve; calculate)

write down (write on paper)

▸▸ Phrasal Verbs: Transitive and Intransitive: See page A10.

📊 Data from the Real World

Research shows that the following transitive phrasal verbs are common in academic writing:

break off	cut off	point out	sum up
carry out	find out	set up	

🖱 Grammar Application

Exercise 3.1 Transitive and Intransitive Phrasal Verbs

Label the phrasal verbs *T* (transitive) or *I* (intransitive) according to their use in the sentences. Circle the objects.

1 Experts say you should work on your money problems now. Don't **put** (them) **off**. ___T___

2 Most experts say it's a good idea to **write down** all your expenses. _____

3 For example, Mariah S., from Chicago, **adds up** everything she's spent at the end of the month. _____

4 After Mariah **worked out** a budget, she changed some of her spending habits. _____

5 She used to pay for an expensive gym membership, but now she **out** at home. _____

6 She also decided to **give up** expensive dinners in order to save money. _____

7 Mariah didn't **give up** and eventually saved enough money to start a business. _____

8 She also **paid back** some money her family had loaned her. _____

Exercise 3.2 Transitive Phrasal Verbs

Listen to the expert give advice about money. Complete the list of advice. Use phrasal verbs.

Dana's Money Advice

1 _Put away_ a little money each month.

2 Even a small amount will _____ over time.

3 You need to _____ a budget.

4 _____ your expenses.

5 Don't _____ receipts.

6 Don't _____ a lot of debt.

7 _____ your credit card every month.

8 You need to _____ the topic _____ and discuss it.

9 Don't _____ money matters.

Exercise 3.3 More Transitive Phrasal Verbs

A Complete the conversations. Unscramble the words in A's questions. Use the verb given and an object pronoun in B's answers.

1 **A** Do you usually _write your expenses down/write down your expenses_ (your expenses/write down)?

   B No, I don't. I _don't add them up_ (not add up) every month, either.

2 **A** Do you _____ (your receipts/throw away), or do you keep them?

   B I usually _____ (throw away).

3 **A** Do you ever _____ (things/put off), like doing your finances?

   B I do. I know I should _____ (sort out).

4 **A** Do you think it's a good idea to _____ (a loan/take out)?

   B Yes, but only if you can _____ (pay off) quickly.

5 **A** Do you think it's difficult to _____ (a budget/work out)?

   B I don't think so. You just need to _____ (figure out).

B Pair Work Ask and answer the questions in A with a partner. Answer with your own opinion or information.

A *Do you usually write down your expenses?*

B *Yes, I do. I write everything down. Then I add it up at the end of the month.*

4 Avoid Common Mistakes ⚠

1   **Don't forget a particle when you need one. Be especially careful with these verbs:** *pick up, break down,* **and** *point out.*

He's picked ^up^ bad spending habits, like eating out every night.

2   **Don't use a particle when you don't need one. Be especially careful with these verbs:** *fall, rise, go, find.*

Gas prices fell ~~down~~, then rose ~~up~~.

Things are going ~~on~~ well for me.

3   **Don't confuse** *grow up* **and** *grow. Grow up* **means to grow from a child to an adult.** *Grow* **means get bigger.**

Before the children grew ^up^, we didn't have any savings.

Now our savings have grown ~~up~~.

4   **Do not put object pronouns after particles. They go before particles.**

She summed ~~up it~~ ^up^ it.

Editing Task

Find and correct eight more mistakes on this website.

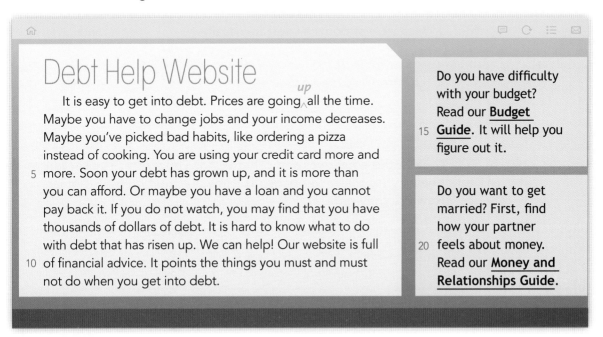

Debt Help Website

It is easy to get into debt. Prices are going ^up^ all the time. Maybe you have to change jobs and your income decreases. Maybe you've picked bad habits, like ordering a pizza instead of cooking. You are using your credit card more and

5   more. Soon your debt has grown up, and it is more than you can afford. Or maybe you have a loan and you cannot pay back it. If you do not watch, you may find that you have thousands of dollars of debt. It is hard to know what to do with debt that has risen up. We can help! Our website is full

10   of financial advice. It points the things you must and must not do when you get into debt.

Do you have difficulty with your budget? Read our **Budget**
15   **Guide**. It will help you figure out it.

Do you want to get married? First, find how your partner
20   feels about money. Read our **Money and Relationships Guide**.

Comparatives

We Are All Different

1 Grammar in the Real World

A Think of a family you know with more than one child. How similar or different are the children's personalities? Read the web article about birth order and personality. Do you agree with the results of the research it describes?

B Comprehension Check Match the child with the description.

1 The first-born child _____   a can be good at resolving conflicts.
2 The younger child _____   b often has an easy time.
3 The middle child _____   c often wants to be a leader.
4 The last-born child _____   d can often be creative and break rules.

C Notice Find the sentences in the article and complete them.

1 Because first-born children are usually _____ and

_____ _____ their younger siblings,

they can try to dominate them.

2 Younger children are often _____ _____ and

_____ _____ _____ older children.

Look at the adjectives and other words you wrote. The sentences show two ways to make comparisons. How are the two ways similar? How are they different?

Does Birth Order[1] Affect Personality?

Some researchers believe that birth order affects people's personalities. According to Dr. Frank Sulloway, professor of psychology, birth order differences are **as strong as** gender differences.[2]

First-born children, he says, are often **more responsible** and **more**
5 **conservative**. They are also **more likely** to be successful, and many first-born children are presidents and CEOs. Because first-born children are usually **bigger** and **stronger** than their **younger** siblings,[3] they can try to dominate[4] them.

As a result, says Sulloway, **younger** children can be rebellious and
10 **less likely** to obey rules. Younger children are often **more adventurous** and **more creative than older** children. They are also **more independent**. They may **try harder** to get attention from their parents, and parents often do not discipline **younger** children **as strictly as** their **older** siblings.

15 Not all researchers agree with these ideas, but most do agree that middle children can have a very difficult time. They are **more likely** to have to repeat a grade in school. Middle children often worry that they are **not** loved **as much as** their siblings. However, middle children are often the peacemakers in the family and are **more easygoing** as
20 a result.

Parents are often **less strict** with the "baby," or last-born child of the family. Last-born children are **more often** spoiled. Parents are usually **more relaxed** with them, and they often seem to have an easy time. However, if you are from a large family, that may be something you
25 already know!

[1] **birth order:** order in which children were born

[2] **gender difference:** difference between men and women

[3] **sibling:** brother or sister

[4] **dominate:** control

We Are All Different   **273**

2 Comparative Adjectives and Adverbs

Grammar Presentation

Comparative adjectives and adverbs show how two things or ideas are different.	COMPARATIVE ADJECTIVE *First-born children are usually bigger than their siblings.* COMPARATIVE ADVERB *Younger children try harder to get their parents' attention.*

2.1 Comparative Adjectives

Subject	Verb	Comparative Adjective	*Than*	
First-born children	are	**stronger** **more responsible** **less easygoing**	**than**	their siblings.

2.2 Comparative Adverbs

Subject	Verb (+ Object)	Comparative Adjective	*Than*	
First-born children	do things obey rules get spoiled	**better** and **more easily** **more often** **less often**	**than**	their siblings.

2.3 The Spelling of Comparative Adjectives and Adverbs

A Add *-er* to one-syllable adjectives and adverbs.	*fast* → *faster* *hard* → *harder* *strong* → *stronger*
For one-syllable adjectives that end in a vowel + consonant, double the consonant. Do not double the consonant *w*.	*big* → *bigger* *hot* → *hotter* *low* → *lower*
B Remove the *-y* and add *-ier* to two-syllable adjectives ending in *-y*.	*early* → *earlier* *funny* → *funnier* *heavy* → *heavier*
C Use *more* with most adjectives and adverbs that have two or more syllables.	*hardworking* → *more hardworking* *intelligent* → *more intelligent* *quickly* → *more quickly* *often* → *more often*

2.3 | The Spelling of Comparative Adjectives and Adverbs *(continued)*

D Some comparative adjectives and adverbs are irregular.

Adjectives			Adverbs		
good	→	better	well	→	better
bad	→	worse	badly	→	worse

➤ Adjectives and Adverbs: Comparative and Superlative Forms. See page A12.

2.4 | Using Comparative Adjectives and Adverbs

A You can use comparative adjectives to describe how two nouns are different.

> NOUN ADJECTIVE NOUN
> *First-born children are sometimes taller than their siblings.*

You can use comparative adverbs to compare the way two people do the same action.

> VERB ADVERB VERB
> *My son works harder in school than my daughter works.*

B *Less* is the opposite of *more*.

> *Julia is more independent than her brother Lucas.*
> *Lucas is less independent than Julia.*
> *He plays more quietly than his sister does.*
> *His sister plays less quietly.*

Less is not usually used with one-syllable adjectives or adverbs, except *clear*, *safe*, and *sure*.

> *My daughter is younger than my son.*
> *My daughter is ~~less old~~ than my son.*

C You can use a pronoun after *than* instead of repeating the noun. In academic writing, use a subject pronoun + verb.

> *Tim's sister is more creative than he is.*

When both verbs are the same, you do not need to repeat the verb after *than*.

> *She works harder than Tim.*

You can also use an auxiliary verb.

> *Tim's sister works harder than he does.*
> *She did better in college than he did.*
> *She's gone further in her career than he has.*

D You do not need *than* plus the second part of the comparison when the meaning is clear.

> *Older children are often more conservative.*
> (than younger children)

E You can also use a comparative adjective without *than* before a noun when the comparison is clear.

> *Parents are strict with older children.*
> (older than other children)

F In speaking, you can use an object pronoun after *than*. In formal speaking or academic writing, use a noun or subject pronoun and a verb or auxiliary verb.	Say: "*Tim's sister works harder than him.*" Write: *Tim's sister works harder than Tim/he does.*

Data from the Real World

Some two-syllable adjectives have two comparative forms. However, one form is usually more frequent, especially in writing.

Use *-er* to form these comparative adjectives: *easier, narrower, quieter, simpler*	Mateo is **quieter** than his sister.
Use *more* to form these comparative adjectives: *more likely, more friendly*	Do you think she is **more friendly** than her brother?

Grammar Application

Exercise 2.1 Comparative Forms

Listen to the news report about birth order and intelligence. Fill in the blanks with the words you hear.

A Norwegian study says that there may be differences in intelligence between brothers. The study showed that older siblings are _more intelligent than_ their
(1)
younger siblings. The researchers gave intelligence tests to 60,000 pairs of brothers.

They found that the older siblings did _____ their brothers
(2)
on the tests. The _____ boys' scores were definitely
(3)
_____ , although not by very much.
(4)

Researchers say one reason for this may be that older siblings have _____
(5)
language skills. Their language may develop _____ because they have
(6)
been in an adult environment _____ . It is possible that younger siblings are
(7)
_____ in other ways, for example, in emotional intelligence.
(8)

The Norwegian study did not look at age differences. However, _____
(9)
research suggests that when the age difference between two brothers is _____ ,
(10)
the difference in intelligence is _____ .
(11)

Exercise 2.2 More Comparative Forms

A Complete the sentences with the correct comparative forms. Use the information in the chart.

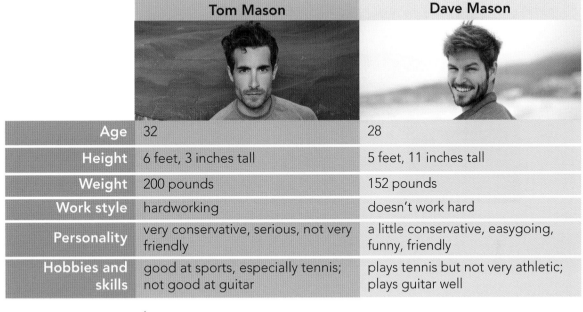

	Tom Mason	Dave Mason
Age	32	28
Height	6 feet, 3 inches tall	5 feet, 11 inches tall
Weight	200 pounds	152 pounds
Work style	hardworking	doesn't work hard
Personality	very conservative, serious, not very friendly	a little conservative, easygoing, funny, friendly
Hobbies and skills	good at sports, especially tennis; not good at guitar	plays tennis but not very athletic; plays guitar well

1 Dave is _younger than_ (young) Tom.

2 Tom is Dave's _____ (old) brother.

3 Tom is _____ (tall) Dave.

4 Tom is _____ (heavy) Dave.

5 Dave is _____ (hardworking) Tom.

6 Tom works _____ (hard).

7 Tom is a _____ (conservative) person.

8 Tom is _____ (athletic) Dave.

9 Tom is _____ (friendly) Dave.

10 Dave plays the guitar _____ (good) Tom.

B Write three more sentences about Tom and Dave. Use comparatives.

Dave is shorter than Tom.
Tom is better at sports than Dave.

_____

_____

_____

A Rewrite the sentences about Sarah and Louisa, two sisters who go to the same college. Use comparatives with the correct form of *be* or *do*.

1 In Biology 101, Sarah works really hard, but Louisa doesn't.
   Sarah works harder than Louisa does.

2 Louisa is very creative. Sarah isn't.

3 Sarah lives very far from school. Louisa doesn't.

4 Louisa is good at writing. Sarah isn't.

5 Sarah learns quickly. Louisa doesn't.

6 Louisa is very quiet. Sarah isn't.

B What happens when you cross out *be* or *do*? Is the meaning still clear?

C Pair Work Rewrite the sentences in A so they are true for you and your partner. Give reasons. Tell the class about your partner.

Virginia works harder than I do. She has three jobs!

A How have you changed? Answer the questions. Use comparatives and try to give extra information.

1 Are you more or less shy than you used to be?
   I'm less shy than I used to be. Now I enjoy parties because I'm more confident.

2 Do you work or study harder than you did when you were younger?

_____

_____

3 What can you do more easily now than last year?

_____

_____

4 What do you do on weekends more often than you used to?

_____

_____

5 What has been more difficult about studying English than you thought?
What has been easier?

_____

_____

B Group Work **Discuss your answers in a group. Have you changed in similar or in different ways?**

I am less shy than I used to be, but Leona is more shy. She doesn't like speaking in front of the class. We've changed in different ways.

3 Comparisons with _As . . . As_

Grammar Presentation

<table>
<tr>
<td>You can use _as . . . as_ to say that two ideas are the same or similar.
Not as . . . as means "less."</td>
<td>Birth order differences are _as strong as_ gender differences.
Older children are sometimes _not as creative as_ younger children. (= Older children are less creative.)</td>
</tr>
</table>

3.1 _As . . . As_ with Adjectives

Subject	Verb	As	Adjective	As	
Younger children	are are not aren't	as	smart creative good	as	older children

3.2 _As . . . As_ with Adverbs

Subject	Verb	As	Adverb	As	
The younger boys	learned didn't learn	as	easily quickly well	as	their older brothers.

3.3 Using (Not) As . . . As

A You can use *as* + adjective + *as* to show that two nouns are similar or the same.	Max is *as intelligent as* his brother.
You can use *as* + adverb + *as* to show that the way two people do things is the same or the way that two events happen is the same.	Max *works as hard as* his brother. (How Max works = how his brother works.)
B *Not as . . . as* shows that two ideas are not similar. It means "less than."	Andreas is *not as ambitious as* his brother. (= Andreas is less ambitious than his brother.)
Use *not as . . . as* instead of *less* with short adjectives and adverbs, such as *bad, easy, high, great,* and *big.*	My brother's test score *was not as high as* my score. (= My brother's score was lower than my score.)
C *As . . . as* can be followed by a noun or a subject pronoun + a verb or auxiliary verb.	Kate's brother is as intelligent as *Kate/she is.* Kate's brother did as well in college as *she did.* He works as hard as *she does.* He's gone as far in his career as *she has.*
D You do not need to use *as* + the second part of the comparison when the meaning is clear.	Middle children feel their parents *don't love them as much* (as the other children).
E In speaking informally, you can use an object pronoun after *as . . . as.*	Say: "Kate's brother isn't as creative as *her.*"
In formal speaking or academic writing, use a noun or subject pronoun and a verb or auxiliary verb.	Write: Kate's brother is not as creative as *Kate/she is.*

Data from the Real World

Research shows that these are some of the most common adjectives and adverbs with (*not*) *as . . . as* in speaking and writing:

adjectives: *bad, big, easy, good, great, hard, high, important, popular, simple, strong*
adverbs: *easily, fast, hard, much, often, quickly, well*

Grammar Application

Exercise 3.1 Forming (Not) As . . . As Sentences

A Rewrite the sentences in the article with (not) as . . . as. Keep the same meaning.

How Much Gender Difference Is There?

The following statements are common beliefs about gender differences:

1 Boys are better than girls at math.

2 Women are better than men at communication.

3 Teenage boys are more confident than teenage girls.

4 Men solve problems more easily than women.

Girls _are not as good as_ boys at math.

Men_____ women at communication.

Teenage girls _____teenage boys.

Women _____ men.

A study by psychologist Janet Shibley Hyde (2007) showed that these beliefs may not all be true. According to her study:

5 People think the differences between boys and girls are big, but they aren't.

6 Young girls and boys do equally well in math.

7 Communication is equally hard for men and women.

8 Girls and boys are equally likely to have low confidence.

The differences _____ people think.

Young girls _____ boys in math.

Communication for women _____ _____ it is for men.

Boys _____ girls to have low confidence.

Hyde found that in 78 percent of tests, men and women were about the same. She did find some differences.

9 Boys are more aggressive than girls.

10 Men get angry more quickly than women.

11 Men can throw objects further than women.

Girls _____ _____ .

Women _____ _____ .

Women _____ _____ .

Hyde's study shows that most differences are in our beliefs, and not really in our gender. She hopes these beliefs will change.

B Pair Work Discuss the information with a partner. What did you know? What surprised you?

A *I didn't know that girls do as well as boys in math.*
B *I know. That surprised me, too.*

Exercise 3.2 Using *As . . . As*

A Pair Work Answer the questions. Then ask and answer the questions with a partner.

What is something . . .

1 you do as often as possible? Why?

I play soccer as often as I can because it is my favorite sport.

_____

2 you can't do as often as you'd like? Why?

_____

3 you do as quickly as you can each day? Why?

_____

Who is . . .

4 as creative as you? Why do you think so?

_____

5 as adventurous as you? Why do you think so?

_____

B Group Work Tell the class about your partner.

A *Agnes plays soccer as often as possible. It's her favorite sport.*
B *Boris visits his parents as often as he can because he misses them.*

Exercise 3.3 Using *(Not) As . . . As*

A Over to You Think of a person you know who fits each description below. Write a sentence about each person using *(not) as . . . as* + a subject pronoun + verb.

1 works as hard as you   *My sister works as hard as I do.*

2 doesn't talk as much as you   _____

3 did as well as you in school   _____

4 isn't as old as you   _____

5 hasn't lived here as long as you _____

6 can speak English as well as you _____

7 doesn't drive as carefully as you _____

8 has studied as much as you   _____

B Pair Work Discuss the people you know with a partner. Are your friends, relatives, and teachers similar or different?

A *My sister works as hard as I do.*

B *What does she do?*

A *She's a nurse. We're both nurses.*

4 Avoid Common Mistakes ⚠

1 Do not use a comparative when you are not comparing two ideas.

young
I have two very ~~younger~~ sons.

2 Use *than*, not *that*, after a comparative.

than
I am more patient now ~~that~~ I was.

3 Do not use *more* and *-er* together.

My work is ~~more~~ better than it used to be.
I work ~~more~~ harder now than I used to.

4 Do not forget the second *as* in *as . . . as* comparisons.

as
I do not see my family now as much ⌃ I did last year.

Editing Task

Find and correct 12 more mistakes in this student's personal essay.

How I Have Changed

I think I have changed in three important ways since high school. First, I have a ~~more~~ kinder personality now. I used to be less patient that I am now, especially with my grandparents. I have spent a lot of time with my grandparents in the last three years, and I have learned to be more patient with them and to understand them more better. I can see that getting old can be more difficult, so I try to

5 help my grandparents as often I can.

Second, I did not use to be as serious I am now about my education. I now realize that I need to study as much possible so I can get a diploma in engineering. Five years ago, I was very younger and did not study a lot. Now I'm studying more harder than I did then, and I do not skip classes as much I did in high school.

10 Finally, I worry less that I did because I have goals now. I know what I want and where I am going. In general, I have grown up and become more clearer about who I am and what I want out of life. I believe I am a better person that I used to be.

27

Superlative Adjectives and Adverbs

The Best and the Worst

1 Grammar in the Real World

A What are some ways we can help people during disasters? Read the web article about technology and disaster relief. What is one way people use technology for disaster relief?

B Comprehension Check **Answer the questions.**

1 When did Hurricane Harvey happen?
2 Which hurricane hit hardest before Hurricane Harvey?
3 What is one way people used social media after the hurricane?
4 How did the Red Cross use social networking sites after the 2010 earthquake in Haiti?
5 What was special about the ice bucket challenge?

C Notice **Read the sentences from the article and answer the questions.**

1 "The heaviest rainfall was 51.88 inches in Cedar Bayou, making it a record for a single storm."

   Was there heavier rain in another city?

   _____

2 "This (social media) seemed to be **the quickest** and **the most efficient** way to give and get information."
   Did there seem to be a quicker and more efficient way to get and give information?

   _____

3 "The ALS ice bucket challenge became one of **the fastest** worldwide money-raising events in history."
   Were there slower money-raising events before?

   _____

The TECHNOLOGY of RELIEF[1]

Natural disasters[2] can strike at any time and with no warning. However, **today's newest** technologies can help disaster victims in new and amazing ways. Here are a few examples.

When Hurricane Harvey hit Texas in August 2017, it was a terrible
5   disaster. It was **the hardest** hurricane to hit the United States since Hurricane Katrina in 2005. **The heaviest** rainfall was 51.88 inches in Cedar Bayou, making it a record for a single storm. TV, newspapers, and radio all covered the storm, but **one of the best** sources of news about the disaster was social media. Soon after the storm hit, people
10   began to post[3] reports of missing persons and to share news and stories. This seemed to be **the quickest** and **the most efficient** way to give and get information. The news on the radio and TV was often not **the most current**.[4] **One of the most important** roles of social media is to help raise money.[5] Soon after the major earthquake in Haiti in 2010, the
15   Red Cross and other organizations that help people in disasters were trending topics on social networking sites. The Red Cross raised more than $8 million in fewer than 48 hours through these sites. Similarly, in 2014, the ALS ice bucket challenge became one of **the fastest** worldwide money-raising events in history. It raised $115 million dollars
20   in just one summer!

Unfortunately, disasters will continue to happen. Hopefully, however, new technologies will continue to develop as well. They can help people to get and to give relief and funding in **the best** ways possible.

[1]**relief:** help
[2]**natural disaster:** a natural event (e.g., hurricane) that causes great damage
[3]**post:** announce; put something on the Internet
[4]**current:** up-to-date, present
[5]**raise money:** convince people to give money, usually for a charity

2 Superlative Adjectives and Adverbs

Grammar Presentation

Superlative adjectives and adverbs compare one idea to other ideas. They mean "more / less than all of the others."	SUPERLATIVE ADJECTIVE *Social networking sites are the newest way to communicate after a disaster.* SUPERLATIVE ADVERB *The rainfall in Cedar Bayou was the heaviest ever recorded.*

2.1 Superlative Adjectives

Subject	Verb	*The*	Superlative Adjective	
The hurricane	was is	**the**	**biggest** **most expensive** **least damaging**	storm of the season.

2.2 Superlative Adverbs

Subject	Verb	(*The*)	Superlative Adjective	
Rescuers	worked	**(the)**	**hardest** **most quickly** **least efficiently**	right after the disaster.

2.3 Forming Superlative Adjectives and Adverbs

A Add *the* and *-est* to one-syllable adjectives and adverbs.	*fast* → *the fastest* *hard* → *the hardest* *strong* → *the strongest*
B For adjectives that end in a vowel + consonant, double the consonant.	*big* → *the biggest* *hot* → *the hottest*
C Remove the *-y* and add *-iest* to two-syllable adjectives ending in *-y*.	*busy* → *the busiest* *early* → *the earliest* *heavy* → *the heaviest*
D Use *the most* with almost all adjectives that have two or more syllables and with adverbs ending in *-ly*.	*expensive* → *the most expensive* *frequently* → *the most frequently*

2.3 Forming Superlative Adjectives and Adverbs *(continued)*

E Some superlative adjectives and adverbs are irregular.	**Adjectives**		**Adverbs**	
	good	→ the best	well	→ the best
	bad	→ the worst	badly	→ the worst

▸▸ Adjectives and Adverbs: Comparative and Superlative Forms: See page A12.

2.4 Using Superlatives

A Superlative adjectives show that a noun has the most or least of a certain quality. They compare one noun to the other nouns in a group.	*It was the biggest forest fire in the state.* (Compares one forest fire to all others in the state.)
B Superlative adverbs show that a verb happens in the most or least of a certain way. They compare one action or situation to others in a group.	*That group worked most effectively after the disaster.* (Compares the way that group worked to the way all other groups worked.)
C *The least* + adjective or adverb is the opposite of *the most* + adjective or adverb.	*This storm was the least dangerous one of the season. There wasn't much damage from it.*
The least is not usually used with one-syllable adjectives or adverbs.	*My daughter is the youngest of my children.* *My daughter is the ~~least old~~ of my children.*
D You do not need to repeat words after the superlative when the meaning is clear.	*That disaster was the biggest (disaster).* *Of all the technologies we use, this is the easiest (technology).*
E You can identify the group being compared with:	
• a prepositional phrase (*in* and *of* are the most common prepositions).	*It was the worst storm in years.*
• a possessive form, like a possessive pronoun or noun. You do not need *the* before the superlative when you use possessives.	*Today's newest technologies help us during disasters.* *Our biggest problem was raising relief money.*

F You can use *one of the* or *some of the* before a superlative adjective.	It is *one of the* best ways to communicate quickly.
Use a plural noun or a noncount noun with these expressions.	These are *some of the* most interesting new technologies.

📊 Data from the Real World

The five most common superlative adjectives with *-est* in writing are *best, biggest, greatest, highest,* and *largest.*	They are **the best** workers to have during a disaster. The disaster struck **the largest** city in the country.
The five most common superlative adjectives with *most* in writing are *most common, most effective, most famous, most important,* and *most popular.*	It's **the most popular** site for social networking. What is **the most common** problem after a disaster?
Research shows that *the* is rarely used before superlative adverbs, except in formal speaking and writing.	Rescue workers worked **fastest** in the first days after the event.

▶ Grammar Application

Exercise 2.1 Superlative Forms

Complete the sentences with the superlative form of the adjectives or adverbs in parentheses. Use *most* or *-est* with ↑. Use *least* with ↓. Some forms are irregular.

1 The flood was *the largest* (↑ large) disaster of the past 10 years.

2 Rescue workers worked _____ (↑ hard) during the first few days.

3 It was one of _____ (↑ big) earthquakes in history.

4 This is _____ (↓ useful) way to help during a disaster.

5 This disaster was the state's _____ (↑ bad) storm.

6 People donated money _____ (↑ quickly) using websites.

7 It was the area's _____ (↓ damaging) hurricane of the year.

8 Medical staff worked _____ (↓ effectively) during the night.

Exercise 2.2 More Superlative Forms

A Write the superlative form of each of the words below. Then listen to the lecture about the eruption of Mount Vesuvius and the Great Chicago Fire. Listen for the superlative forms of the words in the chart, and check (✓) which event they describe.

		Eruption of Mount Vesuvius	Great Chicago Fire
1 bad	*the worst*	☐	☐
2 big		☐	☐
3 famous		☑	☐
4 fast		☐	☐
5 good		☐	☐
6 helpful		☐	☐
7 important		☐	☐
8 interesting		☐	☐
9 popular		☐	☐

B Listen again. Complete the sentences with the words you hear.

1 The eruption of Mount Vesuvius is _____ _____ natural disasters in history.
2 It is also probably _____ disaster in history.
3 However, it has also been _____ events in history for archeologists.
4 It was _____ fire and _____ disaster in the history of the city.
5 _____ story is that a cow kicked over a lantern in a barn and started the fire.
6 The way people worked together after the fire was _____ result.
7 I think that has to be _____ building projects in history.
8 This also shows how people often work together _____ when they are helping one another.

Mount Vesuvius

The Great Chicago Fire

A Look at the information in the chart about three forest fires. Write eight more sentences about the information. Use superlative adjectives and adverbs from the box. Use some words more than once.

| big | damaging | expensive | long | quickly | short | small |

	Westland Fire	Highside Fire	Lakeview Fire
1 Size of fire	100 acres	25 acres	50 acres
2 How long the fire lasted	10 days	3½ days	4 days
3 Damage from the fire (+ = 20 cabins destroyed)	++++	++	+++
4 Cost of fighting the fire	$$$$$	$$	$$$
5 How quickly the firefighters arrived to fight the fire	5 minutes	7 minutes	8 minutes

The Westland fire was the biggest fire. The Highside fire was the smallest.

1 _____
2 _____
3 _____
4 _____
5 _____
6 _____
7 _____
8 _____

B Pair Work Check your partner's sentences. Are they similar or different from yours?

A Over to You Write three superlative sentences about yourself or people you know. In each sentence, use one word or expression from each column.

Expressions	Adjectives		Nouns	
one of the	good	useful	job	technology
some of the	bad	funny	family	life
my friend's/brother's/family's . . .	interesting	enjoyable	story	pet
my/our/your	exciting	unusual	classes	hobby
	difficult		hometown	

This has been one of the least exciting years of my life.
My brother's most unusual pet was a spider.

B Over to You Write three more superlative sentences about yourself or people you know. In each sentence, use one word or expression from each column.

Verbs		Adverbs		Expressions	
study	run	well	easily	I know	in my life
work	speak English	badly	fast	of anyone I know	in my family
play	cook	carefully	quietly	of my life	in the world
learn	drive	quickly	creatively	of the year	
walk		slowly			

My friend Lisa cooks the best of anyone I know.
In my family, my mother drives the most carefully.

3 Avoid Common Mistakes ⚠

1 **Use *the most* with long adjectives. Do not use *-est*.**

most helpful
They were the ~~helpfulest~~ workers after the hurricane.

2 ***Good* and *bad* have irregular superlative adjective and adverb forms.**

worst   *best*
It was the ~~baddest~~ fire of the year.   Everyone worked ~~wellest~~ early in the morning.

3 **Use a possessive pronoun before a superlative. Do not use an object pronoun.**

his
Cleaning up after the storm was ~~him~~ biggest problem.

4 **Do not put a superlative adverb between the verb and the object.**

the fastest
They helped ~~the fastest~~ those people ⁄ after the storm.

Editing Task

Find and correct nine more mistakes in the e-mail.

Hi Miko,

worst
 We had a terrible storm last week. It was the ~~baddest~~ storm of the decade. It was probably the terrifyingest experience of my life. The children were home with me. All three of them were scared, but Alexis behaved the wellest. She was the helpfulest. She kept the other children calm. The dog was
5 probably the difficultest! He barked and barked.
 After the storm, we went outside. The damage to our house is the baddest. Me biggest problem is getting someone to help us fix it. There were some people injured, so rescue workers helped the fastest those people. After that, they started cleaning up the most quickly our neighborhood. A tree fell on our garage and is still there, so that's us biggest problem right now. We hope someone will
10 move it tomorrow.

Pat

Gerunds and Infinitives (1)

Managing Time

1 Grammar in the Real World

A Think of a time when someone made you wait. How did you feel? Read the web article about how different cultures think about time. What are some different ways that people see time?

B Comprehension Check Answer the questions.

1 Why does Joe feel frustrated?
2 If people like to control time, which view do they have?
3 If people don't expect to control time, which view do they have?
4 What are two tips for avoiding time problems with multicultural groups?

C Notice Underline the first verb (main verb) in the sentences below. Circle the second verb.

1 Joe needs to leave soon.
2 People from these cultures do not expect to control time.
3 Joe enjoys keeping a schedule.
4 How can Joe avoid experiencing problems with multicultural meetings?

Look at the second verb in the sentences. How are the second verbs in sentences 1 and 2 different from the ones in sentences 3 and 4?

VIEWS of TIME

Joe is a new manager at his company. He is leading his first team meeting today, and he is feeling frustrated. He **remembered to e-mail** everyone about the meeting, but one person is missing. Did she **forget to come**? Also, Joe **needs to leave** soon, but the group has not

5 discussed everything on the agenda.[1] He **remembers arranging** a two-hour meeting, and he has **tried to keep** the discussion moving forward. However, he has not succeeded. What is the problem? Many of Joe's team members are from different cultures, and different cultures see time very differently.

10 For people in some cultures, like Joe's, time is linear.[2] Events happen one after the other, along a time line, and each one has a beginning and an end point. People in these cultures **like to control** their time. For example, Joe **enjoys keeping** a schedule, and he **likes being** punctual.[3]

15 However, people from other cultures, like some of Joe's team members, see time as a cycle.[4] In this view, events do not have specific beginning and end points – they occur and then reoccur. People from these cultures do not **expect to control** time, so they often do not **like to make** schedules. Instead, they **prefer to be** flexible.

20 How can Joe **avoid experiencing** problems with multicultural meetings? Here are some tips: Get other people on the team to help plan the meeting. If they help create the agenda, it will be more realistic for them. Also, **try to be** flexible. Understand the reasons behind different ideas about time. **Try following** these tips, and you will have

21 more productive meetings.

[1]**agenda:** list of points to discuss
[2]**linear:** following a straight line; continuing in a clear way from one part to the next
[3]**punctual:** on time
[4]**cycle:** a process that repeats

2 Verbs Followed by Gerunds or Infinitives

Grammar Presentation

A gerund is the *-ing* form of a verb, used as a noun.	VERB GERUND *I kept looking at the clock during the meeting.* VERB INFINITIVE *We expected to finish by 4:00 p.m.*
An infinitive is *to* + the base form of a verb.	

2.1 Using Verbs with Gerunds and Infinitives

A Some verbs can be followed by a gerund, but not by an infinitive.	*I kept looking at the clock during the meeting.* *I kept ~~to look~~ at the clock during the meeting.*
B Some verbs can be followed by an infinitive, but not by a gerund.	*We expected to finish by 4:00 p.m.* *We expected ~~finishing~~ by 4:00 p.m.*
C Some verbs can be followed by an infinitive or by an object + an infinitive. These verbs include *expect*, *need*, and *want*.	VERB INFINITIVE *Roberto expects to go soon.* VERB OBJECT INFINITIVE *Roberto expects us to go soon.*
D When a verb is followed by an infinitive or gerund, use *not* before the infinitive or gerund to form a negative statement.	*Jim suggested not leaving early today.* *We agreed not to work after 5 o'clock.*
E You can use *and* or *or* to connect two infinitives or two gerunds. When you connect infinitives, you don't usually repeat *to*, especially when the sentence is short.	*We suggested waiting and going another day.* *I need to stop and think about this for a minute.*

▶▶ Spelling Rules for Verbs Ending in *-ing*: See page A4.

2.2 Verbs Followed by a Gerund Only

avoid	involve
consider	keep (continue)
deny	mind (object to)
enjoy	recall (remember)
finish	suggest

2.3 Verbs Followed by an Infinitive Only

agree	plan
decide	refuse
expect	seem
hope	tend (be likely)
need	want

▶▶ Verbs + Gerunds and Infinitives: See page A5.

📊 Data from the Real World

Research shows that these are the most common verbs followed by a gerund in speaking and writing:			These are the most common verbs followed by an infinitive in speaking and writing:		
avoid	finish	miss	agree	hope	seem
consider	involve	practice	decide	need	tend
deny	keep	risk	expect	plan	want
enjoy	mind	suggest	fail	refuse	

🖥 Grammar Application

Exercise 2.1 Listening for Gerunds and Infinitives

Listen to a podcast about how people think about time. Complete the sentences with the gerund or infinitive you hear.

Most people feel that time speeds up as they get older. At the end of each day, adults often ask themselves: Why haven't I done the things that I planned ___*to do*___ (do) today?
(1)

When you are a child, time seems _____ (go) very slowly. As you get older, time tends
(2)

_____ (pass) more quickly. Why do adults and
(3)
children see time differently?

According to psychologists, one theory is that children tend _____ (look) forward. On a car trip, for
(4)
example, children always want _____ (arrive).
(5)
They ask, "Are we there yet?" Children look forward, so time seems _____ (last) longer. Adults, on the other hand, enjoy
(6)
_____ (look) back and _____ (think) about their
(7)   (8)
memories.

In addition, adults tend _____ (be) busy, so time often passes
(9)
more quickly for them. Also, most adults will keep _____ (look) at
(10)
their watch throughout the day, and as a result, are more aware of time.

Finally, children have a lot of new experiences to process, but as people get older, they do not tend _____ (have) so many new
(11)
experiences. This also speeds time up. Maybe experiencing new adventures as we get older can help us feel as if we can regain a little bit of that childhood sense of time.

Complete the e-mail about problems with time in multicultural business settings.
Circle the correct answer.

To productionteam@cambridge.org
From jj@cambridge.org
Subject Time Management Issues

Dear Team,

As you all know, yesterday morning we had an important meeting. I hoped
(to finish)/ finishing at noon. However, the meeting did not end until 1:30 p.m. In addition,
(1)
we did not finish **to discuss / discussing** everything on the agenda. I do not mind
(2)
to end / ending late. However, we need **to cover / covering** everything on the agenda.
(3)   (4)

At the end of the meeting, some of you suggested **to continue / continuing** our
(5)
discussions over lunch. I usually avoid **to combine / combining** work with meals, so I
(6)
suggested **not to do / not doing** that. We also considered **to stop / stopping** and
(7)   (8)
to continue / continuing another day. In the end, we decided **to arrange / arranging** another
(9)   (10)
meeting for next week.

I want **to feel / you to feel** good about coming to meetings when I ask you to come.
(11)
For this reason, I need **to help / the team to help** me plan meetings from now on. Can we
(12)
agree **to write / writing** the agenda for next week's meeting together? Can I expect
(13)
to participate / everyone to participate with me in this?
(14)

Good time management involves **to agree / agreeing** on an agenda and then
(15)
follow / following it. I hope you all agree.
(16)

Sincerely,

Joe

A What can you tell the people in these situations? Give advice with gerunds or infinitives.

Situation	Advice
1 My friends always come late to my parties.	Your friends need _to call you and tell you that they are going to be late_ .
2 Heather is always late for class.	She should plan _____ .
3 Roberto always turns his homework in late.	He should avoid _____ .
4 Time goes so slowly for me at work. I look at the clock again and again, but it never changes!	You shouldn't keep _____ .
5 Wei doesn't leave me a message when he's going to be late.	He should agree _____ .
6 Lisa refuses to wear a watch.	She needs _____ .

B Pair Work Compare answers in A with a partner. Is your advice similar or different?

A I think Heather should plan to get to class on time.
B I said Heather should plan to have a friend call her one hour before class starts.

3 Verbs Followed by Gerunds and Infinitives

Grammar Presentation

Some verbs can be followed by both a gerund and an infinitive. Sometimes the meaning is the same. Sometimes it is different.	*I stopped e-mailing* the agendas. (For a while, I e-mailed the agendas. Then I stopped doing that.) *I stopped to e-mail* the agendas. (different meaning) (First I stopped what I was doing. Then I e-mailed the agendas.)

A Some verbs can be followed by an infinitive or a gerund without a change in meaning. These verbs include *begin, continue, hate, like, love, prefer,* and *start.*	*Everyone began to speak / speaking at the same time.* *Wei loves to get up / getting up early.*
B Some verbs can be followed by an infinitive or a gerund, but the meaning changes. These verbs include *forget, remember, stop,* and *try.*	*Luis will never forget meeting the president.* (Luis met the president, and he will never forget that he did this.) *Luis must not forget to enclose his résumé with his application.* (Luis has not enclosed his résumé with his application yet, and he must not forget to do this.)
C In sentences with *forget, remember,* or *stop* + a gerund, the gerund tells what happens first.	SECOND EVENT FIRST EVENT *Jim remembered making an appointment.* (First Jim made the appointment. Later, he remembered this.)
In sentences with *forget, remember,* or *stop* + an infinitive, the infinitive tells what happens second, after the action of the main verb.	FIRST EVENT SECOND EVENT *Jim remembered to make an appointment.* (First Jim remembered that he needed to make an appointment. Then he made it.)
D In sentences with *try* + gerund, the action of the gerund generally happens.	*Marta tried setting her alarm for 6:00 a.m., but she was still late.* (She set the alarm.)
In sentences with *try* + infinitive, the action of the infinitive often does not happen or is not successful.	*Marta tried to set her alarm for 6:00 a.m., but the clock wasn't working.* (She didn't set the alarm.)
E You can use *and* or *or* to connect two infinitives or two gerunds. With infinitives, you don't usually repeat *to,* especially when the sentence is short.	*He loves planning and attending meetings.* *He loves to plan and attend meetings.* *I like walking or riding a bike to work.*
With verbs that can be followed by either a gerund or an infinitive, use the same form for both after the verb.	*I like walking and riding a bike to work.* *I like walking and ~~to ride~~ my bike to work.*

Grammar Application

Exercise 3.1 Same or Different Meaning?

A Rewrite the sentences. Change the gerunds in **bold** to infinitives and the infinitives in **bold** to gerunds. If the meaning of the sentence stays the same, write *S* next to the sentence. If the meaning is different, write *D*.

1 I remembered **making** an appointment with the doctor.

   I remembered to make an appointment with the doctor.   *D*

2 My co-workers and I like **to learn** about how different cultures view time.

_____

3 We began **discussing** our plans for next year.

_____

4 To manage her time, our colleague Kelly tried **to buy** a calendar.

_____

5 Our boss started **to accept** that different cultures see time differently.

_____

6 Kelly and I love **having** a very long lunch break.

_____

7 Our colleague Bill hates **mixing** work and social activities.

_____

8 Our co-workers didn't stop **eating** lunch until 4:00 p.m.

_____

9 We continued **to discuss** our problems until very late at night.

_____

10 Jill forgot **to contact** Janet last week.

_____

11 Bo remembered **writing** and **sending** the memo.

_____

B Pair Work In which sentences in A does the meaning change? Explain the difference in meaning to a partner.

The meaning is different in number 1. In the first sentence, he made the appointment and later remembered that. In the second sentence, he first remembered that he needed to make an appointment. Then he made it.

Read the class discussion. Circle the correct answer.

Ms. Vargas Class, tell me how you did research for this assignment. Did most of you use the web?

Laura Well, yes. I tried (reading)/ **to read** a long
(1)
article on the web. The conclusion was good, but I didn't learn much from the rest of the article. I found another article on a website about linear time, but I stopped **reading** / **to**
(2)
read it because it wasn't very academic.

Wendy I tried **getting** / **to get** on to a website about time and psychology, but I
(3)
couldn't make it work. It kept shutting down.

Ms. Vargas Did anyone else have trouble?

Ahmet No. Not really. I remember **reading** / **to read** one article that wasn't very
(4)
good. I found another really good website, though, and I luckily remembered
bookmarking / **to bookmark** it before I closed it.
(5)

Wendy That was a good idea! I found one good site, but I forgot
bookmarking / **to bookmark** it. I was reading an article, but then I stopped
(6)
reading / **to read** and answered the phone. When I got back, my computer was
(7)
off. That was weird because I don't remember it **crashing** / **to crash!**
(8)

Diego I didn't use the web. In fact, I read a book. I prefer books. I read for a while
and take notes, then I stop **thinking** / **to think** for a few minutes about my own
(9)
ideas. Then I add my ideas to the notes.

A Over to You Answer the questions about time. Write complete sentences.

1 Where do you like to go when you have free time?

    I like to go/going to the beach when I have free time.

2 What do you prefer to do after work or school?

    _____

3 What do you try doing when you feel bored?

_____

4 How do you remember not to miss appointments?

_____

B Pair Work Ask and answer the questions in A with a partner. Are your answers similar or different?

4 Avoid Common Mistakes

1 **Do not use gerunds after verbs that require infinitives.**

to discuss

They did not expect ~~discussing~~ work during lunch.

2 **Do not use infinitives after verbs that require gerunds.**

writing

We finished ~~to write~~ our report at 5:00 p.m.

3 **Remember: Infinitives include to.**

_to_

I want ⌄ learn about other cultures.

Editing Task

Find and correct eight more mistakes in this paragraph from a web article about time and boredom.

FIGHTING BOREDOM

looking

Do you keep ~~to look~~ at the clock when you are bored? Does time seem going slowly for you? If you expect having a boring life, you will have a boring life. It is time to make a change! Here are things you can do to avoid to feel bored. First, try look at the clock less often. Time will go more quickly. Next, use your time differently. Start thinking

5 about things that interest you. Try do things that you know will be interesting. If you enjoy to do an activity, time will pass more quickly. In addition, do things that involve changing your daily habits. For example, try wearing your watch on the other wrist or to brush your teeth with the other hand. If your mind is active, time will seem passing more quickly.

Gerunds and Infinitives (2)

Civil Rights

1 Grammar in the Real World

A Are all people treated fairly in the United States today? Read the article about the civil rights movement. What types of discrimination have become illegal since the 1960s?

B Comprehension Check Answer the questions.

1 What kinds of discrimination were there in the United States in the past?
2 What are two examples of segregation?
3 What did civil rights workers want to change?
4 What other groups fought for civil rights after Congress passed the Civil Rights Act of 1964?

C Notice Find the sentences in the reading and complete them.

1 _____ the laws wasn't easy.

2 _____ against people because of their age or for other reasons was common in the United States in the past.

3 Now, because of this law, it is illegal _____ people.

4 Civil rights workers opposed this segregation and worked hard _____ attention to unfair laws.

Look at sentences 1 and 2. You learned that gerunds can come after certain verbs. Where else can gerunds occur in a sentence? Look at sentences 3 and 4. One infinitive shows a purpose or reason for the action. Which one?

The 1960s and Civil Rights

In the 1960s, a 35-year-old American woman applied for a job as a flight attendant. The airline **was not interested in hiring** her. They told her she was too old.

Discriminating[1] against people because of their age or for other
5 reasons was common in the United States in the past. However, certain laws make it less common today. The struggle to pass many of these laws began during the civil rights movement.[2]

In the 1960s, laws in many states segregated[3] African Americans. For example, in some states, African Americans and whites went to
10 separate schools. In addition, African Americans couldn't buy houses in many "white" neighborhoods. Civil rights workers opposed this segregation and worked hard **to call** attention to unfair laws. **Changing** the laws wasn't easy. However, in 1964, the U.S. Congress passed the Civil Rights Act. Now, because of this law,
15 **it is illegal to segregate** people.

After the Civil Rights Act of 1964, other groups became **interested in fighting** for civil rights. These groups included women and people with disabilities.[4] This led to many new laws. Today, for example, **it is against the law to build** a school without access[5] for people in
20 wheelchairs. Not **hiring** people because of their age is also illegal.

Discrimination is still a problem in the United States today. Hopefully, however, people will **keep on working** for equal rights for all groups. **By working** hard, we can **succeed in passing** even more new laws to stop the spread of discrimination.

[1]**discriminate:** treat people differently, in an unfair way

[2]**the civil rights movement:** the struggle for equal rights for African Americans

[3]**segregate:** keep one group of people separate because of race, religion, etc.

[4]**disability:** a physical or mental challenge, such as difficulty walking or seeing

[5]**access:** easy ways to enter

2 More About Gerunds

Grammar Presentation

Gerunds can be the subjects of sentences and the objects of prepositions. They can also come after *be*.

SUBJECT GERUND
Changing the laws wasn't easy.

OBJECT OF A PREPOSITION
We can change the law by working hard.

BE + GERUND
His job is trying to help people fight for their rights.

2.1 Using Gerunds as Subjects, After Prepositions, and After *Be*

A Gerunds can be the subjects of sentences. A gerund subject is singular. It takes third-person singular verb forms.	*Discriminating against people because of age is illegal.*
B Gerunds can be used after prepositions.	*We can succeed in passing more laws against discrimination.*
Note: An infinitive cannot be the object of a preposition.	*They weren't interested in ~~to hire~~ her.*
C Use *by* + gerund to express how something is done.	*You can change laws by voting.*
D Certain verb + preposition + gerund combinations are very common.	**VERB PREP. GERUND** *We believe in fighting for our rights.*
Certain adjective + preposition + gerund combinations are also very common, especially after the verb *be*.	**ADJECTIVE PREP. GERUND** *They weren't interested in hiring her.*
E Gerunds can also come after *be*.	**VERB GERUND** *The worst part of her job was talking to angry customers.*

📊 Data from the Real World

Research shows that these are very common verb + preposition + gerund combinations:

believe in	forget about	succeed in	think about	worry about
disagree with	keep on (continue)	talk about	think of	

Research shows that these are very common adjective + preposition + gerund combinations:

afraid of	good at	important in	involved in	tired of
aware of	important for	interested in	sorry about	worried about

▸▸ Verb + Gerunds and Infinitives: See page A5.
▸▸ Verb and Preposition Combinations: See page A5.

Grammar Application

A Complete the essay on Rosa Parks with the gerund form of the verbs in parentheses.

Rosa Parks is a hero in the American civil rights movement. Her work was important in

_____*ending*_____ (end) segregation in Montgomery, Alabama.
(1)

Parks's major contribution to civil rights was one very simple act. That act

was _____ (refuse) to stand up and move to another seat
(2)

on a bus.

In Montgomery, Alabama, in the 1950s, African Americans had to stand if a white person wanted a seat on a city bus. This was a law. Rosa Parks did not agree with this law. She worked very long hours every day, and she often had to stand up and give her seat to a white person, even though she

was exhausted and her feet hurt. Parks was tired of _____ (do) this. She did not believe in
(3)

_____ (give) her bus seat to a white person for no reason. In addition, she was not afraid
(4)

of _____ (try) to stop something that was wrong. Therefore, one day, Parks refused to
(5)

stand up and move when the bus driver asked her to.

The police arrested Parks. Her arrest angered many African Americans in Alabama. In fact, many

people across the entire United States did not believe in _____ (treat) African Americans
(6)

this way. They were interested in _____ (support) civil rights. These people helped by
(7)

_____ (send) money to the civil rights organizers in Alabama. This support succeeded in
(8)

_____ (pressure) the state of Alabama. As a result, Alabama changed its laws.
(9)

Rosa Parks was involved in _____ (get) an important civil right for African Americans.
(10)

Her one simple act also inspired other people around the country to keep on _____ (work)
(11)

to end discrimination.

B Pair Work Ask and answer questions with a partner about Rosa Parks. Use a form of the words in the box and a gerund, or your own ideas.

be afraid of	be involved in	disagree with
be important in	believe in	keep on
be interested in	be tired of	succeed in

A *What was Rosa Parks tired of doing?*
B *She was tired of giving up her seat on the bus.*

A Complete the sentences in the civil rights time line with the words in parentheses.
Use the gerund form, and add prepositions where needed. Note: All main verbs are in
the present tense.

Civil Rights Time Line – The Early Days

1948 _____*Discriminating*_____ (discriminate) against people in the military because
(1)
of race, religion, or national origin becomes illegal.

1954 After much debate and discussion, the U.S. Supreme Court
_____*agrees to ending*_____ (agree / end) segregation in public schools.
(2)

1955 Martin Luther King Jr. _____ (be involved / start) the
(3)
Montgomery bus boycott.

1957 Martin Luther King Jr. starts a civil rights organization, the Southern Christian
Leadership Conference. King and his organization have many ideas about
_____ (fight) for civil rights peacefully.
(4)

1960 Four African-American students fight segregation by _____ (sit)
(5)
at a lunch counter. No one serves them, but they _____ (keep / sit)
(6)
at the counter. By _____ (do) this, they start the idea of "sit-ins" –
(7)
peaceful demonstrations in the civil rights movement.

1962 James Meredith _____ (succeed / become) the first
(8)
African-American student to enroll at the University of Mississippi.

1963 200,000 people _____ (be involved / march) in
(9)
Washington, D.C. They do this to show their support for civil rights.

1967 _____ (not allow) interracial marriage becomes illegal.
(10)
African Americans and whites can
now marry each other.

1968 More and more Americans

_____
(11)
(be involved / work) for civil rights.

B Group Work **Discuss civil rights in a group. Answer the questions.**

1 Are there civil rights issues you are interested in supporting? If so, which ones?

2 Have you ever been involved in marching or protesting to support a civil right? If so, where and when?

3 More About Infinitives

Grammar Presentation

Infinitives can come after *be*. They are also often used with *in order* to show a purpose.	One idea was to organize farm workers.
	African-American children had to walk (in order) to get to school.
It + infinitive sentences are also very common.	It was difficult to be an African American in the 1960s.

3.1 Using Infinitives After *Be*, to Show Purpose, and in *It* + Infinitive Sentences

A Like gerunds, infinitives can follow *be*.	Her job is to help other people.
	The purpose of the demonstration is to get people's attention.
B *In order* + infinitive expresses a purpose. It answers a "*Why?*" question.	People are fighting in order to change unfair laws.
You can use the infinitive alone when the meaning is clear.	People are fighting to change unfair laws.
	Why are people fighting? To change unfair laws.
When *and* connects two infinitives of purpose, *(in order) to* is usually not repeated.	They were working (in order) to change laws and help people.
C *It* + infinitive sentences are very common. *It* + infinitive sentences often include the verbs *be*, *cost*, *seem*, and *take*.	It is important to fight against discrimination.
	It costs a lot of money to run for office.
	It seems difficult to revise immigration laws.
	It takes time to change people's minds.
An *It* + infinitive sentence usually has the same meaning as a sentence with a gerund subject. The gerund subject is more formal.	It was her dream to have equal rights for everyone.
	Having equal rights for everyone was her dream.

Exercise 3.1 Infinitives After *Be*, to Show Purpose, and with *It*

Listen to a podcast on an early hero in the women's rights movement. Complete the sentences with the words you hear.

It was difficult __*to be*__ a woman in the United States in the early part of the
        (1)
twentieth century. Women did not have many rights. For example, they were not able to vote.

In 1917, Alice Paul organized a group of women _____ for the right
                                                        (2)
to vote in national elections. The group demonstrated in front of the White House in order _____ the president's attention. This angered many people.
        (3)
The police arrested many women_____ the demonstrations. However,
                                        (4)
this didn't work, so they arrested Paul and gave her a seven-month jail sentence in order _____ the other women. This was unfair, but Alice Paul was
        (5)
strong. She stopped eating. She went on a hunger strike _____
                                                                (6)
attention to the issue of women's rights.

Paul suffered in order _____ the right to vote, but in the end, this
                                (7)
and other demonstrations worked. Congress finally gave women the vote in 1920.

Exercise 3.2 More Infinitives

A Complete the textbook passage about César Chávez. Use the correct form of the verbs in the boxes.

focus   get   help   improve

César Chávez was a Mexican-American farm worker. He was also a civil rights worker. He fought _____*to get*_____ equal rights
(1)
for Mexican Americans and _____ the lives of farm
(2)
workers.

Chávez was interested in workers' rights at an early age. He was born in Arizona in 1927. When he was growing up, he experienced discrimination. **For example, it was against school rules to speak Spanish.** If children spoke Spanish, the teacher punished them.

In the 1950s, Chávez joined a civil rights group _____ Mexican Americans
(3)
register and vote in elections. He gave speeches _____ people's attention on
(4)
workers' rights. Later, he started the National Farm Workers Association.

be   help   pay   stop   use

It was difficult _____ **a farm worker in the 1950s. For example, it**
(5)
was common _____ **farm workers very low wages. It was also common**
(6)
_____ **dangerous pesticides (toxic chemicals) on farm crops.**
(7)
It was Chávez's dream _____ **these things.** In the 1960s, he organized a
(8)
strike _____ farm workers.
(9)

convince   get   help   show

The purpose of the strike was _____ higher pay for the workers. The strike
(10)
succeeded, and finally, farm workers got higher wages. In the 1980s, Chávez used another strike
_____ growers to stop the use of pesticides on grapes.
(11)
César Chávez worked all his life _____ Mexican Americans and farm workers.
(12)
Today, his birthday is a state holiday in California and in seven other states. The purpose of César
Chávez Day is _____ respect for his important work.
(13)

B Rewrite each **boldfaced** sentence from the reading. Use a gerund subject.

For example, it was against the rules to speak Spanish.

1   *For example, speaking Spanish was against the rules.*

2   _____

3   _____

4   _____

5   _____

C Pair Work   Ask and answer the questions about César Chávez with a partner. Use infinitives.

1   What did César Chávez work for all his life?

    He worked to improve the lives of Mexican Americans and farm workers.

2   Why did Chávez join a civil rights group in the 1950s?

3   Why did Chávez give speeches in the 1950s?

4   Why was it difficult to be a farm worker?

5   Why did Chávez organize a strike in the 1960s? in the 1980s?

6   What is the purpose of César Chávez Day?

D Over to You   Think about civil rights today. Are there still problems? What do we still need to work on? Complete the following sentences on a separate piece of paper. Then share your sentences with the class.

Today, it is still difficult to help women get the same pay as men.

It still seems hard for [group] to . . .

People are still fighting to . . .

We are still working to . . .

It is my dream to . . .

4 Avoid Common Mistakes ⚠

1 **Gerund subjects take singular verbs.**

is
Changing laws ~~are~~ a slow process.

2 **Use the correct preposition in verb + preposition and adjective + preposition combinations.**

in
They succeeded ~~on~~ getting more rights.

of
Do not be afraid ~~for~~ standing up for your rights.

3 **Do not use an infinitive after a preposition.**

hiring
They weren't interested in ~~to hire~~ her.

4 **Do not use *for* in infinitives of purpose.**
He worked hard ~~for~~ to help workers with disabilities.

5 **Don't forget *It* or *to* in *It* sentences.**

It is *to*
~~Is~~ important ∧ attend the march this weekend.

Editing Task

Find and correct 10 more mistakes in this paragraph.

to
It was more difficult ∧ be disabled in the United States in the past.
It was hard do things like enter buildings or cross the street if you
were in a wheelchair. In many places, it was impossible bring a guide
dog into a restaurant. Many people were interested in to help the

5   disabled. They worked hard for to help people with disabilities.
They finally succeeded on passing an important law. It was the
Americans with Disabilities Act of 1990. Today, sight-impaired people
are not afraid for bringing their dogs into any building. Making streets
accessible to people with physical disabilities are another result of

10   the 1990 law. For example, adding gentle slopes to the edges of
sidewalks help the disabled. Now a person in a wheelchair doesn't
worry about to get from one side of the street to the other.
Making changes like these are a slow process, but an important one.

30 Subject Relative Clauses (Adjective Clauses with Subject Relative Pronouns)

Sleep

1 Grammar in the Real World

A How many hours a night do you sleep? Read the article about scientific research on sleep. Why do some people need only a few hours of sleep?

B Comprehension Check **Answer the questions.**

1 What might control how much sleep we get?
2 What do scientists call people who do not need a lot of sleep?
3 Why did scientists study a mother and her daughter?
4 What did the experiment with mice show?

C Notice **Find the sentences in the article and complete them.**

1 There are many people _____ need eight or more hours of sleep a night.

2 Researchers recently found a gene mutation _____ might control our sleep.

3 The researchers then created mice _____ had the same hDEC2 gene mutation.

4 The mice _____ did not have the mutation needed extra sleep.

Look at the words you wrote. Circle the noun that each one refers to.

SLEEP & SCIENCE

Sleep is important. We need it to live, but not everyone gets the same amount of sleep each night. There are many people **who need eight or more hours of sleep a night**. However, there are also others **who are happy with only four or five hours**. Scientists call these

5 people "short sleepers." Is this simply a lifestyle choice? Not necessarily. Researchers recently found a gene mutation[1] **that might control our sleep**.

Recently, a research team studied a mother and her daughter **who are short sleepers**. They only sleep about six hours a night.

10 The researchers analyzed the DNA[2] of the entire family, and they found a gene mutation in both the mother and daughter. The team already knew about this gene, the hDEC2 gene. It controls sleep in animals. They made a guess: People **who have the mutation** might need less sleep than other people.

15 The researchers then created mice **that had the same hDEC2 gene mutation**. The mice **that had the gene mutation** slept less at night than mice **that didn't have the mutation**. After that, the researchers forced both kinds of mice to stay awake. The mice **that did not have the mutation needed extra sleep**. The mice **that had the mutation did not**.

20 These researchers think genetics might be more important for our sleeping patterns than lifestyle. If you only sleep four or five hours a night, your lifestyle might not be to blame. Perhaps it's just in your genes!

[1] **gene mutation:** a change in the structure of a gene, the pattern of cell structure that we get from our parents

[2] **DNA:** chemical in the cells of living things that controls the structure of each cell

2 Subject Relative Clauses

Grammar Presentation

Relative clauses define, describe, identify, or give more information about nouns. Like all clauses, relative clauses have both a subject and a verb.

RELATIVE CLAUSE

| SUBJECT | VERB |

The team studied people *who slept only four to six hours.* (**who** = *people*)

2.1 Subject Relative Clauses

	RELATIVE CLAUSE			
	Subject Relative Pronoun	**Verb**		
The scientists studied people	**who**	**slept**	**only four to six hours.**	
The mice	**that**	**had**	**the gene mutation**	slept less at night.
It is a gene	**which**	**controls**	**sleep in animals.**	

2.2 Using Subject Relative Clauses

A In a subject relative clause, the relative pronoun is the subject of the clause.	RELATIVE CLAUSE RELATIVE PRONOUN *There are people who only need about six hours of sleep.* RELATIVE CLAUSE RELATIVE PRONOUN *A mouse that had a mutated gene needed less sleep.*
B The subject relative pronouns are *who*, *which*, and *that*.	
Use *who* or *that* for people.	*She's the researcher who/that heads the sleep project.*
Use *which* or *that* for things and animals.	*They created a mouse which/that had the same gene.*
C Subject relative clauses combine two ideas.	*The scientists studied mice.* + *The mice had a gene mutation.* *The scientists studied mice that had a gene mutation.*

2.2 Using Subject Relative Clauses (continued)

D The verb after the relative pronoun agrees with the noun or pronoun before the relative pronoun.	*People who have the hDEC2 gene need less sleep.* *I know a woman who sleeps only four hours a night.*
E A subject relative clause usually comes right after the word it modifies. It can modify any noun or pronoun in a sentence.	SUBJECT *Someone who has the hDEC2 gene sleeps less.* *The scientists studied mice who had a mutated gene.* *The women participated in a study that ended last year.*

Grammar Application

Exercise 2.1 Subject Relative Clauses

Read the student summary of a science article. Circle the relative pronouns and underline the relative clauses.

> Many researchers have done studies (that) look at sleep. This article
> is about a study that compares the habits of good sleepers and bad
> sleepers. A group of scientists who specialize in sleep research did
> the study. First, the scientists studied people who sleep well. They
> 5   learned about the habits that might make these people good sleepers.
> Then the scientists studied people who do not sleep well. These short
> sleepers often have habits which are very different from the habits of
> good sleepers. From this study, the researchers have developed the
> following tips for people who cannot sleep. First, do not drink caffeinated
> 10   beverages like tea or coffee after noon. In addition, eat dinner at least
> three hours before going to bed, and, finally, get some exercise every
> day. These are three habits of good sleepers. If you are a person who
> does not sleep well at night, try to start doing these things. They could
> help you change your sleep patterns.

Data from the Real World

Research shows that in informal speaking and writing, people use either *who* or *that* to refer to people.	**A** *Do you know the woman **who / that participated in the study**?* **B** *Yes. She's my aunt.*
In formal writing, people use *who* to refer to people and *that* or *which* to refer to things. *Which* is more formal.	*Participants **who had the hDEC2 gene** slept less.* *A report on the study **that / which showed a genetic basis for sleep patterns** appears in the journal Genetics Today.*

Complete the article about sleep with the correct **formal** relative pronouns. Circle the noun that each relative pronoun refers to.

A Good Night's Sleep

Everyone needs a good night's sleep. This is important for staying healthy. However, (people)

_____who_____ have trouble sleeping often worry about their health. Troubled sleepers can get help
(1)

from recent studies. Researchers _____ study sleep have good advice for people with sleep
(2)

problems. A study _____ appeared recently showed some interesting results. Not everyone
(3)

needs the same amount of sleep. Most people need 8 to 8½ hours of sleep a night. However, some people

_____ have a special gene need less sleep. People _____ have this gene probably
(4)   (5)

cannot change their sleep habits. They should not worry about sleeping less. However, sleep researchers

have some advice for people _____ do not have this gene.
(6)

People _____ have trouble sleeping should avoid caffeine after noon. Some men and women
(7)

_____ have trouble sleeping have found it helps to exercise. Even walking 20 minutes every
(8)

day can help. One idea _____ has helped many people is for them to go to bed only when
(9)

they are tired. This might mean going to bed at 2:00 a.m. and waking up at 7:00 a.m. Another strategy

_____ has helped people is moving bedtime back 15 minutes each night until it is 8 hours
(10)

before it is time to wake up.

A Complete the questions with a relative pronoun and the correct form of the verb.

1 Do you know someone _who/that_ _has_ (have) trouble sleeping? Who?

2 Do you know someone _____ _____ (sleep) nine hours most nights? Who?

3 Do you read websites or articles _____ _____ (give) tips on sleeping? Which websites or articles?

4 Do you have a friend _____ _____ (stay) up late? Who?

5 Do you have a relative _____ _____ (wake up)
early most days? Who?

6 Do you have friends _____ _____ (take) naps? Who?

7 Do you have a favorite sleeping position _____ _____
(help) you get to sleep? What position is it?

8 Do you have tips _____ _____ (help) you get to
sleep? What are they?

B Group Work **Ask and answer the questions in A in a small group.
Compare answers.**

    A   *Do you have a favorite sleeping position that helps you get to sleep?*
    B   *Yes, I do.*
    A   *What position is it?*
    B   *I sleep on my back. What about you?*

Exercise 2.4 Sentence Combining

A Complete the questions with a relative pronoun and the correct form of the verb.

What's Your Position?

1 A study linked sleep positions with personality. The study looked at how people sleep.

   A study that looked at how people sleep linked sleep positions with personality.

2 In this study, a sleep expert studied people. The people sleep in several different positions.

   _____

3 The expert learned many things. These things surprised her.

   _____

4 People tend to be shy and sensitive. These people sleep in a fetal position.
(*fetal position* = curled up on your side)

   _____

5 People are sociable and relaxed. The people sleep on their sides and have their arms at their sides.

   _____

6 People sleep on their backs and have their arms at their sides. The people are quiet and shy.

   _____

7 People are friendly and helpful. The people sleep on their backs and have their arms up near their pillows.

   _____

8 People sleep on their stomachs and hug their pillows. The people are easily upset.

   _____

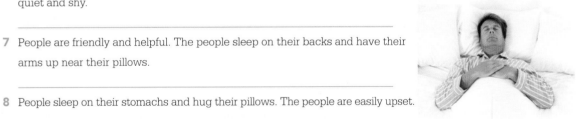

Sleep   **317**

B Underline the subject relative clauses in your new sentences. Circle the noun in the main clause that the relative pronoun refers to.

(A study) that looked at how people sleep linked sleep positions with personality.

C Group Work Take a survey of sleeping positions in your group. What is everyone's usual sleeping position and personality? Talk about your group. Give examples. Use subject relative clauses.

I don't think all people who sleep on their backs are quiet. For example, Marcelo sleeps on his back, and he's outgoing and friendly.

3 More About Subject Relative Clauses

Grammar Presentation

Subject relative clauses can use a variety of verb forms. They can also show possession.	*People who have sleep problems can join the study.* *People who are having sleep problems can join the study.* *People who have had sleep problems can join the study.* *Sally is a scientist whose discoveries have helped many people.* (Sally's discoveries have helped many people.)

3.1 More About Subject Relative Clauses

A Verbs in subject relative clauses can take a variety of verb forms.	*The woman who <u>was participating</u> in the study was my aunt.* *People that <u>have participated</u> in the study receive a payment.*
B The possessive form of *who* is *whose*. *Whose* + a noun shows possession in a subject relative clause. A noun always follows *whose*.	NOUN WHOSE + NOUN SUBJECT *The <u>scientist</u> whose work has helped many people won an award.*
C *Whose* can combine two sentences. *Whose* replaces the possessive form in the second sentence.	*The woman is my neighbor. + ~~Her~~ daughter was in a sleep study.* *The <u>woman</u> whose daughter was in a sleep study is my neighbor.* *They are the scientists. + ~~Their~~ study was on the news last night.* *They are <u>the scientists</u> whose study was on the news last night.*

Grammar Application

Exercise 3.1 Verbs in Subject Relative Clauses

Listen to a student podcast about sleeping. Complete the sentences with the relative pronoun and the correct form of the verb you hear.

Why do we sleep? This is still a mystery. Scientists _who study_ (study) sleep are still not
(1)
completely sure of the reasons. They know some things about sleep, however. Here are some facts:

- People _____ (be) asleep have active brains. Their brains are
(2)
most active during the "rapid eye movement," or REM, phase of sleep.

- Different animals sleep in different ways. For example, a dolphin
_____ (sleep) may continue to swim.
(3)

- Humans and animals _____ (lose) sleep need to make it up later on.
(4)

- A person _____ (need) less than eight hours of sleep should not worry about
(5)
sleeping less than other people.

- There are animals _____ (sleep) very little. For example, a horse only sleeps
(6)
three hours a day. There are other animals _____ (sleep) a lot. For example, a
(7)
small animal called a ferret sleeps about 15 hours a day.

Scientists _____ (study) sleep also have a few guesses about the
(8)
reasons for sleep. There is a study _____ (show)
(9)
REM sleep helps learning and memory. However, there are other studies
_____ (show) the opposite results. For example, certain drugs
(10)
shorten REM sleep. A group of people _____ (take) these drugs
(11)
showed no memory problems in a recent study.

Most scientists agree on one thing. They need to do more research to solve the
mysteries of sleep.

A Combine the sentences to complete a web article about interpreting (giving meaning to) dreams. Make the second sentence a relative clause. Use *who*, *that*, or *whose*.

What Do Dreams Mean?

What do your dreams mean? Interpreting dreams is an important part of many cultures.

whose goal is to understand dreams

1 Some specialists study dream symbols. ~~Their goal is to understand dreams~~.

2 They believe dreams are about certain things. These things represent important ideas or feelings in our lives. Here are some examples of dream symbols and their meanings:

3 People dream about losing a tooth. They are worried about something.

4 People may have a special wish for freedom. Their dreams are about flying.

5 People dream about falling. They have a fear of losing control of something.

6 People sometimes dream about a frightening dog. They have trouble with friends.

7 A dream can represent extreme emotions. The dream focuses on fire.

8 Some other meanings seem obvious. For example, a person might also dream of fire. This person's room is too hot.

9 In any case, most people do not see symbols in a simple way. These people analyze dreams. Instead, they believe in looking at how the dreamer *feels* about the object in the dream.

B Group Work Discuss dream symbols in a group. Use the ones in A or your own ideas. Discuss possible interpretations for each symbol. Use subject relative pronouns. Present your ideas to the class. Use these questions to guide you.

- Which dream symbols are important in a culture you know well?
  Dream symbols that include animals are important in my culture.

- What are some interpretations of these symbols?

- Do you dream about any of these symbols? Which ones?

- What are some positive dream symbols?

- What are some negative dream symbols?

- Whose cultures have similar dream symbols?

- Do they have similar interpretations?

4 Avoid Common Mistakes ⚠

1 **Use *who* or *that* for people and *which* or *that* for things.**

which/that

The scientists studied a woman ~~which~~ never sleeps.

which/that

The research ~~who~~ proved the scientist's theory was interesting.

2 **Do not use a subject pronoun after a subject relative pronoun.**

Scientists study people who ~~they~~ sleep a short amount of time.

3 **The verb after the relative pronoun agrees with the noun before the relative pronoun.**

have

People who ~~has~~ the hDEC2 gene need less sleep.

4 **Do not omit the relative pronoun in a subject relative clause.**

who

Two women ᠕were "short sleepers" participated in a study.

5 **Remember to spell *whose* correctly.**

whose

The scientist ~~who's/whoes~~ work has helped many people won an award.

Editing Task

Find and correct nine more mistakes in a web article about colors in dreams.

Dreaming in **Color**

Can dreams give us insights into our feelings? Some people who ~~they~~ analyze dreams believe

this. There are dream analysts who's interest is the colors that they are in our dreams. In their

opinion, these colors provide clues about our lives. For example, dreams about people which

are wearing black represent sadness. Dreams who have a lot of gray, brown, or tan in them can

5 represent happiness. A dream who's main color is orange can represent boldness. Many people

who analyzes dreams think green represents life or new beginnings. On the other hand, there are

some people do not dream in color. These people dream in black and white.

Do you remember the colors that was in your dreams last night? The next time you dream, try

to remember the colors. Write down the colors appear in your dream, and think about how they

10 made you feel.

Object Relative Clauses (Adjective Clauses with Object Relative Pronouns)

Viruses

1 Grammar in the Real World

A How do you feel when you get a cold or the flu? Read the article from a health website. Why is it so easy to get a virus?

B Comprehension Check **Answer the questions.**

1 What are two illnesses that viruses cause?

2 How do viruses spread?

3 How long can viruses live on a surface?

4 What are three things you should do to protect yourself and others against viral infection?

C Notice **Look at the underlined words in these sentences from the article. Circle the nouns that the underlined words refer to.**

1 The common cold and the flu are two well-known illnesses that viruses cause.

2 Infected people can pass viruses easily to others who they interact with.

VIRUSES

When was the last time you had a viral infection?[1] Almost everyone has at least one a year. If you are like most people **that viruses attack**, you feel
5 pretty miserable once they enter your body. In addition, it can take several days or even weeks to get better. Therefore, it is a good idea to avoid catching or spreading viruses.

10 Viruses are tiny disease-causing particles.[2] The common cold and the flu are two well-known illnesses **that viruses cause**. Infected people can pass viruses easily to others **who they**
15 **interact with**. This is because they blow small drops of liquid into the air when they cough or sneeze. These drops contain viruses. You can catch a virus from a person **that you touch** or even
20 from someone **that you stand near** if these drops enter your mouth or nose.

Viruses can also live on surfaces[3] from a few minutes to many hours. This means you can also catch viruses from things
25 **you touch**. This is especially true if you then touch your face before washing your hands.

There are ways to avoid spreading viruses. First, always wash items such as dishes and towels **that an infected**
30 **person has used**. Cover your mouth and nose when you cough or sneeze. Wash your hands frequently. Also, try to stay home if you get sick, so the people
35 **who you work with** can stay healthy.

Viruses are difficult to control. However, knowing more about them and following the tips above can help you slow the cycle of viral infection.

---

[1]**viral infection:** illness caused by a virus

[2]**particle:** a very small piece of something

[3]**surface:** the top or outside of something

2 Object Relative Clauses

Grammar Presentation

Object relative clauses describe, identify, or give more information about nouns. In an object relative clause, the relative pronoun is the object.	RELATIVE CLAUSE OBJECT SUBJECT VERB *There are many diseases* *that viruses cause.*

2.1 Object Relative Clauses

	RELATIVE CLAUSE			
	Object Relative Pronoun	Subject	Verb	
You can infect people	**that** **who / whom**	**you**	**meet.**	
The virus	**that** **which**	**the scientist**	**studied**	was a type of flu.

2.2 Using Object Relative Clauses

A In an object relative clause, the relative pronoun is the object of the clause.	RELATIVE CLAUSE OBJECT *Cold and flu are illnesses* *that viruses cause.*
B The object relative pronouns are *who*, *whom*, *which*, and *that*.	
Use *that*, *who*, or *whom* for people.	RELATIVE CLAUSE OBJECT *The professor* *that I met yesterday has the flu.*
Use *that*, *who*, or *whom* for people.	RELATIVE CLAUSE OBJECT *She has a virus* *that young people often get.*
C Object relative clauses can combine two ideas.	*That is the virus.* + *Rob gave me the ~~virus~~.* *That is the* <u>virus</u> *that Rob gave me.*
D You can omit the relative pronoun in an object relative clause.	*The doctor (who) she spoke with had a cold himself!* *Wash the things (that) you touch if you are infected.*
E The object relative pronoun is followed by a subject and a verb.	SUBJECT VERB *I wash the towels that she uses.* SUBJECT VERB *The flu vaccine that they use didn't work.*

2.2 Using Object Relative Clauses (*continued*)

F An object relative clause usually comes right after the word it modifies. It can modify any noun or pronoun in a sentence.

SUBJECT
The virus that she studied was a type of flu.

SUBJECT
She washed the towels that she used.

PRONOUN
He's the one who I contacted on the phone.

2.3 Comparing Subject and Object Relative Clauses

	Subject Relative Clauses	Object Relative Clauses
In a relative clause, the relative pronoun is . . .	the subject.	the object.
In a sentence, the relative pronoun modifies . . .	any noun or pronoun.	
In a sentence, the relative pronoun usually comes . . .	right after the word it modifies.	
In a sentence, the relative clause has . . .	a new verb.	a new subject and verb.
The relative pronoun can be omitted.	no	yes, except for *whose*
The relative pronouns include . . .	*who, which, that, whose.*	*who, whom, which, that, whose.*

2.4 Using Subject and Object Relative Clauses

Subject relative clause	*The doctor who treated her had a cold.* SUBJECT *The doctor had a cold.* + *The doctor treated her.*
Object relative clause	*The doctor who she visited had a cold.* OBJECT *The doctor had a cold.* + *She visited the doctor.*

📊 Data from the Real World

Which is common in academic writing. It is much less common in informal language.	*The virus copies the host cell which it has invaded.*
In informal speaking and writing, *that* is more common in object relative clauses than *who* to refer to people. *Whom* is only used in rather formal situations.	**A** *Is she the scientist that you met at the lab?* **B** *Yes, she is.*

Grammar Application

A Read a passage from a history textbook about an epidemic (a disease that spreads quickly). Underline seven more relative clauses. Circle the relative pronouns. Three of the relative clauses do not have relative pronouns. Put a check (✓) above them.

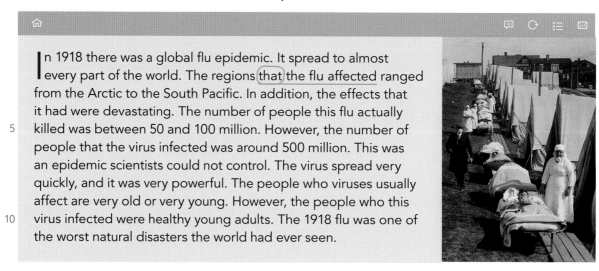

In 1918 there was a global flu epidemic. It spread to almost every part of the world. The regions (that) the flu affected ranged from the Arctic to the South Pacific. In addition, the effects that it had were devastating. The number of people this flu actually
5   killed was between 50 and 100 million. However, the number of people that the virus infected was around 500 million. This was an epidemic scientists could not control. The virus spread very quickly, and it was very powerful. The people who viruses usually affect are very old or very young. However, the people who this
10   virus infected were healthy young adults. The 1918 flu was one of the worst natural disasters the world had ever seen.

B Pair Work Compare answers with a partner. Which relative clauses do not have a relative pronoun?

Combine the sentences using object relative clauses with *who*, *that*, and *which*.

1   Another name for the flu epidemic was the "Spanish flu." The world experienced this flu epidemic in 1918.

Another name for the flu epidemic _that the world experienced in_ 1918 was the "Spanish flu."

2   The people were mostly young adults. The flu killed them.

The people _____ were mostly young adults.

3   The people are typically elderly. The flu usually affects these people.

The people _____ are typically elderly.

4   The countries were very far apart. The flu affected countries.

The countries _____ were very far apart.

5   The 1918 flu was an unusual virus. Scientists could not control the virus.

The 1918 flu was an unusual virus _____ .

6   Strange flu viruses also occur today. Scientists do not understand these strange flu viruses.

Strange flu viruses _____ also occur today.

7 SARS, bird flu, and swine flu are recent examples of strange new viruses. Many people fear these viruses.

SARS, bird flu, and swine flu are recent examples of strange new viruses

_____ .

8. Scientists are interested in people. These strange new viruses affect these people.

Scientists are interested in people _____ .

Exercise 2.3 Using Object Relative Clauses

A Over to You Complete the sentences about getting sick. Use your own ideas. Write a correct relative pronoun, or Ø for no relative pronoun.

1 The thing _that /which/Ø_ I usually do when I have a cold is ___drink hot lemon juice with honey___ .

2 The thing _____ I usually do when I have the flu is _____ .

3 I like the doctor _____ I go to when I get sick because he/she

_____ .

4 The best cold medicine _____ I know is

_____ .

5 _____

was the cold remedy _____ my family used

when I was a child.

6 _____ is the flu remedy

_____ my friend uses.

7 _____ is something _____ I avoid when I get sick.

B Pair Work Compare the sentences in A with a partner. Then tell the class about some of the interesting home remedies you discussed.

A _The thing that I usually do when I have a cold is drink hot lemon juice with honey. What about you?_

B _The thing that I usually do is . . ._

A Complete the article about swine flu. Use the correct relative pronoun and the correct form of the verb in parentheses. Use Ø for no relative pronoun. If more than one pronoun is possible, write them all in the blank.

🏠

A NEW FLU

The flu is one of the most common diseases __that/which/Ø__
(1)

viruses __cause__ (cause). Sometimes the virus _____
(2)   (3)

_____ (cause) the flu isn't serious.
(4)

Other times, it is. The number of people _____ it
(5)

_____ (attack) determines this. The number of places
(6)

around the world _____ it _____
(7)   (8)

(affect) also decides this. A disease _____
(9)

_____ (attack) a large number of people and areas
(10)

is an epidemic. For example, the 1918 flu was an epidemic. In 2009,

another flu, swine flu, became an epidemic. Some people feel swine flu

is still a serious threat. Regions _____ swine flu still
(11)

_____ (affect) include Europe, Africa, North and South
(12)

America, the Middle East, and Asia. A lot of people _____
(13)

_____ (have) swine flu have mild symptoms. Others
(14)

_____ _____ (have) the disease
(15)   (16)

have more serious symptoms. Swine flu became less serious after the 2009

outbreak, but it could return at any time.

B Pair Work Compare answers in A with your partner. Which sentences have subject relative pronouns?

3 More About Object Relative Clauses

Grammar Presentation

Object relative clauses can use a variety of verb forms.	*He doesn't touch surfaces that the patient touches.* *He didn't touch the surfaces that the patient touched.* *He hasn't touched the surfaces that the patient has touched.*
They can also show possession.	*The student whose towel she used had the flu.* (It was the student's towel.)

3.1 More About Object Relative Clauses

A *Whose* + a noun shows possession in an object relative clause.	WHOSE + NOUN The woman *whose husband* the doctor saw also needs an appointment.
A noun always follows *whose*.	WHOSE + NOUN The scientist *whose article* we read is giving a lecture.
Do not omit *whose*.	WHOSE The scientist ~~article~~ we read is giving a lecture.
B *Whose* can combine two sentences.	The woman is sick. + The doctor saw ~~her~~ children. The woman *whose children* the doctor saw is sick.
Whose replaces the possessive form in the second sentence.	That is the scientist. + We read ~~his~~ article. That is the scientist *whose article* we read.

Grammar Application

Exercise 3.1 Verbs in Object Relative Clauses

A Listen to a podcast about the flu vaccine. Complete the sentences with the relative pronoun or Ø (for no relative pronoun) and the correct form of the verb.

A vaccine is a substance _____*that*_____ a health practitioner _____
(1)   (2)
(give) to help a person avoid getting a disease. There are two types of flu vaccines. One is a

shot _____ a practitioner usually _____ (give) the patient in the arm.
(3)   (4)
The other type is a nasal spray _____ the practitioner _____ (spray)
(5)   (6)
directly into the patient's nose. Scientists develop new flu vaccines every year.

They study flu viruses _____ people around the world
(7)
_____ (had) the previous year. Then they choose three
(8)
critical viruses and make vaccines for them. For example, in 2009,

the viruses _____ they _____ (choose) were
(9)   (10)
the most likely to continue to cause disease in 2010.

People often don't like to get their flu shots. However, the flu shot _____
(11)
scientists _____ (develop) for 2009 was in high demand in the United States.
(12)
More people than usual received that shot. According to doctors, getting a flu shot each

year is the most important thing _____ a person _____ (do) to
(13)   (14)
prevent the flu. Maybe their message is now being heard.

B Listen again, and check your answers.

C Pair Work Compare answers with a partner.

Combine the sentences about Louis Pasteur. Use *that, which, who(m), Ø,* **or** *whose.*

1 A biologist of the nineteenth century was Louis Pasteur. Doctors today still value his research.
A biologist of the nineteenth century *whose research doctors today still value*
was Louis Pasteur.

2 Pasteur was a scientist. We still use his vaccines.
Pasteur is a scientist _____ .

3 Pasteur developed vaccines to prevent diseases. Farm animals often get the diseases.
Pasteur developed vaccines to prevent the diseases
_____ .

4 He also developed a vaccine to prevent a disease. People get the disease from dogs and other animals.
He also developed a vaccine to prevent a disease
_____ .

5 This is a disease. People get it from animal bites. The name of the disease is rabies.
This is a disease _____ .
The name of the disease is rabies.

6 Pasteur first tried his rabies vaccine on a young boy.
A dog bit the boy.
Pasteur first tried his rabies vaccine on a young boy
_____ .

7 The vaccine worked. He cured the boy. The boy became his friend.
The vaccine worked. The boy
_____ became his friend.

8 Another disease is called anthrax. A lot of farm animals still get the disease.
Another disease _____ is called anthrax.

A Over to You **Answer the questions. Use object relative clauses.**

1 In your opinion, what is the best thing that you can do to prevent the flu? Why?
The best thing that you *can do to prevent the flu is get a flu shot. If you get a flu shot, you won't get the flu, and you won't give it to other people* .

2 What is the best thing that you can do to prevent the common cold? Why?
The best thing that you _____ .

3 When you get the flu or a cold, what is the remedy that you use? Why?
The remedy that I _____ .

4 What disease worries you the most? Why?
The disease that I _____ .

5 What is the thing you worry about the most when you get sick? Why?
When I get sick, the thing that I _____ .

B Pair Work Discuss your answers with a partner. What do you agree or disagree about?

4 Avoid Common Mistakes ⚠

1 Use *that* / *who* / *whom* / Ø to refer to people in object relative clauses; use *which* / *that* to refer to things.

        that / who / whom / Ø

The scientist ~~which~~ I remember reading about was Louis Pasteur.

2 Do not confuse *whose* with *who*. *Whose* is possessive.

    whose

A person ~~who~~ computer is infected with a virus can use software to solve the problem.

3 Use *whom* in object relative clauses only (and in rather formal situations).

    who

The man ~~whom~~ had the virus was very ill.

4 Do not use an object pronoun at the end of an object relative clause.

The articles that I read ~~them~~ are about Louis Pasteur.

Editing Task

Find and correct eight more mistakes in the web article about computer viruses.

A New Kind of Epidemic

Are computer viruses similar to human viruses? In some ways, they are. A virus that invades your computer sometimes behaves like a virus that infects your body.

                                   that / Ø

Computer viruses became a serious problem in the 1990s. One of the first types of virus ~~who~~ computer scientists created was a "worm." A worm is a computer virus that a computer receives ~~it~~ without

5 the user's knowledge. A user ~~who~~ computer is attacked by a worm may lose data or suffer damage to his or her computer system.

The people ~~which~~ we must blame for the very first worm developed it in 1979. Much like a human virus, the worm of 1979 gradually spread until it became an "epidemic." A virus ~~who~~ thousands of computers received very rapidly was the famous "Melissa" virus of 1999. Luckily, someone developed a

10 "vaccine" for this virus, and it is no longer the cause of a computer virus epidemic.

However, people continue to create viruses of different kinds. For example, one virus attacks people's electronic address lists and sends e-mails to everyone ~~who~~ name is on a list. The people who you know ~~them~~ may be surprised when they get an e-mail from you that is really an advertisement!

People ~~who~~ computers were infected with viruses needed protection, so companies began to

15 produce anti-virus software in the 1990s. Nowadays, a user ~~whom~~ has good anti-virus software doesn't need to worry about a sick computer. However, people create new viruses all the time. Viruses will continue to be a problem, and new computer virus "vaccines" will need to be developed to fight them.

1 Grammar in the Real World

A What holidays do you celebrate each year? Which are your favorite days? Read the magazine article about "Black Friday" (the day after Thanksgiving). What's good and bad about Black Friday?

B Comprehension Check **Answer the questions.**

1 Why is the holiday shopping season important?

2 Why do people want to shop on Black Friday?

3 What are the problems with shopping on Black Friday?

4 What are some ways to avoid the problems of Black Friday?

C Notice **Complete the sentences from the article. Circle the correct words.**

1 It is the start of the holiday shopping season, **but / so** it is an important day for retailers.

2 For instance, a store will advertise a big-screen TV at a very low price, **but / because** there may be only one in the store.

3 Shoppers occasionally get into arguments **and / so** even fistfights.

4 They shop on the weekend after, **since / or** they stay home and buy online.

Think about the meaning of each word you circled. In which sentence above does the word express these meanings?

a a result _1_   **b** an addition ___   **c** an alternative ___   **d** a contrast ___

Black FRIDAY

Black Friday is the Friday after Thanksgiving Day in the United States. It is the start of the holiday shopping season, so it is an important day for retailers.[1] It is called "Black Friday" **because**
5 it is the day when retailers go "into the black." That is, they make a profit. Retailers can make 18 percent to 40 percent of their yearly sales in the month between Thanksgiving and Christmas, **so** the holiday shopping season is crucial for them
10 **and** the U.S. economy in general.

Although Black Friday is not an official holiday, many workers have the day off and start their holiday shopping. Shopping on this day is popular **because** retailers offer very low prices on
15 items such as electronics.

There is a sense of excitement about Black Friday. Stores advertise their prices in advance and open their doors at 5:00 a.m. Shoppers often line up outside a store hours before it opens **so** they
20 can be the first ones in. Some people even camp in the parking lot the night before.

However, Black Friday shopping is not without its problems. **Even though** the deals sound fantastic, they are often not as good as they seem.
25 For instance, a store will advertise a big screen TV at a very low price, **but** there may be only one in the store. **Since** there are not enough low-priced items for everyone, sometimes people get stressed **and** angry. Shoppers occasionally get
30 into arguments **and** even fistfights. In addition, **since** people are excited and stores are crowded, there are sometimes accidents on Black Friday.

Some people avoid the problems of Black Friday. They shop on the weekend after, or they
35 stay home and buy online. Black Friday can mean crowds and bad deals, **and yet** it remains one of the busiest shopping days of the year.

---

[1]**retailer:** store owner

2 Conjunctions

Grammar Presentation

<table>
<tr>
<td>The conjunctions and, or, but, so, and yet can connect single words, phrases, or clauses.</td>
<td>

WORD   WORD
Black Friday causes problems for <u>shoppers</u> and <u>stores</u>.

PHRASE   PHRASE
They shop <u>on weekends</u> but not <u>on weekdays</u>.

CLAUSE   CLAUSE
<u>He wanted to save money</u>, so <u>he shopped on Black Friday</u>.
</td>
</tr>
</table>

2.1 Conjunctions

A You can use *and* to connect related information and add ideas.	*The shoppers were tired and hungry.* (words) *People go out and spend money.* (phrases) *The store opened at 5:00 a.m., and shoppers were waiting outside.* (clauses)
B You can use *or* to give alternatives or choices.	*You can shop today or tomorrow.* (words) *They camp in the parking lot or in front of the store.* (phrases) *You can shop today, or you can wait until tomorrow.* (clauses)
C You can use *but (not)* to connect contrasting ideas.	*The store is small but successful.* (words) *They liked the clothes but not the high prices.* (phrases) *She has invited Jim for the holiday, but she has never invited us.* (clauses)
D You can use *so* to connect causes and results.	*The stores are crowded, so I'll stay home.* (clauses)
You can use *and* before *so* to show a result.	*Stores cut their prices, and so they make less money.* (clauses)
It is not common to use *so* to connect words and phrases.	

2.2 Using Conjunctions

A Use a comma when you connect two long clauses. However, you do not need a comma when the clauses are short.	*This is an important day, and it is the busiest shopping day.* *Stores cut prices and people save money.*
B When you connect two clauses and the subject is the same, you do not need to repeat the subject.	*People go shopping and (people) buy holiday gifts on this day.* *They save money but (they) don't realize the items aren't new.*
If the verb is the same, you do not need to repeat it.	*People can shop online or (can shop) at the mall.* *Shoppers start arguments and even (start) fistfights.* *Stores are cutting prices and (are) hoping to sell more.*
In addition, you often do not need to repeat prepositions after conjunctions.	*People are not at work on Thursday and (on) Friday.*
C You can often use *but + not* to shorten contrasting clauses to words or phrases.	*They shop on Friday but not Thursday.* (= They shop on Friday, but they do not shop on Thursday.) *They liked the clothes but not the high prices.* (= They liked the clothes, but they did not like the high prices.)
Do not use *not* if the contrasting ideas are both affirmative.	*The store is small but successful.* (= The store is small, but it is successful.)

2.3 Yet, And Yet

A *Yet* is a formal word. It has a similar meaning to *but*. *Yet* connects strongly contrasting ideas or surprising information.	*It is often cold, yet shoppers still sleep in doorways.* *The deals are often not good, yet people still go shopping.*
B You can use *and* with *yet*.	*There is a downside, and yet it is a popular shopping day.*

Grammar Application

Complete a news article about the holiday shopping season. Circle the correct words.

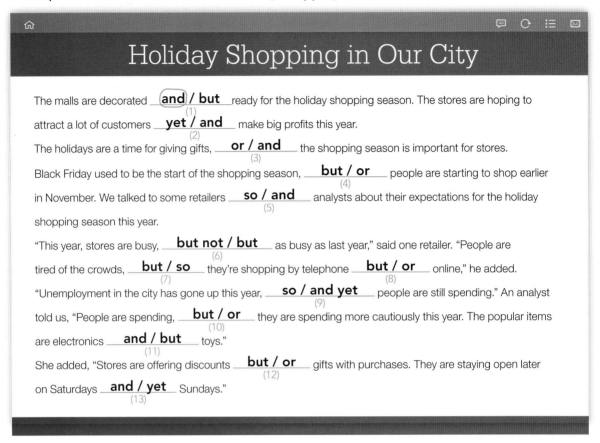

Holiday Shopping in Our City

The malls are decorated __(and) / but__ ready for the holiday shopping season. The stores are hoping to
(1)
attract a lot of customers __yet / and__ make big profits this year.
(2)
The holidays are a time for giving gifts, __or / and__ the shopping season is important for stores.
(3)
Black Friday used to be the start of the shopping season, __but / or__ people are starting to shop earlier
(4)
in November. We talked to some retailers __so / and__ analysts about their expectations for the holiday
(5)
shopping season this year.

"This year, stores are busy, __but not / but__ as busy as last year," said one retailer. "People are
(6)
tired of the crowds, __but / so__ they're shopping by telephone __but / or__ online," he added.
(7)   (8)
"Unemployment in the city has gone up this year, __so / and yet__ people are still spending." An analyst
(9)
told us, "People are spending, __but / or__ they are spending more cautiously this year. The popular items
(10)
are electronics __and / but__ toys."
(11)
She added, "Stores are offering discounts __but / or__ gifts with purchases. They are staying open later
(12)
on Saturdays __and / yet__ Sundays."
(13)

Read an online interview with shoppers about Black Friday. If you do not need to
repeat a subject or verb, cross it out.

Alex B., Detroit: (1) Black Friday can be a good thing or ~~Black Friday
can be~~ a bad thing. (2) There are good deals and there are special
offers. (3) For example, at a lot of stores, I can choose free shipping
or I can choose a gift with my purchase. (4) I love the deals but I hate
the crowds.

Maria S., Chicago: (5) People become over-excited and people become aggressive on Black Friday. (6) People push and people fight to get to the deals. (7) I stay home and I shop online, or I order things over the phone.

Wei P., San Francisco: (8) I can buy all of my gifts and I can save money, too. (9) We go shopping as a family and we enjoy our day out together.

Exercise 2.3 Using *And, Or, But,* and *So*

A Pair Work What do you know about Thanksgiving in the United States and Canada? When are the two holidays? How do people celebrate them? How did the holidays start? Make a list of facts with a partner.

B Listen to a radio show about Thanksgiving in the United States and Canada. Complete the chart below.

	Canada	The United States
1 What year was the first Thanksgiving Day?	1578	
2 Who started it (according to history books)?		
3 What month is it in?		
4 What day of the week is it on?		
5 What do people eat on Thanksgiving?		
6 What day of the week do they eat Thanksgiving dinner?		
7 What is the big shopping day?		

C Complete these sentences about Thanksgiving in the United States and Canada. Use the information in the chart to help you. Circle the correct conjunctions.

1 Thanksgiving is a holiday in ___the United States___ (**and**)/ **but** Canada.

2 Thanksgiving is in November in the United States, **but** / **so** the Canadian Thanksgiving is in _____ .

3 In the United States, Thanksgiving Day is always on a _____ , **or** / **but** in Canada, it's on a Monday.

4 In _____ , people get together with family **and** / **but** have a traditional Thanksgiving dinner.

5 People eat turkey **and** / **or** _____ .

6 In the United States, the meal is always on Thanksgiving Day, **but** / **so** in Canada, the meal can be on _____ .

7 Canadians can have Thanksgiving dinner on Saturday, Sunday, **or** / **but** _____ .

8 In the United States, Black Friday is the big shopping day, **but** / **and** in Canada, the big sales are on _____ .

Exercise 2.4 More Conjunctions

Group Work Make a list of favorite holidays and special days in your group. Talk about why the day exists, how people celebrate it, what they wear, what they eat or drink, where they go, and so on. Then discuss the similarities and differences among the days on your list. Use *and*, *but*, *or*, *so*, and *yet*.

3 Adverb Clauses

Grammar Presentation

Adverb clauses show how ideas are connected. They begin with conjunctions such as *because*, *since*, *although*, and *even though*.

| MAIN CLAUSE | ADVERB CLAUSE |
| | CONJUNCTION |

Many people have the day off work   *even though it's not an official holiday*.

3.1 Adverb Clauses

Adverb Clause		Main Clause
Because Since	there is a big sale today,	the stores are crowded.
Although Even though	it is not a holiday,	a lot of people have the day off.

3.1 Adverb Clauses *(continued)*

	Main Clause	Adverb Clause	
The stores are crowded	**because** **since**		**there is a big sale today.**
Many people have the day off	**although** **even though**		**it isn't a holiday.**

3.2 Using Adverb Clauses

A Like most other clauses, an adverb clause must have a subject and a verb.

People shop on Black Friday because prices are lower.

ADVERB CLAUSE — SUBJ. VERB

B An adverb clause on its own is not a sentence. It is a fragment.

They have the day off work although it's not a holiday.
They have the day off work. Although it's not a holiday.

C An adverb clause can come before or after the main clause. Use a comma when the adverb clause comes first.

Black Friday is an important day for retailers because it is the start of the holiday shopping season.
Because Black Friday is the start of the holiday shopping season, it is an important day for retailers.

D *Although, even though,* and *though* connect contrasting ideas.

Although it is not a holiday, workers have the day off.
Even though some deals sound fantastic, they are not.
Though prices are low, the deals are often not good.

E *Because* and *since* introduce reasons or causes and connect them with results.

RESULT CAUSE
It's a popular day since stores offer special deals.

CAUSE RESULT
Because prices are low, the stores are crowded.

REASON RESULT
Because stores are crowded, many people stay home.

You can use *since* when the reader or listener knows about the reason from general knowledge, or because you have explained it.

Most stores cut their prices on Black Friday. Since prices are lower, it is a popular shopping day.

F *So* introduces results.

The stores are crowded, so many people stay home.

So can also introduce a purpose or reason.

They camp in the parking lot so they can be first in the store.

Do not start a sentence with *so.*

Data from the Real World

Research shows that *since* is more common in formal writing than in speaking.

Writing
Speaking

Grammar Application

Exercise 3.1 *Because, Since, Although, and Even Though*

Complete the magazine article about "Cyber Monday" (the Monday after Thanksgiving in the United States). Circle the best conjunctions.

CYBER MONDAY

The holiday shopping season is important for the U.S. economy **(since)/although** a high percentage of retail sales
(1)
occur between Thanksgiving and Christmas. **Although / Because**
(2)
Black Friday is an important day for retailers, Cyber Monday has become equally important. Cyber Monday is the first Monday after Thanksgiving Day. It's called "Cyber Monday" **although / because** a
(3)
lot of retailers have online sales on that day.

There are a number of reasons why so many people shop on Cyber Monday, **even though / because** they cannot touch or
(4)
handle the items they are buying. For one thing, it's convenient. **Even though / Because** most companies have rules against online
(5)
shopping, millions of people still shop online on Cyber Monday while they're at work and sitting in front of computers. Also, Cyber Monday deals are sometimes even better than Black Friday deals. **Although / Because** Monday is often the last chance for retailers
(6)
to get rid of all the items they had for Black Friday, they often cut prices on Cyber Monday. In addition, some people prefer to buy online **because / although** shipping is usually free, and they don't
(7)
have to carry heavy items home.

Since / Although most people think of the Friday after
(8)
Thanksgiving as the biggest shopping day in the United States, Cyber Monday is now almost as important for retailers as Black Friday.

Exercise 3.2 Adverb Clauses

Combine the sentences to make one sentence. Use *because, since, so, although, even though,* **or** *though.* **Sometimes there is more than one correct answer.**

1 Researchers study the psychology of giving gifts. Gift giving is an important part of life.

Researchers study the psychology of giving gifts because / since gift giving is an important part of life.
Gift giving is an important part of life, so many experts study the psychology of giving gifts.

2 Stores are crowded during the holiday shopping period. Some people decide not to give gifts.

_____

_____

3 Holiday shopping can be unpleasant and expensive. Sometimes people feel like they can't avoid gift giving.

_____

_____

4 Gift giving in the right situations can make our relationships with people stronger. It can be a nice reminder of how we feel about other people.

_____

_____

5 Gift giving varies from culture to culture. It's a good idea to learn about cultural rules for gift giving.

_____

_____

6 In some cultures, you open a gift as soon as you get it. You wait until the giver has left in other cultures.

_____

_____

7 A certain color can mean bad luck in some cultures. People will avoid using the color as a gift wrap.

_____

_____

8 Both men and women enjoy gifts. Researchers say that gift giving is more important for females.

_____

_____

A Complete the questions about gift-giving habits with an appropriate conjunction.

1 Do you ever buy gifts for people _**because**_ you want to say "thank you"?

2 Do you ever feel you have to buy gifts _____ you can't really afford them?

3 Have you ever given a gift to someone _____ you felt you had to?

4 Have you ever taken a gift back to the store for a refund or exchange

_____ you didn't like it?

5 Have you bought a gift for someone _____ you didn't like that person?

6 Have you bought a gift for someone _____ you wanted to say "I'm sorry"?

7 Have you ever given someone a gift _____ you had no reason?

8 Have you ever pretended to like a gift _____ you didn't like it?

B Pair Work Ask and answer the questions in A with a partner. Do you have the same gift-giving habits?

A *Do you ever buy gifts for people because you want to say "thank you"?*

B *Yes, I sometimes buy a small gift for my neighbor when she waters my plants for me.*

4 Avoid Common Mistakes ⚠

1 **Check the spelling of _although_.**
Although
~~Althought~~ *the stores are crowded, it's my favorite day to shop.*

2 **Do not link three or more clauses with _although_, _though_, or _even though_.**
I like Black Friday. Although it is very tiring, it's a lot of fun.
~~I like Black Friday although it is very tiring it's a lot of fun.~~

3 **Do not forget to use a comma after the adverb clause when it is first.**
Although we think it is a modern celebration, it is an ancient tradition.

Editing Task

Find and correct seven more mistakes in these paragraphs.

Although
    ~~Allthough~~ Mother's Day is an old holiday it may surprise you to know that
Father's Day is a modern holiday. Some people say the first modern Father's Day
was in 1908, althought most people agree it started in 1910. Father's Day was
born in Spokane, Washington, on June 19, 1910. Father's Day was partly the idea
5 of Mrs. Sonora Smart Dodd. Because her father was a single parent and raised six
children, she wanted to honor him. Although she suggested her father's June 5
birthday she did not give the organizers enough time to make arrangements. The
holiday moved from June 5 to the third Sunday in June. Father's Day is now a popular
holiday. Althogh people laughed at the idea of Father's Day at first it gradually
10 became popular.

    Because retailers saw an opportunity to increase sales in the 1930s, they started
to advertise Father's Day gifts. People then felt that they had to buy gifts for their
fathers even though they realized this was commercialization, they still bought them.
Father's Day is an international holiday. Even though people celebrate it on different
15 dates it is an important day in many cultures.

Appendices

1 Capitalization and Punctuation Rules

Capitalize	Examples
1. The first letter of the first word of a sentence	*Today is a great day.*
2. The pronoun *I*	*After class, I want to go to the movies.*
3. Names of people	*Simon Bolivar, Joseph Chung*
4. Names of buildings, streets, geographic locations, and organizations	*Taj Mahal, Main Street, Mt. Everest, United Nations*
5. Titles of people	*Dr., Mr., Mrs., Ms.*
6. Days, months, and holidays	*Tuesday, April, Valentine's Day*
7. Names of courses or classes	*Biology 101, English Composition II*
8. Titles of books, movies, and plays	*Crime and Punishment, Avatar, Hamlet*
9. States, countries, languages, and nationalities	*California, Mexico, Spanish, South Korean, Canadian*
10. Names of religions	*Hinduism, Catholicism, Islam, Judaism*

Punctuation	Examples
1. Use a period (.) at the end of a sentence.	*I think I can pass this class.*
2. Use a question mark (?) at the end of a question.	*Why do you want to buy a car?*
3. Use an exclamation point (!) to show strong emotion (e.g., surprise, anger, shock).	*Wait! I'm not ready yet.* *I can't believe it!*
4. Use an apostrophe (') for possessive nouns. Add 's for singular nouns. Add s' for plural nouns. Add ' or 's for nouns that end in -s. Add 's for irregular plural nouns. Use an apostrophe (') for contractions.	*That's Sue's umbrella.* *Those are the students' books.* *It is Wes' house. It is Wes's house.* *Bring me the children's shoes.* *I'll be back next week. He can't drive a car.*

1 Capitalization and Punctuation Rules (*Continued*)

Punctuation	Examples
5. Use a comma (,): between words in a series of three or more items. (Place *and* before the last item.)	*I like fish, chicken, turkey, and mashed potatoes.*
after a time clause when it begins a sentence.	*Before I play soccer, I do my stretching exercises.*
after a prepositional phrase when it begins a sentence.	*Next to my house, there's a beautiful little park.*
after an adverb clause when it begins a sentence.	*Because she got a job, she was able to get her own apartment.*
before *and, or, but,* and *so* to connect two or more main clauses.	*You can watch TV, but I have to study for a test.*

2 Stative (Non-Action) Verbs

Stative verbs do not describe actions. They describe states or situations. Stative verbs are not usually used in the present progressive, even if we are talking about right now. Some are occasionally used in the present progressive, but often with a different meaning.

Research shows that the 25 most common stative verbs in spoken and written English are:

agree	dislike	hope	love	see
believe	expect	hurt	need	seem
care (about)	hate	know	notice	think
cost	have	like	own	understand
disagree	hear	look like	prefer	want

Other stative verbs are:

be	feel	matter	recognize	sound
belong	forgive	mean	remember	taste
concern	look	owe	smell	weigh
deserve				

Using the present progressive of these verbs sometimes changes the meaning to an action.

Can you see the red car?   (= use your eyes to be aware of something)

I'm seeing an old friend tomorrow.   (= meeting someone)

I think you're right.   (= believe)

Dina is thinking of taking a vacation soon.   (= considering)

I have two sisters.   (= be related to)

We're having eggs for breakfast.   (= eating)

3 Irregular Verbs

Base Form	Simple Past	Past Participle	Base Form	Simple Past	Past Participle
be	was / were	been	keep	kept	kept
become	became	become	know	knew	known
begin	began	begun	leave	left	left
bite	bit	bitten	lose	lost	lost
blow	blew	blown	make	made	made
break	broke	broken	meet	met	met
bring	brought	brought	pay	paid	paid
build	built	built	put	put	put
buy	bought	bought	read	read [red]*	read [red]*
catch	caught	caught	ride	rode	ridden
choose	chose	chosen	run	ran	run
come	came	come	say	said	said
cost	cost	cost	see	saw	seen
cut	cut	cut	sell	sold	sold
do	did	done	send	sent	sent
draw	drew	drawn	set	set	set
drink	drank	drunk	shake	shook	shaken
drive	drove	driven	show	showed	shown
eat	ate	eaten	shut	shut	shut
fall	fell	fallen	sing	sang	sung
feed	fed	fed	sit	sat	sat
feel	felt	felt	sleep	slept	slept
fight	fought	fought	speak	spoke	spoken
find	found	found	spend	spent	spent
fly	flew	flown	stand	stood	stood
forget	forgot	forgotten	steal	stole	stolen
forgive	forgave	forgiven	swim	swam	swum
get	got	gotten	take	took	taken
give	gave	given	teach	taught	taught
go	went	gone	tell	told	told
grow	grew	grown	think	thought	thought
have	had	had	throw	threw	thrown
hear	heard	heard	understand	understood	understood
hide	hid	hidden	wake	woke	woken
hit	hit	hit	wear	wore	worn
hold	held	held	win	won	won
hurt	hurt	hurt	write	wrote	written

*pronunciation

4 Spelling Rules for Verbs Ending in *-ing*

1. For verbs ending in a vowel-consonant combination, repeat the consonant before adding *-ing*.
   get → *getting*   *swim* → *swimming*

2. However, if the verb has more than one syllable, repeat the consonant only if the final syllable is stressed.
   beGIN → *beginning*   BUT   *HAPpen* → *happening (no doubling of consonant)*

3. For verbs ending in a silent *e*, drop the *e* before adding *-ing*.
   move → *moving*   *drive* → *driving*

   For *be* and *see*, don't drop the *e* because it is not silent.
   be → *being*   *see* → *seeing*

   For verbs ending in *-ie*, change *ie* to *y* before adding *-ing*.
   die → *dying*   *lie* → *lying*

Verbs that end in *-ing* are also called *gerunds* when they are used as nouns. The same spelling rules above apply to gerunds as well.

5 Spelling Rules for Regular Verbs in the Simple Past

1. To form the simple past of regular verbs, add *-ed* to the base form of the verb.
   work → *worked*   *wash* → *washed*

2. For regular verbs that end in *-e*, add *-d* only.
   live → *lived*   *like* → *liked*

3. For regular verbs ending in a consonant + *-y*, change *y* to *i* and add *-ed*.
   study → *studied*   *hurry* → *hurried*

4. For regular verbs that end in a vowel + *-y*, add *-ed*.
   stay → *stayed*   *enjoy* → *enjoyed*

5. For regular verbs that end in a vowel-consonant combination, repeat the consonant before adding *-ed*. Exception: Do not double the last consonant for verbs that end with *-w*, *-x*, or *-y*.
   stop → *stopped*   *plan* → *planned*   BUT   *fix* → *fixed*

6. However, if the verb has more than one syllable, repeat the consonant only if the final syllable is stressed.
   preFER → *preferred*   BUT   *Visit* → *visited (no doubling of consonant)*

6 Verbs + Gerunds and Infinitives

Verbs Followed by a Gerund Only

admit	keep (= *continue*)
avoid	mind (= *object to*)
consider	miss
delay	postpone
deny	practice
discuss	quit
enjoy	recall (= *remember*)
finish	risk
imagine	suggest
involve	understand

Verbs Followed by an Infinitive Only

afford	hope	pretend
agree	intend	promise
arrange	learn	refuse
attempt	manage	seem
decide	need	tend (= *be likely*)
deserve	offer	threaten
expect	plan	volunteer
fail	prepare	want
help		

Verbs Followed by a Gerund or an Infinitive

begin	like	start
continue	love	stop*
forget*	prefer	try*
hate	remember*	

*The meanings of these verbs are different when they are followed by a gerund or an infinitive. See Unit 28.

7 Verb and Preposition Combinations

Verb + *about*	Verb + *for*	Verb + *of*	Verb + *to*
ask about	apologize for	approve of	admit to
complain about	ask for	dream of	belong to
talk about	look for	think of	listen to
think about	pay for	**Verb + *on***	look forward to
worry about	wait for	count on	talk to
Verb + *against*	**Verb + *in***	decide on	**Verb + *with***
advise against	believe in	depend on	agree with
decide against	succeed in	insist on	argue with
Verb + *at*		plan on	bother with
look at		rely on	deal with
smile at			

8 Adjective and Preposition Combinations

Adjective + *of*
    afraid of
    ashamed of
    aware of
    careful of
    full of
    sick of
    tired of

Adjective + *by*
    amazed by
    bored by
    surprised by

Adjective + *at*
    amazed at
    angry at
    bad at
    good at
    surprised at

Adjective + *from*
    different from
    separate from

Adjective + *with*
    bored with
    familiar with
    satisfied with
    wrong with

Adjective + *in*
    interested in

Adjective + *for*
    bad for
    good for
    responsible for

Adjective + *about*
    concerned about
    excited about
    happy about
    nervous about
    pleased about
    sad about
    sorry about
    surprised about
    upset about
    worried about

Adjective + *to*
    similar to

9 Modal Verbs and Modal-like Expressions

Most modals have multiple meanings.

Function	Modal Verb or Modal-like Expression	Time	Example
Ability / Possibility	can	present, future	I can speak three languages. I can help you tomorrow.
	could	present, past	She could play an excellent game of tennis when she was young.
	be able to	past, present, future	I won't be able to help you tomorrow. I'm not able to help you today.
Permission less formal more formal	can could	present, future	Yes, you can watch TV now. You could give me your answer next week.
	may	present, future	You may leave now.
Requests less formal	can will	present, future	Can you stop that noise now? Will you please visit me tonight?
more formal	could would	present, future	Could you turn off your cell phone please? Would you please come for your interview this afternoon?
Offers	can could may will	present, future	I can help you paint your room. I could drive you to work next week. May I carry that for you? We'll help you find your wallet.
Invitations	would you like	present, future	Would you like to come to my graduation tomorrow?
Advice less strong	ought to should	present, future	You really ought to save your money. She shouldn't go to school today.
stronger	had better	present, future	They had better be very careful in the park tomorrow.
Suggestions	could might want to	present, future	He could take a train instead of the bus. You might want to wait until next month.

Function	Modal Verb or Modal-like Expression	Time	Example
Preferences	*would like* *would prefer* *would rather*	present, future	I *would like* to take a trip next year. We *would prefer* to go on a cruise. They *would rather* eat at home than in a restaurant.
Necessity less formal	*have / has to* *need to*	past, present, future	We *had to* cancel our date at the last minute. She *needs to* quit her stressful job.
more formal	*have / has got to* *must*	past, present, future present, future	They've *got to* study harder if they want to pass. You *must* be more serious about your future.
Lack of Necessity	*don't / doesn't have to* *don't / doesn't need to*	past, present, future	I *didn't have to* renew my driver's license. You *don't need to* worry about your brother.
Prohibition	*can't* *must not* *may not*	present, future	You *can't* attend tonight without an invitation. You *must not* fish without a license. You *may not* board the plane before going through security.
Speculation / Probability	*could* *may* *might* *should*	present, future	He *could* be late because he missed his train. I *may* stay home. It *might* rain later because I see dark clouds. We *should* probably leave now.
	must	present only	She *must* be sick because she didn't come to work today.

10 Adjectives: Order Before Nouns

When you use two (or more) adjectives before a noun, use the order in the chart below.

Opinion	Size	Quality	Age	Shape	Color	Origin	Material	Nouns as Adjectives
beautiful comfortable delicious expensive interesting nice pretty reasonable special ugly	big fat huge large long short small tall thin wide	cold free heavy hot safe	ancient new old young	rectangular round square triangular	black blue gold green orange purple red silver yellow white	American Canadian Chinese European Japanese Mexican Peruvian Thai	cotton glass leather metal paper plastic stone wooden woolen	computer evening rose safety software summer training

Examples:

I bought a beautiful, new, purple and gold Indian scarf.

There is a tall, young woman sitting next to that handsome man.

We're going to learn an interesting, new software program.

The museum has expensive glass jewelry.

11 Conditionals

The factual conditional describes general truths, habits, and things that happen routinely.
The simple present is used in both clauses. You can use modals in the result clause, too.

    IF CLAUSE   RESULT CLAUSE
If you use the highway, the drive is much faster.   (general truth)
If you enter before 11:00 a.m., you can get a discount.   (general truth)
Use the imperative in the result clause to give instructions or commands.
If you don't like the oranges, give them to me.   (command)
The future conditional describes things that will happen under certain conditions in the future.
The simple present is used in the *if* clause and a future form is used in the result clause. You can
use modals in the result clause, too.

    IF CLAUSE   RESULT CLAUSE
If it rains tomorrow, they're going to cancel the game.
If I finish my homework early, I'll go to the movies.
If she works hard, she could get a promotion.

You can begin a conditional sentence with the *if* clause or the result clause. It doesn't change the meaning. Use a comma between the two clauses if you begin your sentence with the *if* clause.

RESULT CLAUSE   IF CLAUSE
They're going to cancel the game if it rains tomorrow.

     IF CLAUSE   RESULT CLAUSE
If it rains tomorrow, they're going to cancel the game.

12 Phrasal Verbs: Transitive and Intransitive

Transitive (Separable) Phrasal Verbs

Phrasal Verb	Meaning	Phrasal Verb	Meaning
add up	add together, combine	*give up*	quit
blow up	explode	*hang up*	end a phone call
bring back	return something or someone	*help out*	assist someone
bring up	(1) raise a child, (2) introduce a topic	*lay off*	lose a job, end employment
build up	accumulate	*leave on*	keep on (a light, clothing, jewelry)
call back	return a phone call	*let in*	allow someone to enter
call off	cancel	*look over*	examine
cheer up	make someone happy	*look up*	find information
clear up	resolve a problem or situation, explain	*make up*	create or invent (a story, a lie)
do over	do again	*pass out*	distribute (paper, a test, material, homework)
figure out	find an answer, understand	*pay back*	repay money
fill in	write in blank spaces	*pay off*	repay completely
fill out	complete an application or form	*pick up*	(1) go get someone or something, (2) lift
find out	look for or seek information, learn	*point out*	call attention to something
give away	donate, give for free	*put away*	(1) save for the future, (2) put in the correct place
give back	return		

Transitive (Separable) Phrasal Verbs *(continued)*

Phrasal Verb	Meaning	Phrasal Verb	Meaning
put back	return something to its usual place	*talk over*	discuss
put off	delay, postpone	*think over*	consider
put out	(1) extinguish, stop the burning of a fire or cigarette, (2) place outside	*throw away / throw out*	get rid of something; discard
put together	assemble	*try on*	put on clothing to see if it fits
set up	(1) arrange, (2) plan, (3) build	*turn down*	(1) lower the volume, (2) reject
shut off / turn off	stop (a machine, a light, a TV)	*turn on*	start (a machine, a light, a TV)
sort out	(1) organize, (2) solve	*turn up*	increase the volume
straighten up	(1) make something look neat, (2) stand tall	*wake up*	stop sleeping
take back	return something	*work out*	(1) solve, (2) calculate
take out	(1) remove, (2) obtain something officially	*write down*	write on paper

Intransitive (Inseparable) Phrasal Verbs

Phrasal Verb	Meaning	Phrasal Verb	Meaning
break down	(1) stop working, (2) lose control	*fall down*	fall to the ground
break up	end a relationship, separate	*fool around*	act playfully
come back	return	*get ahead*	succeed, make progress
come from	originate	*get along*	have a good relationship
come on	(1) hurry, (2) start	*get over*	recover from an illness or a shock
dress up	put on nice or formal clothes	*get up*	arise from bed
drop in	visit without advance notice	*give up*	stop
drop out	quit (school, a race, a club)	*go ahead*	start or continue
eat out	eat in a restaurant	*go away*	leave; go to another place

Phrasal Verb	Meaning	Phrasal Verb	Meaning
go on	continue	*run out*	(1) leave, (2) be completely used
go out	not stay home	*set in*	begin and continue for a long time
go up	rise, go higher	*show up*	appear
grow up	become an adult	*sign up*	register for a class or event
hang on	(1) wait, (2) keep going	*sit down*	sit; take a seat
hold on	(1) wait, (2) persist	*slip up*	make a mistake
look into	investigate	*speak up*	talk louder
look out	be careful	*stand up*	stand; rise
make up	end a disagreement	*stay up*	remain awake
move in (to)	(1) take your things to a new home, (2) begin living somewhere	*take off*	(1) leave on an airplane, (2) grow; be successful
move out (of)	leave a place you live in	*watch out*	be careful
run into	meet someone by chance or unexpectedly	*work out*	(1) exercise, (2) go as planned

13 Adjectives and Adverbs: Comparative and Superlative Forms

		Adjective	Comparative	Superlative
1	**One-Syllable Adjectives**			
a	Add *-er* and *-est* to one syllable adjectives.	cheap	cheaper	the cheapest
		high	higher	the highest
		large	larger	the largest
		long	longer	the longest
		new	newer	the newest
		old	older	the oldest
		small	smaller	the smallest
		strong	stronger	the strongest
		tall	taller	the tallest
b	For one-syllable adjectives that end in a vowel + consonant, double the final consonant and add *-er* or *-est*.	big	bigger	the biggest
		hot	hotter	the hottest
		sad	sadder	the saddest
		thin	thinner	the thinnest
	Do not double the consonant *w*.	low	lower	the lowest

Adjectives and Adverbs: Comparative and Superlative Forms *(continued)*

		Adjective	Comparative	Superlative
2	**Two-Syllable Adjectives** **a** Add *more* or *most* to most adjectives.	boring famous handsome patient	more boring more famous more handsome more patient	the most boring the most famous the most handsome the most patient
	b Some two-syllable adjectives have two forms.	friendly narrow simple strict quiet	friendlier more friendly narrower more narrow simpler more simple stricter more strict quieter more quiet	the friendliest the most friendly the narrowest the most narrow the simplest the most simple the strictest the most strict the quietest the most quiet
	c Remove the -y and add -*ier* or -*iest* to two-syllable adjectives ending in -y.	angry easy friendly happy lucky pretty silly	angrier easier friendlier happier luckier prettier sillier	the angriest the easiest the friendliest the happiest the luckiest the prettiest the silliest
3	**Three or More Syllable Adjectives** Add *more* or *most* to adjectives with three or more syllables.	beautiful comfortable creative difficult enjoyable expensive important independent relaxing responsible serious	more beautiful more comfortable more creative more difficult more enjoyable more expensive more important more independent more relaxing more responsible more serious	the most beautiful the most comfortable the most creative the most difficult the most enjoyable the most expensive the most important the most independent the most relaxing the most responsible the most serious
4	**Irregular Adjectives** Some adjectives have irregular forms.	bad far good	worse farther / further better	the worst the farthest / the furthest the best

Adjectives and Adverbs: Comparative and Superlative Forms *(continued)*

	Adjective	Comparative	Superlative
5 *-ly* Adverbs Most adverbs end in *-ly*. Add *more* or *most*. People usually only use *the* with superlative adverbs in formal writing and speaking.	dangerously patiently quickly quietly slowly	more dangerously more patiently more quickly more quietly more slowly	(the) most dangerously (the) most patiently (the) most quickly (the) most quietly (the) most slowly
6 One-Syllable Adverbs A few adverbs do not end in *-ly*. Add *-er* and *-est* to these adverbs.	fast hard	faster harder	(the) fastest (the) hardest
7 Irregular Adverbs Some adverbs have irregular forms.	badly far well	worse farther / further better	(the) worst (the) farthest / furthest (the) best

Index

Art Credits

The following images are sourced from Getty Images.

The following images are sourced from Getty Images.

U1: Antonio_Diaz/Istock; Wavebreak Media; Jgi/Tom Grill/Blend Images; Dolgachov/Istock; U2: Lilechka75/Istock; Jgi/Tom Grill/Tetra Images; Ariel Skelley/Digitalvision; Aldomurillo/Istock; U3: M-Imagephotography/Istock; Dstarky/Istock; Fuse/Corbis; Clerkenwell/Vetta; Gareth Brown/Cultura; Jeff Greenough/Blend Images; U4: Ralph Orlowski; Afp; Jean Baptiste Lacroix/Wireimage; Michael Ochs Archives; U5: Vincenzo Assenza/Eyeem; Bettmann; Jenifoto/Istock; Mimi Haddon/Photodisc; U6: Marvin E. Newman/Photographer'S Choice; Afp Contributor; Klaus Vedfelt/Taxi; Shannon Fagan/The Image Bank; Ajr_Images/Istock; Mauro_Repossini/Istock; Otto Greule Jr; Warren Faidley/Corbis; Nasa/Handout/Hulton Archive; U7: Corbis/Vcg; Mistikas/Istock; Alexandr Dubovitskiy/Istock; Zak00/Digitalvision Vectors; Joern Pollex; U8: Ezra Bailey/Taxi; U9: Geber86/E+; Peopleimages/Digitalvision; Stocknroll/E+; Hoxton/Ryan Lees; U10: Ariel Skelley/Photodisc; Georgette Douwma/Photographer'S Choice; Zubin Shroff/The Image Bank; Encyclopaedia Britannica/Universal Images Group; Barcroft; Wolfgang Poelzer/Waterframe; Universal History Archive; U11: Peter Chadwick Lrps/Moment Open; Dndavis/Istock; Afp Contributor; Vm/Istock; Westend61; U12: Didier Marti/Moment; Yuji Kotani/Taxi Japan; Brittak/Istock Unrelease; Jose Luis Pelaez Inc/Blend Images; Masuti/Istock; U13: Maximilian Stock Ltd/The Image Bank; Digitalvision; Steve Cole/The Image Bank; Juice Images/Cultura; U14: Monkeybusinessimages/Istock; U15: Visionsofamerica/Joe Sohm/Digitalvision; Elena_Danileiko/Istock; Peter Dazeley/Photographer'S Choice; Sawitree Pamee/Eyeem; Roberto Machado Noa/Lightrocket; U16: Istvan Kadar Photography/Moment Open; Paul Bradbury/The Image Bank; Juanmonino/Istock; Gary John Norman/The Image Bank; U17: Westend61; Catherine Macbride/Moment; Baona/E+; Maria Taglienti-Molinari/Stockbyte; R_Type/Istock; Alan Bailey/Rubberball Productions; U18: Monkeybusinessimages/Istock; Kidstock/Blend Image; Bettmann; Wedwam/Istock; U19: Robert Lachman; Jiji Press/Afp; Pasieka/Science Photo Library; U20: Saul Loeb/Afp; Tetra Images; Aldomurillo/E+; Klaus Vedfelt/Digitalvision; U21: Daniloandjus/E+; George Doyle/Stockbyte; Eva-Katalin/E+; U22: Emirmemedovski/E+; U23: Hero Images; Monkeybusinessimages/Istock; Ariel Skelley/Digitalvision; U24: Sam Edwards/Caiaimage; Fuse/Corbis; Anchiy/E+; Moodboard Brand X Pictures; U25: Ktsdesign/Science Photo Library; David Arky/Tetra Images; U26: Thomas Barwick/Taxi; Robin Skjoldborg/Cultura; Peopleimages/E+; Dragonimages/Istock; U27: Parkerdeen/Istock; Dea/A. Dagli Orti/De Agostini Picture Library; Chicago History Museum/Archive Photos; Cameron Davidson/Photolibrary; U28: Westend61; Sue Barr/Image Source; Hill Street Studios/Blend Images; Vvoevale/Istock; Andersen Ross/Blend Images; U29: Universal Images Group; Universal Images Group; Bob Riha Jr; Fotosearch; Jim Craigmyle/Corbis; U30: Michael H/Photodisc; Romolotavani/Istock; Moncherie/E+; Robert Decelis Ltd/Stockbyte; U31: Jose Luis Pelaez Inc/Blend Images; Photoquest/Archive Photos; Tim Hale/Photographer'S Choice; Garo/Canopy; Hero Images; Paul Nadar/Hulton Archive; U32: Mandel Ngan/Afp; Lívia Fernandes - Brazil/Moment; Ajr_Images/Istock; Shannon Fagan/Taxi; Jgi/Tetra Images; Jose Luis Pelaez Inc/Blend Images.

Images from other sources

U4: A'Lelia Bundles/Madam Walker Family Archives/Washington, D.C; U19: Steven Senne/Shutterstock; Jeff Morgan 09/Alamy Stock Photo; U22: J.R. Bale/Alamy Stock Photo; U27: Cal Sport Media/Alamy Stock Photo; U29: Digital Image Library/Alamy Stock Photo; Library of Congress Washington, D.C. 20540 USA.

sit	sat	think	thought
sleep	slept	throw	threw
speak	spoke	understand	understood
spend	spent	wake	woke
stand	stood	wear	wore
steal	stole	win	won
swim	swam	white	wrote
take	took		
teach	taught		
tell	told		